We Are What We Eat

We Are What We Eat

Ethnic Food and the Making of Americans

Donna R. Gabaccia

Harvard University Press
Cambridge, Massachusetts
London, England
1998

Illustrations by Susan Keller

Library of Congress Cataloging-in-Publication Data

Gabaccia, Donna R., 1949–
We are what we eat : ethnic food and the making of Americans /
Donna R. Gabaccia.
p.   cm.
Includes bibliographical references and index.
ISBN 0-674-94860-2 (cloth)
ISBN 0-674-00190-7 (pbk)
1. Food habits—United States. 2. Ethnic food industry—United
States. 3. Ethnic attitudes—United States. 4. United States—
Social life and customs. I. Title.
GT2853.U5G33   1998
394.1'2'0973—dc21
97-52712

Mangiando, ricordo:
Dedicated to Tamino,
my German-speaking,
Italo-Polish-American child,
who eats Ethiopian and cooks Cuban
and who grew up with this book

The Mexican Sangwitch

Is it a tortilla with peanut butter and jelly,
or jalapeños piled on Wonder Bread?
Is it a coney made with tortillas,
or a Kaiser roll smothered
with salchiches y salsa mayonesa?
Is it chorizo con huevo on whole wheat,
or refried beans on white bread?
Is it the patron saint of botanas,
or a Mexican who can only speak English?
Is it the same as an American Taco?
Is it a Mexican playing tic-tac-toe?
Is it carne asada on rye,
or guacamole on toast?
Do you really want to know why?
Is it me inside of you,
or you wrapped around me?
Is it a güera dancing with two Mexicans,
or two gringos putting the make on my sister?
Is it a super sandwich, with the official
ingredients labeled: HECHO EN MEXICO!
Is it a plain sandwich
made by authentic Mexican hands?
Is it true Juan de la Raza invented it?
Is it a moot question?
Are you a lawyer or a poet?
Does the judge really care?

Detroit 7/1990

Trinidad Sánchez, Jr., "Why Am I So Brown?" from the
book of the same title, copyright 1991. Reprinted by
permission of MARCH Abrazo Press, Chicago, Illinois.

Contents

What Do We Eat?

In 1989, hungry Houstonians learned they could buy "New York deli" without leaving town—at the newly opened Guggenheim's Delicatessen. The restaurateur offering bagels, rugelach, herring, corned beef, and cheese cake at Guggenheim's was Ghulam Bombaywala, an immigrant from Pakistan. Bombaywala had already worked for years in a Houston steakhouse and a local Italian restaurant and had also operated a small chain of Mexican restaurants. Before opening Guggenheim's, Bombaywala went to New York to do his own research, eating in different delis three meals a day for five days. Back in Houston, Bombaywala sought partners, and he borrowed the recipes for Guggenheim's from one of them, a Mrs. Katz.[1] Bombaywala did not seem to know that Germans, not Eastern European Jews, had opened New York's first delicatessens. And needless to say, most Houstonians devouring Guggenheim's New York deli were neither Germans, Eastern Europeans, Jews, nor New Yorkers. But then neither was Bombaywala.

The same year, three transplanted easterners with suspiciously Italian-sounding names—Paul Sorrentino, Rob Geresi, and Vince Vrana—opened their own New York Bagel Shop and Delicatessen in Oklahoma. Bagels packaged by Lender's had been available for years in local frozen food compartments, as were advertisements offering recipes for "pizzels," made of frozen bagels topped with canned tomato sauce. As businessmen looking for a market niche, Sorrentino, Geresi, and Vrana wagered that the most knowledgeable and sophisticated of Oklahoman consumers would enjoy freshly baked "New-York-style" bagels, which were chewier than their frozen counterparts. Like many retailers in the South and West, however, their New York Bagel Shop and Delicatessen offered bagels with sandwich fillings—everything from cream cheese to "California-style" avocado and sprouts.[2]

Meanwhile, in far-off Jerusalem, a New Yorker, Gary Heller, concluded that Israelis too could appreciate bagels, given an opportunity. Importing frozen dough from Manhattan's Upper West Side H & H Bagels (begun in 1972 by the brothers-in-law Helmer Toro and Hector Hernandez), Heller did the final baking of his bagels in Israel. He quickly acquired orders from a national supermarket chain and from Dunkin' Donuts, which was about to open its first Tel Aviv franchise. After a long journey from Eastern European bakeries through the multi-ethnic delis of New York and the factories of a modern food industry, the bagel had arrived in the new Jewish homeland.

Heller knew that Americans transplanted to Israel would buy his bagels, but to make a profit, he had to sell 160,000 of them to native consumers, in competition with a local brand under license from Lender's Bagels. As Heller noted, Jews born in Israel (sabras) "think bagels are American, not Jewish." Israelis knew "bagele"—the closest local products—only as hard, salt-covered rounds, unlike Heller's product, or as soft sesame ellipses. And these, ironically, were baked and sold by Arabs.[3]

A grumpy cultural observer pauses at this point, well-armed for a diatribe on the annoying confusions of postmodern identities in the 1990s. It is easy to harrumph, as Octavio Paz once did, that "the melting pot is a social ideal that, when applied to culinary art, produces abominations"—bagel pizzas and bagels topped with avocado and sprouts surely qualify.[4] Paz would find a typical American's eating day an equally abominable multi-ethnic smorgasbord. The menu might include a bagel, cream cheese, and cappuccino at breakfast; a soft drink with hamburger and corn chips, or pizza and Greek salad, at lunch; and meat loaf, stir-fried "vegetables orientale" (from the frozen foods section of the supermarket), and apple pie for dinner. Wasn't eating better when delicatessens served sausages to Germans, when Bubbie purchased bagels at a kosher bakery, and when only her Jewish children and grandchildren ate them, uncorrupted by Philadelphia cream cheese? When Houston savored chili from "Tex-Mex" vendors? When only Oklahomans ate their beef and barbecue? And when neither pizza, tacos, nor bagels came from corporate "huts" or "bells," let alone a Dunkin' Donuts in Tel Aviv?

As a historian of American eating habits, I must quickly answer any potentially grumpy critics with a resounding no. The American penchant to experiment with foods, to combine and mix the foods of many cultural traditions into blended gumbos or stews, and to create "smorgasbords" is scarcely new but is rather a recurring theme in our history as eaters.

Consider, for example, the earlier history of the bagel. It is true that in the 1890s in the United States only Jews from Eastern Europe ate bagels. In thousands of nondescript bakeries—including the one founded in New Haven around 1926 by Harry Lender from Lublin, Poland—Jewish bakers sold bagels to Jewish consumers. The bagel was not a central culinary icon for Jewish immigrants; even before Polish and Russian Jews left their ethnic enclaves or ghettoes, their memories exalted gefilte fish and chicken soup prepared by their mothers, but not the humble, hard rolls purchased from the immigrant baker. As eaters, Jewish immigrants were initially far more concerned with the purity of their kosher meat, their challah, and their matzos, and with the satisfactions of their sabbath and holiday meals, than with their morning hard roll. They and their children seemed more interested in learning to use Crisco or eat egg rolls and chicken chow mein than in affirming the bagel as a symbol of Jewish life or as a contribution to American cuisine.

Still, the bagel did become an icon of urban, northeastern eating, a key ingredient of the multi-ethnic mix that in this century became known as "New York deli." The immigrant neighbors of Eastern European Jewish bakers were among the first to discover the bagel and to begin its transformation from a Jewish specialty into an American food. Unconvinced by the turn-of-the-century arguments of home economists that Americanization required them to adopt recipes for codfish and other New-England-inspired delicacies, consumers from many backgrounds began instead to sample culinary treats, like the bagel, for sale in their own multi-ethnic home cities. In New Haven, by the mid-1940s, for example, the Lenders' bakery employed six family workers, including Harry's sons Murray and Markin, who still lived at home behind the store. Hand-rolling bagels and boiling them before baking, two workers could produce about 120 bagels an hour, enough to allow the Lenders to meet expanding demand from their curious Italian, Irish, and Russian neighbors. The Lenders soon produced 200 dozen bagels daily.

No one knows who first slathered bagels with cream cheese—a product introduced and developed by English Quakers in their settlements in the Delaware Valley and Philadelphia in the eighteenth century. The blend of old and new, however, proved popular with a wide range of American consumers. With a firm grasp on regional marketing, Harry Lender's sons reorganized the family business in 1962 and decided to seek a national market. They purchased new machines that could produce 400 bagels an hour. The machines eliminated hand-rolling and substituted steaming for boiling. Flash-freezing and packaging in plastic bags for distribution to supermarkets around the country soon followed.

When union bagel bakers protested the introduction of the new machines, bagel manufacturers responded by moving production outside the Northeast. Along with the manufacturers of "Jewish" rye bread and other products common to deli display cases, the Lenders had learned "You don't have to be Jewish" to purchase and enjoy Jewish foods. With mass production for a mass market, they learned "You don't have to be Jewish" to produce them, either. In the late 1970s, Lender's was still family-owned and managed, but it employed 300 nonunionized and mainly non-Jewish workers.

In 1984 Kraft purchased Lender's as a corporate companion for its Philadelphia brand cream cheese. All over the country, consumers could now buy a totally standardized, mass-produced bagel under the Lender's label. A bagel, complained Nach Waxman, owner of a New York cookbook store, with "no crust, no character, no nothing."[5] This was a softer bagel, and—like most American breads—sweetened with sugar. Following in the tradition of the long-popular breakfast muffin, bagels emerged from factories in a variety of flavors associated with desserts and breakfast cereals—honey, raisin, blueberry, cinnamon.[6] Sun-dried tomato bagels followed in the 1990s, along with other popular flavors inspired by Mediterranean cuisines. Broney Gadman, a Long Island manufacturer of bagel-steaming equipment, believed that American consumers wanted a bland bagel.

They were "used to hamburger rolls, hot-dog buns and white bread," he explained. "They prefer a less crusty, less chewy, less tough product—You needed good teeth" to eat hand-rolled and boiled bagels.[7]

Waxman and Gadman made a sharp distinction between mass-produced factory bagels (or cinnamon and sun-dried-tomato bagels) and "the real thing." They preferred authenticity, as defined by their memories of bagels in the Jewish ghettoes of the past. As millions of Americans with no bagel eaters in their family trees snapped up Kraft's Lender's brand, and as sabras came to appreciate American bagels at Dunkin' Donuts in Tel Aviv, Bubbie's descendants, along with a multi-ethnic crowd of well-educated Americans fascinated with traditional ethnic foods, searched elsewhere for their culinary roots and a chewier bagel.

Some of them found authenticity with Bombaywala's renditions of Mrs. Katz's recipes. Others discovered they could buy "real" bagels again from the Lenders. For Murray and Markin Lender chose not to follow their family brand into employment with corporate Kraft. Instead, they opened a suburban restaurant that offered, among other things, a bagel of crust and character, ideal for Nach Waxman. A host of small businessmen like Bombaywala and the Lender brothers revived hand-rolling and boiling, sometimes in full view of their customers.

The history of the bagel suggests that Americans' shifting, blended, multi-ethnic eating habits are signs neither of postmodern decadence, ethnic fragmentation, nor corporate hegemony. If we do not understand how a bagel could sometimes be Jewish, sometimes be "New York," and sometimes be American, or why it is that Pakistanis now sell bagels to both Anglos and Tejanos in Houston, it is in part because we have too hastily assumed that our tendency to cross cultural boundaries in order to eat ethnic foods is a recent development—and a culinary symptom of all that has gone wrong with contemporary culture.

It is not. The bagel tells a different kind of American tale. It highlights ways that the production, exchange, marketing, and consumption of food have generated new identities—for foods and eaters alike. Looking at bagels in this light, we see that they became firmly identified as "Jewish" only as Jewish bakers began selling them to their multi-ethnic urban neighbors. When bagels emerged from ghetto stores as a Jewish novelty, bagels with cream cheese quickly became a staple of the cuisine known as "New York deli," and was marketed and mass-produced throughout the country under this new regional identity. When international trade brought bagels to Israel, they acquired a third identity as "American." And finally, coming full circle, so to speak, the bagel's Americanization sent purists off in search of bagels that seemed more authentically "New York Jewish."

If the identity of bagels emerged from an evolving marketplace, can we say the same of bagel eaters' identities? What, after all, does "what we eat" tell us about "who we are"? Again, too easily, we assume a recent, sharp departure into culinary eclecticism or consumerist individualism from the natural, conservative, and ethnically rigid eating habits of the past. In fact, eating habits changed and evolved long before the rise of a modern consumer market for food. Human eating habits originate in a paradoxical, and perhaps universal, tension between a preference for the culinarily familiar and the equally human pursuit of pleasure in the forms of culinary novelty, creativity, and variety.

Neither the anthropologist nor the man on the street doubts that humans can be picky eaters, or that humans can exhibit considerable conservatism in their food choices. If you doubt popular wisdom, imagine serving a plate of tripe, corn fungus, or caterpillars at a diner in Garrison Keillor's Lake Woebegone. Psychologists tell us that food and language are the cultural traits humans learn first, and the ones that they change with the greatest reluctance. Humans cannot easily lose their accents when they learn new languages after the age of about twelve; similarly, the food they ate as children forever defines familiarity and comfort.

But cultural conservatism, while it cannot be ignored, cannot explain the history of the bagel, where instead we see evidence of human adaptability and curiosity. Cooks know this combination well: they substitute ingredients when necessary, even in well-loved recipes; they "play with their food" on occasion, just for the pleasure of finding new tastes. When people of differing foodways come together, whether cooks or merely eaters, they will almost invariably peek into one another's kitchens. They will not like all they find, but they are usually curious and excited to try some of it.

Two closely related histories—of recurring human migrations and of changes in the production and marketing of food—help us to understand why and how American eating habits, and identities, have evolved over time. The migrations sparked by the European empires of the sixteenth and seventeenth centuries mixed the foodways of Spanish and indigenous Americans in today's Southwest and Florida; English, French, Dutch, or German culinary traditions were combined with Indian practices in the Northeast; and African, English, Scotch-Irish, French, and native American eating habits influenced the cuisine of the Southeast. During the long nineteenth century, successive waves of Irish, British, German, Scandinavians, Slavs, Italians, Jews, Chinese, Japanese, and Mexicans changed the face, and the eating patterns, of American farmlands and cities. In the early decades of this century, though restrictive laws lessened immigration from Europe and Asia, internal migrations of southern white and black sharecroppers to Detroit and New York, and of foreclosed "Okies" and "Arkies" to the West, transferred eating habits from one American region to another. And in today's world, again, new immigrants from Asia, the Caribbean, and Latin America bring the smells and tastes of their homeland cuisines to Miami, New York, Minneapolis, and Los Angeles.

Four hundred years ago climate and terrain placed harsh restraints on local eaters, reinforcing regional identities, and even today we do not expect Iowans to fish for cod, or eat much of it. The United States remains a nation of many regional environments, and its culinary and ethnic history has been shaped by regionalism, reinforced by territorial expansion from the Atlantic to the Pacific, and then beyond to Alaska and Hawaii. Already in 1550, however, sugar traveled the world because merchants could make huge profits by offering it for sale in nontropical climes. Today, changing technology, the use of fertilizer, and plant and animal breeding have vastly altered any local environment's impact on farming and consuming. Although regional eating habits persist in the United States, they are no longer straightforward reflections of a seaside location or a prairie continental climate.

If our eating is more homogeneous today than in the past, we can thank (or blame) a national marketplace through which the standardized foods of modern food industries have circulated. As farms gave way to "factories in the field," as huge canneries replaced women's domestic labor, and as the corner grocery store gradually gave way to supermarkets, the most ambitious businessmen, regardless of cultural origin, dreamed of capturing regional, and then national, markets by producing a few food items in massive quantities. Corporate food business fostered standardized foods and national connections, while migrations repeatedly introduced new sources of culinary diversity. Migrations also produced new "communities of consumption," which generated small businesses to serve their taste for distinctive foods.[8] Today, food corporations position themselves to compete in a wide variety of market segments defined by ethnicity, gender, age, and income. Yet their most successful competitors are small businessmen like Ghulam Bombaywala and the Lenders, whom many consumers trust to deliver "the real thing."

Commercial food exchanges neither created nor eliminated the fundamental tension between our longing for both familiar and novel foods. While mass production delivered huge quantities of a few standardized, processed foods, expanding markets also linked producers and consumers of diverse backgrounds and tastes, opening opportunities for new blends, new juxtapositions, new borrowing. Food businesses large and small have lured adventurous consumers with novelties while soothing others with traditional foods. American eaters' search for the familiar and the novel became matters of consumer choice, just as producers' and retailers' experiments with both innovation and traditional techniques became marketing strategies.

It is easiest to see how food choices reflect the eater's identity when we focus on culinary conservatism. Humans cling tenaciously to familiar foods because they become associated with nearly every dimension of human social and cultural life. Whether in New Guinea or New Bedford, humans share particular foods with families and friends; they pursue good health through unique diets; they pass on food lore, and create stories and myths about food's meaning and taste; they celebrate rites of passage and religious beliefs with distinctive dishes. Food thus entwines intimately with much that makes a culture unique, binding taste and satiety to group loyalties. Eating habits both symbolize and mark the boundaries of cultures. Scholars and ordinary people alike have long seen food habits, both positively and negatively, as concrete symbols of human culture and identity. When we want to celebrate, or elevate, our own group, we usually praise its superior cuisine. And when we want to demean one another, often we turn to eating habits; in the United States we have labeled

Germans as "krauts," Italians as "spaghetti-benders," Frenchmen as "frogs," and British as "limeys."

To understand changing American identities, we must explore also the symbolic power of food to reflect cultural or social affinities in moments of change or transformation. Today, as in the days of the Columbian exchanges, Americans eat what students of linguistics call a "creole," or what cooks describe as a gumbo or a stew. We quite willingly "eat the other"—or at least some parts of some others, some of the time. Eating habits like these suggest tolerance and curiosity, and a willingness to digest, and to make part of one's individual identity, the multi-ethnic dishes Paz deplored. As food consumers, Americans seem as interested in idiosyncratic and individualistic affiliations to the foodways of their neighbors as they are in their own ethnic and regional roots. Ultimately, then, as students of American eating we must not only understand what we eat, and celebrate the many ethnic reflections of who we are, but we must also understand the roots of our multi-ethnic creole foodways, and ask of them, too, "If we are what we eat, who are we?"

CHAPTER ONE

Colonial Creoles

In 1770, in South Carolina, Harriott Horry wrote down her instructions for preparing "pompion [pumpkin] chips." "Shave your Pompion thin with a plain and cut it in slips about the width of your finger, put shreds of Lemon peel among it, wet your sugar with orange Juice and boil it into Syrup. Then put in your chips and lemon peel and let them boil till done."[1] If we were to follow Horry's recipe today, we would probably call the product pumpkin marmalade.

Horry's was a thoroughly European technique for preserving fruit in sugar, but it made use of a North American fruit—the pumpkin—much prized by natives but unknown to the English before they came to the Americas. Horry's recipe was also distinctive to its region. It included tropical fruits, reminding us that the Carolinas of the eighteenth century were the northernmost reaches of the British Caribbean, with which it shared a plantation-based economy and a semitropical climate.

In 1796, nine hundred miles north of Horry, in New Haven, Amelia Simmons also used "Pompkin," but she put in a pastry shell. Her instructions called for "one quart stewed and strained, 3 pints cream, 9 beaten eggs, sugar, mace, nutmet and ginger, laid into paste no. 7 or 3 [pastry recipes presented earlier in her collection] and with a dough spurt, cross and chequer it, and baked in dishes three quarters of an hour."[2] Simmons's dish is quite identifiable as pumpkin pie, well known to many Americans today as a treat for Thanksgiving—a national holiday commemorating the survival of English settlers, with the assistance of Native Americans, in New England.

Simmons's recipe, like Horry's, applied an English technique (pie-making) to local ingredients. But unlike bakers of today's pumpkin pies, Simmons used cream and eggs lavishly, while treating sugar as a minor ingredient, just one of the spices ("sugar, mace, nutmet and ginger") that flavored her pie. Here we see the influence of region again. Cows, and dairy production, flourished in New England's cool climate, as they did not in coastal South Carolina.

The recipes of Horry and Simmons reflect the distinctive environments and economies of America's many regions. But colonial cooks did not limit themselves to local products, although these were the main ingredients. Long before the thirteen North American states formed their "more perfect union," colonial eating had already become a creole blend of the products and traditions of many interacting cultures from around the world. Unlike Horry, whose flavorings came from the tropical Caribbean, Simmons used the spices of the East, available in port cities like Boston through the merchant trade of the British Empire. As every school child once learned, Europeans' tastes for these spices, first acquired from the Arab world during the Crusades of the Middle Ages, played a far from indirect role in motivating their exploratory sea voyages outward around Africa and westward into the Atlantic. Recipes like Horry's and Simmons's indicate that trade in food—sugar, spices, and tropical fruits—was an integral part of Europe's conquest of the New World.

Within a century of Columbus's arrival, European ships were already transporting the curious plants of the Americas—potatoes, corn, tomatoes, peppers, and peanuts—to Europe, Africa, and Asia. But trade routes are usually a two-way street. Outward from Europe and Africa, flocks of chickens and herds of pigs, cattle, and sheep, along with the seeds of common weeds and food crops (coffee, rice, sesame, sugar, yams), reached the Americas and the Pacific world. Sugar cane, transported initially from Asia throughout the Mediterranean, eventually transformed the ecology and economy of the islands of the Caribbean, while dramatically altering the tastes of Europe and the Americas.

Here was an era of rapid dietary change, and not just in the American colonies. By the eighteenth century the Aztecs were eating pork, the Iroquois were drinking rum, and West Africans were enjoying corn. By the nineteenth century the Chinese were consuming sweet potatoes and pea-nuts, the Irish had abandoned their traditional porridge and bread for potatoes, and Italians had built a new cuisine around tomatoes. Most people were not well informed about the sources of their new foods: the Italians, for example, called corn "Turkish grain," and other Europeans—thinking that corn originated in Africa—called it "Guinea corn."

The rise of a global food marketplace did not, however, produce culinary homogeneity. Crops and animals flourished selectively in differing envi-ronments. Local foodways easily incorporated some new ingredients, while eaters adamantly rejected others. Peoples around the world could take the exact same imported ingredients—tomatoes or sugar or peppers—and prepare them in wildly diverging ways, depending upon their distinctive tastes, cooking techniques, and native staples, which might be as different as rice, corn, rye, and cassava.

Though very much a part of this global exchange of foods, many Ameri-cans provisioned themselves by hunting, raising, gathering, and processing most of the foods they ate—much more so than most Americans do today. Africans and Englishmen alike incorporated maple syrup, beans, turkeys, berries, and other local foodstuffs into their traditional meals, adapting and inventing as they went along. Few Americans in the colonial era depended on the marketplace for their major staples. Yet, because trans-portation across oceans sometimes occurred with greater ease than trans-portation overland within small regions, many colonists sought special pleasures and familiar treats from their European homelands at stores or taverns.

Colonial America provides an excellent starting place for a study of multi-ethnic American eating and its relationship to commerce and iden-tity. In it we can see American eating habits before modern advertising and other marketing strategies pressured consumers always to "want some-thing new." The colonial era provides evidence of the pleasure most peo-ple took not only in consuming the familiar comfort foods of their child-hoods but in adopting new foods and incorporating new ingredients and techniques into their traditions. As the blending of European and native foods in Horry's and Simmons's recipes makes plain, curiosity about new ingredients required no extensive market exchanges—just a local abundance of pumpkin. Furthermore, the market exchanges of the colonial era as often delivered familiar items as novelties, especially to European colonists who were far from their homelands and unable to reproduce all the agricultural and herding practices that their traditional cuisine required.

In colonial America, consumer choice did not yet mediate the linkage of food and human identity as completely as it does in our own times. Necessity more than choice dictated ingredients and methods of preparation. But food nevertheless symbolized changing identities even then. In 1943 Stephen Vincent Benét poetically imagined Europeans newly arrived in the New World undergoing an immediate, if unreflective, shift in their identities. As they ate "the white corn-kernels parched in the sun . . . they knew it not, but they'd not be English again."[3] Indeed, Amelia Simmons's cookbook is considered by historians to be the first American cookbook not because it was the first one published or distributed on American soil but because it is the first to make use of native ingredients like corn and pumpkin. Benét, furthermore, might just as easily have written a similar poem about America's original inhabitants and their first taste of pork. The Columbian exchanges of the colonial era quickly blended the meat of the Old World with the grain and vegetables of the New: their preparation, however, varied from region to region, and from ethnic group to ethnic group.

W hat made American creole dishes vary so by region? Beginning with the founding of St. Augustine, three expanding European empires—centered in France, England, and Spain—pushed their way from opposing directions into the territories already inhabited by approximately four million natives on the continent of North America. A fourth empire, the Dutch, took up temporary residence along the Hudson River. Dutch and English traders in turn transported ten million West Africans to the Americas over the next two hundred years, selling most of them into slavery. All of these groups had developed traditions of eating that marked them as culturally different one from the other. All, on the other hand, had a recent history of selectively adapting new foods even before they confronted one another on North American soil.

As eaters deeply familiar with their natural environments, Native Americans enjoyed tremendous advantages in the culinary exchanges of the colonial period: centuries of adaptation to a variety of natural environments in North America had already shaped their foodways. If any group involved in the Columbian exchanges might have held firmly to tradition, it was Native Americans, with their vast knowledge of their own land and climate.

In most places in North America, native survival had depended on the successful cultivation of the "three sisters": corn, beans, and squashes. Of these, corn and squashes, including the pumpkin, seemed most distinctively American to newer arrivals, since they were unknown in Europe. Corn is a remarkable grain: it has been called "a machine of marvelous efficiency," so bountifully does the plant produce digestible calories from even small tracts of land, and under a wide range of ecological conditions.[4] From Mexico's central valley, corn had spread as far as the eastern woodlands but had faltered in the arid highlands of northern New Mexico and southern Colorado. Nor could corn prosper along the Pacific coast, on the dry prairies of the Great Plains, or in the coldest reaches of northern Minnesota or Maine. Instead of cultivating corn, nomadic natives in California gathered nuts and seeds; those on the Great Plains stalked herds of bison for their meat and hides; and tribes in Oregon and Maine made fish and shellfish a major part of their diet.

Still, corn was North America's staple grain, providing two thirds of Native Americans' calories and influencing every dimension of their cultures. Among the Pueblos in their large New Mexico villages, corn consumption and spirituality were one, for the Pueblo dwellers believed that Mother Earth had literally made humans out of corn, with the help of the male forces of sun and rain. For the Iroquois in the Northeast, as well as the Pueblos, corn cultivation facilitated dense settlement—in large palisaded villages, surrounded by up to one hundred acres of corn fields. Settled agriculture, corn cultivation, and dense settlements of related clans established an important precondition for the complex political confederations of the Iroquois, a form of political organization unimaginable among more nomadic hunters and gatherers without a corn diet.

Almost everywhere, it was women's responsibility to cultivate and process the corn. Natives in the East prepared the grain in an astonishing number of ways, from breadlike concoctions and popped corn, through puddings, dumplings, porridges, stews, and thin, gruel-like drinks. Still, nutritional variety was sought by hunting and gathering wild meats, fish, fowl, insects, seeds, berries, nuts, oils, roots, and vegetables. Animal foods, hunted by men—meat and, in some areas, fish—generally enjoyed higher status as foods, but women's gathering of vegetables was more important as a source of dietary variety. A list of the wild greens gathered by Iroquois women would include milkweed stems, immature flower clusters, marigold, waterleaf, yellow dock, pigweed, lambsquarters, mustard, purslane, dandelion, burdock, nettle, skunk cabbage, leek, wild garlic, sensitive fern, and others.[5] Adding fungus varieties, roots, and berries would easily expand the list to several hundred items, all eaten over the course of a year. Few modern eaters consume such a wide range of plants, fruits, and animals, even when provisioned by a vast international or multi-ethnic marketplace.

Natives' love of variety fostered definitions of "good taste" that differed somewhat by tribe and even more noticeably by region. In the northern forests, natives flavored their staples with the sap from maples and with animal fats and greases (especially bear grease). In New Mexico and Arizona, by contrast, natives developed a special taste for six colors of corn (yellow, white, blue, black, red, speckled), and four varieties (flint, dent, pop, sweet). Processing their corn in a multitude of ways—adding ash to make hominies, grinding different varieties to different consistencies of meal, eating corn green, fresh, parched, boiled, baked, steamed, and roasted—fundamentally altered the texture and taste of their staple grain.

Women in the Southwest worked with their metate (grinding stone) and comal (flat rock griddle) to produce a wide variety of flat corn crisps and softer breads later called tortillas and piki breads. Beans of various colors, shapes, and sizes supplemented corn as staple ingredients, as did local game—rabbits, boars, snakes, deer, antelope, beaver—and wild vegetables, fruits, and seeds. Fifty different varieties of wild seed grains, along with piñon nuts, sunflower seeds, curly dock, lambsquarters, wild mustard, purslane, wild celery, yucca fruits, prickly pear, juniper, and chokecherries, rounded out their diet. Natives also brewed an alcoholic drink similar to the agave-based pulque of Mexico.

While corn provided the basis for both eastern and southwestern foodways, environmental variation thus rendered native diets quite different in the two places. Though varied, natives' comfortable subsistence regularly faced harsh challenges. However sophisticated their familiarity with the natural environment, they could scarcely preclude natural and often extreme fluctuations in food supplies. During good harvest and hunting seasons, natives transformed bounty into occasions for pleasurable gift-giving and overeating. Seasonal surpluses expressed power, as tribal leaders distributed foods or as women working in communal groups prepared festivals featuring massive consumption of desirable foods. Among the Sake Indians, for example, guests greeted the chief sponsoring a festival by saying, "Let your guests die of vomiting, chief, Let your guests die of overfeeding, true chief."[6]

Bounty gave way to want frequently enough that Indian groups developed strategies for managing it. The Pueblos in the Southwest stored up to three years of dried grain underground to prepare for natural fluctuations. Other tribes, like the Ojibway, migrated seasonally through their environmentally varied homeland in order to ensure sufficient food throughout the year. The southern Ojibway trapped and hunted in south Minnesota forests from November until February; in March they drained sap for sugar; in April they traveled to lakes farther north to fish for suckers during their annual run. Returning to their home base south of St. Cloud in May, they cultivated corn, potatoes, and squash, and in August they moved to northern rice camps, harvesting and then duck hunting, before again returning south to the forests and hills for the winter meat hunt.

In a limited number of cases, Native Americans turned to trade to solve their food shortages. The most likely tribes to enter into trade were hunters and gatherers who raised no corn and who lived in particularly cold or dry environments that posed regular, and even predictable, shortages of food. In the Southwest, the roving Comanches and Utes came to Taos and Abiquiú, and Pueblo settlements, to barter their buffalo, elk, and deer hides for corn flour and woven blankets. In New England, upland tribes exchanged acorns for the shellfish found in abundance along the coasts; Indians from northern Maine also regularly exchanged fur and skins for the corn and beans raised by their southern neighbors.

Europeans and Africans faced much larger challenges than natives simply because they had to adapt to a new environment; their survival required it. Europeans were advantaged in many ways by their material and technical culture—guns, ships, animal husbandry, agriculture, salting and preserving, ironware. But the flora, fauna, and native diet of this new land was quite unlike their own. Since they were already accustomed to trading for some part of their food supply, simple common sense would predict that European eating would change more quickly, and more thoroughly, than that of North America's natives during the colonial era.

Still, in most cases Europeans settled in regions not totally unlike their home country, at least in terms of land and climate. The French and English had left behind a land of forests, with changing seasons and a climate that already supported permanent agriculture; the eastern sea-board of the New World was quite similar. The Spanish in the north of Mexico encountered a drier, warmer treeless environment more familiar to them than it might have been to residents of northern France or southern England. While this rough "match" of settlers and environment was not enough to eliminate all the challenges of settlement, it did ease European adjustments, facilitating the introduction and cultivation of familiar foods.

Today we see sharp contrasts between the plain food of the English and the haute cuisine of the French. In fact, the humble English and French who settled the East Coast of North America brought with them remarkably similar experiences as agriculturalists and eaters from relatively cool, damp climates. Few Englishmen or Frenchmen knew much about hunting or fishing from their homelands—these were aristocratic privileges—but most were quite familiar with a mixed, and somewhat similar, agriculture based on grain, beans and peas, dairying, and animal husbandry. Settlers from the south of England and from France's Atlantic provinces both ate a largely wet diet of potages or soups, porridges of grain and beans, stews of meats and vegetables, and breads and dairy products, mainly butter and cheese (called "white meat" in England). The better off and urban among them ate more bread, whiter bread, and more meat, cheese, and butter. With a few important exceptions, English and French traditions of mixed agriculture proved quite transplantable to the East Coast of North America, allowing European settlers to continue to eat many of their familiar foods.

But not all. The English drank more ale and beer, while the French consumed more brandy and wine, and settlers from both backgrounds were broadly familiar with brewing, fermenting, and distilling to supplement their diet. In England, wine had recently become popular among urban and elite drinkers. Unfortunately, religious wars and the accompanying destruction of England's monasteries, where most wine had been produced, left English drinkers in the uncomfortable position of having to import wine from their imperial competitors, France, Portugal, and Spain. English mercantilists hoped that the Americas would become a dependable supplier of wines. In this, however, they would be disappointed.

The Spanish, too, quickly saw in the New World possible solutions to dietary change at home. Although altered somewhat by years of Arab occupation, the Spanish diet in the late Middle Ages still reflected the grain, oil, and wine culinary complex spread by the Romans throughout their Mediterranean empire centuries before. Wheat bread had been the staff of Spanish life for centuries, supplemented by oil, olives, wine, garbanzos, fish, and fowl. Arab conquest had added a taste for sugar, spices, and dried fruits. In the sixteenth century, as Spain sought land and power in the Americas, the rise of extensive sheep herding to supply Flanders' expanding textile industry sparked a precipitous decline in Spanish acreage devoted to wheat production. One consequence was that poorer Spaniards soon found themselves eating gruels and breads of lesser grains (notably barley) to survive. The Spanish would find the dry climate of their new homes suitable for herding and for the cultivation of grains, including wheat and barley, especially as they ventured northward from Mexico's central valley into what is now southern California and the Southwest of the United States.

Far to the south of these European settlers, the Africans who would be snatched away to work on the plantations of the English colonies had already adapted their eating to New World crops before they left home. By 1700 West Africans regularly ate and cultivated corn, cassava, peppers, sweet potatoes, pineapples, and peanuts from the Americas as well as rice and coconuts from Asia. These relatively new imports supplemented native staples like millet, beans, watermelons, palm oil, and yams. Provisioners of slave ships in Africa often loaded foods of Central and South American origin to feed slaves en route, thus facilitating their transplantation to North America's warm southeastern colonies. Africans rarely enjoyed much control over their destinations in the Americas. But Europeans enslaved them in part because they believed Africans adjusted with greater ease and could perform more work in warm climates. Thus, like the English, French, and Spanish, African traditions of agriculture and their foodways prepared them relatively well for provisioning themselves (and their owners) in the tropical and subtropical regions of the New World.

Of all the groups involved in the settlement of the Americas, Europeans and Africans had depended most heavily on trade and commerce to provide at least some of their food in the Old World. Leaving to settle the New World, Europeans worried about traveling well beyond familiar supply lines. One guide warned, "You shall meete neither markets nor fayres to buy what you want. Therefore be sure to furnish yourselves with things fitting . . . as meale for bread, malt for drinke." Another advisor recommended packing "8 Bushels of meale, 2 Bushels of pease, 2 Bushels of Otemeale, 1 Gallon of Aquavitae, 1 Gallon of Oyle, 2 Gallons of Veinegar, 1 Firkin of Butter; also Cheese, Bacon, Sugar, Pepper, Cloves, Mace, Cinnamon, Nutmegs and Fruit." The *Mayflower* itself carried "15,000 brown biscuit, 5000 white (crackers); half-cooked bacon, dried salted codfish, smoked herring; cabbages, turnips, onions, parsnips." By journey's end, its diminishing human cargo had devoured these and had started to eat the less desirable stores of oatmeal, pease puddings, and beer.[7] As a wry food historian later noted, "When the Pilgrims landed at Plymouth in 1620 they brought with them European habits of eating but most of the food they had carried with them was gone."[8] Since trade with the homeland was not a viable option, at least not right away, these settlers had to learn, and learn quickly, how to provision themselves in a new world.

Most of the early English settlers faced a brief starving time amidst the natural plenty of the Americas. Everywhere, Europeans noted the bounty of American nature, yet hesitated to partake of it, even when natives offered food and hospitality, as they often did. Although starving, the Englishmen of Jamestown at first refused to eat oysters. The missionary fathers in the Southwest found the Indians' consumption of grubs and insects revolting. Hunger, not the search for novelty or pleasure, clearly motivated Europeans' earliest exchanges with Native Americans. But even then culture imposed limits on what Europeans would accept. A

French Jesuit priest, otherwise predisposed to study and adopt elements of native culture, found some native cooking techniques unacceptable: "When they have filled their kettle with meat, they boil it, at most, three-quarters of an hour . . . Each one bites into this meat as one would into a piece of bread . . . they very soon perceived my repugnance." (The food this missionary preferred was also native, however—a simple corn broth sweetened with maple sugar.)[9] Catawba hospitality in the Southeast similarly nauseated Europeans: it included "fawns taken out of the Doe's Bellies, and boil'd in the same slimy Bags Nature had placed them in" and rabbits boiled with their hair and guts intact.[10]

Natives, who usually were spared the motive of starvation, had less reason to be interested in Europeans' foods, at least initially. In fact, they seemed far more attracted to the weapons and cooking pots of the Spanish and English than to the foods cooked in them. Indians enthusiastically adopted European horses to replace dogs as beasts of burdens, but they had less use for cows, their meat or their milk. As late as the nineteenth century, one Pacific Coast Indian boy described disgracing himself in his father's eyes when he threatened to vomit after a white explorer offered him rice cooked in milk.[11]

Where they monopolized power, European culinary conservatism could, on occasion, overwhelm the natives' superior knowledge of American environments. In Spanish New Mexico, Texas, and California, Franciscan padres forced natives to tend their European herds and crops, much as they forced them to build their churches. Franciscans introduced European ox, sheep, and pigs to the natives for food; they reserved chickens for their own consumption. In this case, however, their Indian workers cultivated—and also quickly learned to eat—wheat and Spanish fruits, including apricots, peaches, and plums. Spanish soldiers also demanded regular tribute from the natives in the form of corn, which they ate when wheat supplies dwindled. Still, in California, at the twenty-one missions started between 1769 and 1823, native workers raised four times as much wheat as maize; they herded over 150,000 cattle and 150,000 sheep but only 839 swine. California's Franciscans also introduced grapes and vineyards, planting the so-called mission grape from 1767 and producing the wine that was so much a part of the Spanish diet. The Fathers—many of them Germans—and their native workers became the only successful vintners in colonial North America, trading their wines (which were greatly in demand) within the Spanish empire.

Because English settlers lacked a strong desire to live among the natives, cultural conservatism might have brought an end to Indian trade on the East Coast once the Europeans' starving time had passed. But even as European farming in the East became more self-sufficient, the small but growing urban population, combined with Europeans' long history of obtaining at least some of their food through trade, encouraged the colonists to continue to look to natives as provisioners and to exchange what they could for the foods natives could grow. For their part, Indians showed little reluctance to trade with Europeans. Even in a world dominated by subsistence production, trade—whether in the form of barter or monetary exchanges—became the most common way for new foods and cooking techniques to spread, however gradually, from one group to another. Trade facilitated, if it did not always motivate, the creation of America's first multi-ethnic regional cuisines, especially the incorporation of alcohol and European meats into native diets and the incorporation of corn and squashes into European ones.

Native Americans responded quickly to Europeans' continued demand for food, expanding their cultivation of corn in order to provision their new neighbors. In the Southeast, the Cherokees rapidly learned the rules of commercial exchange; when they sold corn, they sold it at a high price even while continuing to give away large quantities of corn to guests, as an act of hospitality. In New England, settlers learned to hunt and fish right away, but they needed more time to adapt familiar grains to a new environment; Massachusetts Bay acquired 100 bushels of corn from natives in 1630; four years later they bought 500 bushels from the Narragansetts alone. In Spanish Florida as late as the 1780s, Seminoles and Creeks organized corn, rice, and ground nut plantations to sell food to the Europeans. As natives devoted ever more time to corn cultivation, they abandoned their seasonal migrations, and they too began to eat more of the corn they raised and stored.

On the East Coast, Europeans also eagerly sought a marketable food surplus for trade with their homelands. Breton, Portuguese, and Bristol fisherman had begun visiting the coastal waters of New England even before 1500. Fishing for the Lenten markets of Europe then drew Europeans to the Gulf of the St. Lawrence River. After 1497 European fishermen began to process and dry fish onshore and to export it to the Caribbean islands, where it was exchanged for sugar, molasses, and rum to feed the growing slave population. In Massachusetts, 10 percent of the population combined farming with fishing. Fishing in turn encouraged Europeans to depend still longer on native food provisioners. Thus in Northeast fishing camps, as in Florida, food became a source of wealth and, as a historian has noted, "Corn was the vital golden fuel of the invaders, even if it was not their primary objective."[12] Eating corn raised by natives allowed newer arrivals to export fish, and to finance their own settlement.

The French and English fur trade encouraged similar food exchanges. In the North, the French fur trade drew traders and voyagers far from their own provisioners. Consequently, native women increasingly farmed and gathered for the traders, while native men hunted for them. In some parts of northern New England, natives themselves bought corn supplies for winter from other tribes, freeing the purchasers to trap and hunt the furs European traders desired. If nothing else, the fur trade created a constant incentive for natives to modify their traditional habits of subsistence. It also quickly introduced them to a European food they enjoyed more than many others—alcohol.

In the Southeast, traders sought deer hides rather than fur, while the natives wanted weapons, traps, kettles, clothing, and alcohol. And they expanded their hunts into month-long campaigns in order to participate in this exchange. Cherokee women in the Carolinas provisioned the English with corn, while trying to prevent soldiers from acquiring land to raise their own supplies. At the same time, the Creeks in Georgia and Florida became "a vast forest proletariat," producing furs and skins in exchange for guns, horses, and liquor.[13] Native women intermarried with trappers and traders and learned to churn butter and make cheese and to prepare pork and beef instead of venison and bear. They then introduced natives to European imports like chocolate, coffee, sugar, apples, peaches, pies, puddings, and pastries.

While native women learned to enjoy European sweets, native men hunted and traded, in part to obtain alcohol. Among the Creeks, Europeans reported, love of spirits knew no bounds, and dependency on alcohol made them ever more dependent on trade. Choctaw men spoke freely of their love of spirits, comparing their desire for imported liquor to their sexual need for women. As one historian noted, the Choctaws, like the Creeks, soon "hunted for liquor. Drunkenness was the final product of their hunt."[14]

Only in the Southwest, where natives had long brewed their own alcohol, did trade in skins produce no obvious rise in either alcohol abuse or social disorder. Having consumed fermented cactus drinks for centuries, natives there had less incentive to exchange skins for alcohol, and they had developed their own cultural and social customs to accommodate and contain the negative consequences of alcohol consumption. No censorious Europeans in the West resembled Ben Franklin, who saw natives, unlike Europeans, as "extreamly apt to get drunk" and to become "very quarrelsome and disorderly." Eastern natives recognized rum as "the water that takes away one's wits." At the same time, they found in intoxication a sense of power. Alcohol allowed natives to enter states of delirium and trance which many perceived as spiritually elevating and empowering.[15] Women, however, quickly learned to associate male drinking with sexual and physical violence, and they often fled from all-male drinking parties. Alcohol was attractive to the men of the eastern woodlands in ways that the European grains, and even many European meats, were not.

In addition to trade between Europeans and Native Americans, trade among different European groups also increased gradually as colonists found marketable food products. After 1700, the coastal Carolinas began exporting rice, a new grain for most English eaters; Carolinians and their slaves consumed 20 percent of the local crop, while exporting 70 percent to England and 10 percent to the Mediterranean. The Carolinas also exported beef cattle to the Caribbean sugar islands, in exchange for tropical fruits, sugar, and rum. New England exported fish, along with some cheese and beef, to the British Caribbean and imported corn and wheat from Virginia and the Middle Colonies. Butter and cheese remained important imports into this region, and so much rum and tea entered New England from the British Empire that fewer New Englanders than Englishmen brewed or made cider at home. The rich agricultural lands of New York, Pennsylvania, and Maryland specialized in the commercial farming of grains, and exported corn, wheat, and rye to the Dutch, French, and English sugar islands in the Caribbean, as well as to New England.

Stores, taverns, and urban markets became centers of food trade for Europeans. In the North, every village had its little store, where women traded salted, pickled, and smoked meat, eggs, butter, and cheese for salt, molasses, sugar, rum, tea, coffee, chocolate, and small household necessities. In New England, maple sugar was an important trade item. In the most rural areas, however, subsistence farming prevailed, and local stores sold only imported goods like spices, tea, sugar, and rum.

Taverns were just as important as stores, and perhaps more common. Alcohol addiction was widespread among Europeans throughout the colonial era, and the tavern provided drink, conviviality, and the only place where travelers could purchase a meal—usually simple and poorly prepared—while on the road. Europeans showed little concern about their own drinking excesses, since they believed they possessed what James Boswell called "the art of getting drunk"—which Indians did not.[16]

By the eighteenth century, coffee houses offered nonalcoholic alternatives in the largest cities, but these never became as popular in Boston or Philadelphia as they did in London or Paris. In 1773 New York had 396 licensed taverns, and many illegal "groggeries" sold liquor. Alexander Hamilton estimated that Americans consumed on average 2.5 gallons yearly of alcohol, while other estimates after 1800 were as high as 7.5 gallons.[17] Although the Puritans in Massachusetts emphasized moderation and self-control in drink, Boston in 1714, with only 10,000 inhabitants, had 34 "ordinaries" and 41 retailers of liquor. English settlers consumed alcohol in the form of rum and other hard liquors; punch, a drink which originated in British India but whose American version incorporated tropical juices and rums produced in the Caribbean, also became popular in the eighteenth century.

With its populations of subsistence farmers, the British colonies in North America never developed true market towns on the British model. Still, urban dwellers had better access to the food marketplace and to the variety it could deliver. Only major coastal cities like Philadelphia, New York, Charleston, and Boston created extensive home markets for farm products. In New England and New York, market days and informal huckstering door to door became common, as small populations of truck farmers (many of them women specializing in dairy production) came in from outlying districts. In Charleston, it was African-American slaves, working on their own account and with the approval of their owners, who provisioned urban consumers with fish and garden vegetables. New York already had three meat markets by 1830. Charleston had two markets by 1800, one for meat and one for general produce. In the Chesapeake, by contrast, chain stores opened by Scottish traders connected international, regional, and local traders in food, while in the Carolinas "factors"—again, usually British or Scottish immigrants connected through family ties to London merchants—purchased planters' crops and ordered and delivered their tropical food supplies, wines, and liquors.

The expansion of trade within and between the colonies was considerable. It guaranteed the circulation of at least some crops and foods well beyond their geographical origins, and well beyond the cultural group most familiar with their cultivation, processing, and cooking. Patterns of trade alone suggest that French, English, Spanish, African, and native had ample opportunities to begin tasting and experimenting with one another's foods.

B y the time of U.S. independence, we have even better evidence that, indeed, all Americans ate hybrid, creole diets that blended the techniques and ingredients of two or more cultures. Each colonial creole diet was, however, distinctive to its particular region. Within each region, furthermore, ethnic variations sometimes remained quite pronounced.

The regional cuisine of the American Southwest—"El Norte" of the Spanish Empire until 1821—reflected its status as a frontier outpost. Although Spanish missionaries introduced wheat quite early to the Southwest, the grain made few inroads among the Pueblo-dwelling natives during the colonial period; in fact, the Pueblos hated wheat, which symbolized Spanish conquest, and they burned the missions' wheat crops during their last major revolt in 1680 against Spanish domination. By contrast, the Pueblos readily adopted the chile peppers brought north from central Mexico by Hispanic settlers, the iron cooking pots, ovens, and garbanzos from Spain, and the many domestic and herd animals introduced by the missions. Pork soon became a stuffing for tamales; pigs feet, rinds or ribs, and beef tripe found their way into stews made with posole (limed hominy). The Pueblo Indians, who had enjoyed sweet fruits and vegetables from desert plants, also quickly adopted Spanish melons (which they called horse pumpkins), and by 1700 they had even incorporated European-origin fruits into their religious rituals.

Of peoples native to Arizona and New Mexico, the Zunis, Pimas, and Papagos seem to have adopted European wheat most readily, perhaps because they lived at altitudes or in climates where corn was more difficult to cultivate. They prepared the wheat into mush and unleavened breads baked on a stone griddle—the forerunners of today's flour tortillas—and eventually developed their own leavenings (mainly soured dough) for wheaten adobe breads and sweets baked in local horno (bee-hive-shaped) ovens. Even before white settlers arrived in Pima territory, in fact, the Pimas may have acquired wheat from Mexico and had to some extent begun to substitute this new grain for the corn they had raised, with irrigation, for centuries. The missionary Father Kino certainly distributed wheat among them in the 1700s. Wheat became popular enough that it eventually distinguished Sonoran and Southwest cuisines from that of central Mexico; scholars have to remind modern readers that corn once absolutely dominated diets in this region, so completely has the wheat-flour tortilla come to symbolize the cuisine of this borderland.[18]

No other native people of the Southwest changed their way of life and eating habits as extensively in response to colonial change and exchange as did the Navajo. Originally sedentary farmers and hunters, the Navajo increasingly dedicated themselves to herding European animals after 1750. Pastoralism gave the Navajo foods to exchange with the Pueblos for corn, which did not grow well in the cold Navajo territories. By the early 1800s a prosperous Navajo herder might care for 2,000 sheep, 100 Mexican goats, 50 cattle, and 200 horses. The Navajo diet became rich in mutton, beef, and animal fats; unlike most indigenous Americans, Navajo people even drank goat's milk.

For the small southwestern farming populations of Hispanics and mestizos (individuals of mixed Spanish and Indian ancestry), a multi-ethnic mix of corn, wheat, frijoles, a few vegetables, and a few European fruits provided the staples for a simple, hybrid diet. Even before they had left central Mexico, the settlers had abandoned the olive oil and wine of their Spanish ancestors to cook with pork lard and to drink pulque or aguardiente manufactured in the colonies. They had learned how to raise corn before they arrived in El Norte. Once there, however, they learned the making of meat jerky from New Mexico Indians and the cultivation of blue corn and the preparation of atole (corn gruel) from the Tewas. They sometimes ate corn tortillas and chiles stewed with meat or with beans; their baked goods more often reflected Spanish traditions and were based on wheat, fruit, and sugar. Like the Navajos, Hispanics drank milk and made cheese, but they ate more beef and less mutton than their Spanish ancestors.

In California, mestizo settlers from Mexico brought corn, beans, chiles, and irrigation, introducing them to the migratory natives, who had depended on acorns as their staple food. For Indians laboring at California missions, breakfast in the early nineteenth century meant boiled barley (a European grain), native beans, and meat; they ate posole with meat and vegetables or atole and meat for lunch. Holiday celebrations included chocolate drinks native to Central America. California's native peoples often fled mission lands and agriculture when they could and returned to their oak forests. And even those who labored in the missions, or converted to Christianity, continued to forage for traditional nuts and berries, comparing the pleasures of gathering their foods to the monotony of raising it by work in the wheat fields.

The colonies of the Southwest, as part of the Spanish Empire, rarely traded with their fellow British colonists to the east. In the absence of trade, the unique ecology and a differing mix of native and European settlers guaranteed that the Northeast would develop a creole diet different from that of the Southwest. Among northeastern tribes, the Iroquois alone proved large, settled, and populous enough to maintain most elements of their own foodways in the face of English incursions. Their success, however, required them to retreat into a backwoods subsistence, and into shifting political alliances with a new trading partner to the north, the French. In New England, English settlers quickly cleared land and fenced it as their own property, making war on local tribes and restricting their access to hunting lands in the process. They forbade migratory Indians to cross private lands and chased diminishing native populations into "praying villages" of converts who practiced settled agriculture along European models. Heavy involvement in the fur trade and heavy use of alcohol further disrupted native diets, which became less diverse and increasingly dominated by corn and the meat of European domesticated animals.

Given the choice, New Englanders of English descent might have preferred a diet of wheat bread, which they were beginning to eat prior to their departure from England. Wheat bread symbolized high status and had recently become a perquisite of urban life in England. Unfortunately, after some initial successes, New England's wheat crops repeatedly succumbed to wheat blast, a fungal plant disease. After 1660 the farmers of New England fell back on the more reliable native corn, supplemented by European rye and peas and the beans of two continents. England's pease porridge began a quick evolution into New England's baked beans, sweetened by maple syrup or molasses. Meanwhile, Puritan cooks, adding a more familiar grain to the coarse corn cakes of natives, produced rye'n'injun bread, which became popular in the eighteenth century.

English settlers also produced English pies made of native pumpkins and hasty puddings made of maize. Settlers of Massachusetts borrowed the French Canadian's cooking pot, the chaudière, to prepare the stew of native clams, cider, cream, salt pork, and onions they called chowder. Observers often attributed the somewhat austere character of the New England colonial diet to the Puritanism of the region's settlers. As one New Englander noted, "Our food was plain, but very good in quality and abundant in quantity."[19] In fact, the same was true of the diet of their French Catholic neighbors to the north. In the Americas, at least, visitors could find no sharp contrast between "plain English" and "French haute cuisine." Both groups also drank home-raised and fermented cider in great quantities.

Amelia Simmons's *American Cookery*, published in 1796, revealed New England's settlers to be more dependent on the food marketplace than most of the colonists further down the East Coast. Simmons included lengthy advice on selecting the best raw ingredients from local markets, and she warned about the quality problems introduced by transporting fish and meat considerable distances to those markets. Simmons's cookbook also provides an early example of the use of ash as baking soda, a blending of native and European cooking techniques. Native Americans used ash to make hominy and to flavor corn dishes and meat stews, but it was European-Americans who first applied it to baking. With the addition of this new leavening (which, in much refined form, we know as baking powder), American gingerbread soon evolved toward a light, cake-like dessert, quite unlike its heavier medieval predecessor, which depended on eggs to raise the dough. Ultimately, all American breads followed gingerbread's evolution and gradually acquired the lightness associated with "quick breads." Later arrivals in the United States, accustomed to the textures and long fermentation of yeast-baked European breads, would note this change as a distinctive, if negative, American trait.

Elsewhere in the Northeast, other early printed cookbooks documented the widespread borrowing that was occurring among European settlers and between Europeans and the natives. In the Middle Atlantic region, English Quakers adopted Indian corn and other native ingredients, along with some home remedies (especially the use of sassafras); they borrowed apple butter, bacon dumplings, bologna sausage, sauerkraut, and liver sausage from their German neighbors in Pennsylvania. Dutch coleslaw and buckwheat cakes appeared as recipes in the first Quaker cookbook, as they did in Amelia Simmons's collection. Remnants of the Quakers' western English origins persisted, however, in their preference for cream cheeses and for "lemon butter"—a thick custard of milk, eggs, butter, sugar, and lemon.[20]

Visitors from England, accustomed to the austerity of the New England cuisine, often emphasized the ease and wealth of agriculture among the German settlers of Pennsylvania—called "the Pennsylvania Dutch"—and their bountiful, rich cooking. Unlike the English settlers, Germans cooked on stoves rather than over the open fire, and they were more likely to stew than to roast native meats. They also devoted more attention to their kitchen gardens—cultivating a wider range of cabbages and other vegetables—and they ate less corn than their English neighbors. Germans built more substantial farm buildings, in order to house and fodder their cows through the winter (allowing them to produce butter year round). They cared for a broader range of domestic animals, and expected more field work from the women of their families.

The first German-language cookbook from this region reflected this group's elaborate sausage culture, strong yeast baking tradition, and hot salads, but it also printed recipes for New England puddings and included much corn—in the form of samp, hominy, gritted bread, and dried grain.[21] In an interesting twist, Germans even roasted corn to make it taste more like their favored grain—rye.

The Dutch settlers of New York, like the German settlers in Pennsylvania, also gained a reputation for the pleasure they took in bounteous meals, and they too contributed a number of distinctive dishes—cookies and coleslaw—to regional food repertoires. Observers often commented on the wealth and diversity of Dutch farmers' larders, especially in the rich fruit and farm lands of the Hudson Valley. The Dutch made corn an ingredient in their native dish of hutespot, by adding salt beef or pork, potatoes, carrots, and turnips to samp (corn) porridge.[22] Perhaps because they cultivated so many other vegetables and fruits, the Dutch ate less pumpkin and squash than New Englanders. Like the Germans, the Dutch struck observers as particularly fond of their cakes and breads, and they seemed to take more pleasure in eating, especially on holidays, than their Puritan neighbors to the north and east.

Africans too left their mark on regional American eating. Indeed, their presence forged a culinary dividing line between the coastal regions of the Carolinas and Georgia (where they settled among English, Caribbean, and French Huguenot planters) and the mountainous regions of these colonies, where native American foodways blended with frontier Scotch-Irish customs. Despite their low social status, Africans were perhaps the main shapers of eating customs in colonial areas where slavery flourished. This was especially clear in the lowland regions of the Carolinas and Georgia, where Africans often outnumbered whites. Not only did they adapt more easily to the semitropical climate, but they also possessed expertise for cultivating and cooking what would become the most important commercial crop of the region, rice. They were without doubt the most important cooks in a society where the wealthiest whites avoided physical labor.

Historians have established through careful research that a significant proportion of the slaves of the Carolina Low Country came from the small but important rice-cultivating districts in western Africa. Some evidence even suggests that planters consciously imported their slaves from this region once rice cultivation became successful. African techniques of sowing, flailing, and storing rice persisted into the nineteenth century.

African cooks also developed the "rice kitchen" of the Georgia and Carolina coasts. Here, rice appeared on the planters' table daily, prepared by black hands. Humbler eaters, notably African and African-American slaves, came to enjoy hoppin' john—a blend of cowpeas or beans and rice similar to dishes found elsewhere in the African Caribbean.

English settlers and their descendants liked to believe that Europeans had brought "Carolina gold" rice from Madagascar, and then learned rice cultivation from the Chinese. Indeed, humorists compared the lives of the privileged rice planters of the coastal Carolinas and Georgia to the Chinese, noting that "they eat rice and they worship their ancestors."[23] It is possible that Europeans invented the rice bread popular in the region, which was made two ways: with rice flour, and with whole rice grains incorporated into a wheaten loaf. Cooked by Africans, the Carolina "pilau" and the method of its preparation (which originated in India, not China) more likely first became popular among the French Huguenots of the region. Planters of English descent intermarried with the Huguenots, and like Harriott Horry, soon enjoyed pilau, daubes, and ragouts.

The eating habits of this colonial elite—like that of Virginia's planters—struck visitors as far more concerned with refinement and hedonistic enjoyment than were New England's prosperous Puritan merchants or the hearty but stolid *bürgerliche* Germans and Dutch of New York and Pennsylvania. Many have attributed this to the French presence in the area. Early visitors rarely mentioned the possibility that African women, who actually did almost all the cooking in elite families, shaped the eating habits of Charleston's and Savannah's wealthy Europeans. This blind spot in descriptions of the elite diet of the Southeast has persisted well into the twentieth century.

Ironically, perhaps, slaves and the European captains and provisioners of the ships that transported them had introduced into the Carolinas and Georgia the central American crops of peppers and peanuts which had been cultivated successfully in western Africa after first being transplanted there. Slave ships brought with them the seeds of benne (sesame) and African yams and watermelons, all of which became well known to eaters, white and black, in the region. Some students of regional cooking do attribute the coastal taste for hot, peppery flavors in local seafood dishes to the hand of generations of African-American cooks—a plausible interpretation, since neither English nor French settlers knew this combination of tomato, onion, and hot red peppers from their homelands.

English and French settlers along the Carolina and Georgia coast could not easily satisfy one important taste they had brought with them. Though living at the same latitude as Italy and blessed with native grapes in profusion, the planters of the coastal Southeast nevertheless found themselves unhappily in the same position as their English counterparts in the eighteenth century. To indulge their taste for wines—especially their preference for port—they had to import them from abroad. Repeated efforts to produce acceptable wines from local grapes, or to import European grape varieties for production in the Americas, met with little success in the Southeast. (Frenchmen trying to make wines with local Missouri grapes in New France enjoyed little more.) Fortunately for the planters, the exorbitant profits to be made in rice export allowed the wealthiest Charlestonians to indulge their taste for wines: visitors commented on the profusion of bottles that accompanied the lavish hospitality and fine dining enjoyed among planters there.

No such lavishness characterized Up Country eating. The hills of the Piedmont, and the mountains beyond, remained the frontier, and a land of Indian-influenced eating. Settled in the 1700s by Scotch-Irishmen, frontiersman in western parts of the Carolinas and in northern Georgia lived and ate much as their Native American neighbors did. They obtained almost all of their meat from hunting local wild animals and birds, and their meal came exclusively from corn (since wheat and other European grains did not flourish in the South's humid summers). Less familiar than natives with gathering local wild plants, these European settlers ate fewer vegetables and even less fruit. Like Native Americans, the men often drank heavily, and many knew how to distill their own liquors, a technique they quickly applied to corn to create the ubiquitous corn liquor. Like Native Americans, too, Up Country settlers cooked and ate their meals from a single pot, without benefit of individual eating utensils.

With time, pork gradually replaced venison, rabbit, and bear in the diet of these backwoodsmen, and they began to purchase molasses, sugar, and salt. The Virginia patrician William Byrd commented that the Carolinians he encountered had developed pig-like snouts, so much pork did they consume.[24] Well into the twentieth century, uplanders' preference for corn bread, their limited consumption of milk (which spoiled easily in the heat), and their love of game and salted hog meat defined simple, frontier eating, untouched by the gentle climate or African hands that produced the coastal cuisine.

With large upland areas but sparsely settled by Europeans in this era, Native Americans of the Southeast defended their culinary autonomy with some success. At the same time, however, they selectively adopted not just imported rum but some European crops and animals as well. In the early 1800s the Catawbas ate basically as their ancestors had, yet even they found the settlers' free-ranging animals hard to resist. Even horse meat quickly found a place in native cooking pots. The Cherokees adopted pig meat, but ambivalently, disparaging the hog itself as an unattractive and dirty animal; beef cattle they might herd and trade, but they adamantly rejected eating them. They appreciated chickens as much for their fine feathers as for their flesh. Sharing the same hilly environment with recent arrivals from Scotland and England, Native Americans of the Piedmont and the Blue Ridge and Smoky Mountains continued to eat in a fashion that marked them as distinctive.

Comparing the eating habits of Americans in the Northeast, Southeast, and Southwest at the end of the colonial era, we see that in none of these cases did one culture's food habits completely conquer or obliterate another's. Imperial conquest determined political and economic relationships far more thoroughly than they could shape the cultural dynamics of New World eating. Three centuries of food exchanges occasionally obscured the ethnic origins of some favorites like brown bread or hoppin' john. More often, however, the mixed cultural origins of multi-ethnic blends remained visible—as in the rye'n'injun bread of New England or the flour tortillas of New Mexico.

With the possible exception of the ubiquitous popularity of corn and beans in all regions and among all groups, the only American eating habits of the colonial era were regional ones. No single American cuisine emerged from these exchanges. At the same time, no group's foodways survived the era completely unchanged. An individual did not have to abandon a connection to a tribal, Spanish, or English past in order to become a Southwesterner or a New Englander, at least not in culinary terms: multi-ethnic blends and regional specialties were synonymous. The only way to become an American, at least as an eater, was to eat creole—the multi-ethnic cuisine of a particular region.

The relationship of region and ethnicity in American eating was thus quite complex. Eating chicken did not transform Cherokees automatically into Englishmen, any more than eating corn made Englishmen into Narragansetts. The Spanish-speaking settlers of New Mexico adopted the corn of the Pueblos without adopting with it native beliefs about the creation of humans from masa dough; they remained Christians even though they ate corn. Similarly, Europeans learned to cultivate corn without—as natives did—either assigning the task to the women of their communities or adopting the communal fields of the Iroquois village. And Cherokees drank European alcohol without opening taverns or aping many other European drinking traditions. Borrowing and commercial exchange alike stripped foods from the myriad associations that tied them in unique fashion to their cultures of origin. Similarly, the adoption of pork, corn, rum, or ash leavening only gradually forged new cultural associations among the people who learned to eat new foods together with their family and friends. Aside from the meal memorialized in Thanksgiving lore, the usual group of people who ate together in the colonial world did not include members of the group from whom corn and pumpkin originated.

It is useful to consider also the new associations that emerged around foods newly adopted from other peoples. The Cherokees did not adopt pork in order to become English, nor drink rum because they wanted closer ties to them. More often, drinking rum or eating corn reflected rather than motivated already-existing connections among groups. Still, the pueblo-dwellers continued to eat pork, and the English settlers continued to eat corn because these new foods tasted good and complemented traditional tastes. Food was not so much a common ground on which people declared themselves alike; rather, it provided a visceral record of a shared history of meeting and interaction across cultural and social boundaries. Because the new foods people incorporated into their everyday meals, family rituals, and religious practices were a source of pleasure and variety, neither Europeans, Africans, nor natives seemed inclined to deny or to reject foods of foreign origin once they had adopted them. While we know the colonial era was one of sharp, and often violent, interethnic conflict and warfare, this history did not adhere to the symbolism of food and eating.

I do not mean to suggest that shared foods and everyday exchanges could eliminate the cultural, social, and economic differences between African slave and Charlestonian Huguenot slaveowner, or between Spanish missionary and Pueblo native. Yet all these groups by the end of the colonial era shared eating habits that were characteristic of their home region, and each seemed quite American in having departed substantially from the eating habits of their ancestors. At least in the world of eating and food, region more than ethnicity defined American identities at the end of the colonial era, and pleasure more than pain marked the interactions between the participants in the colonial food exchanges.

As Americans entered their own era of independence and nationalism, they carried with them eating habits and identities that incorporated in pleasurable ways a long history of multi-ethnic interaction and a strong set of ties to American, rather than European or African, home places. The identities, and the eating habits, of Americans in this era little resemble those of the modern world: no colonial-era American of any cultural background, north, south, or west, ate as any American does today. To understand what happened to the regional creoles of the colonial era, and to trace their further evolution, one must understand the expansion and consolidation of the United States as a nation, the gradual formation of a national food marketplace, and the transportation and corporate revolutions of the nineteenth century, as well as the new migrations that changed the demographic face of much of the new nation.

Ironically, culinary nationalism would not characterize the age of American nationalism. Physical expansion, civil war, and internal and international migrations generated ever new sources of culinary diversity. The United States remained one nation divided into many eating communities, each forming its own distinctive market or "enclave." National homogeneity in eating would prove more elusive than political independence or national unity. In many respects, in fact, Americans of the nineteenth and early twentieth centuries, while living amid an expanding and presumably enticing national marketplace, seem more conservative in their eating habits, and more committed to preserving them, than Americans of the colonial era.

CHAPTER TWO

Immigration, Isolation, and Industry

The first meal," Jewish immigrant Mary Antin noted of her arrival in Boston in the 1890s "was an object lesson of much variety. My father produced several kinds of food, ready to eat, without any cooking, from little tin cans that had printing all over them. He attempted to introduce us to a queer, slippery kind of fruit, which he called 'banana,' but had to give it up."[1] Putting behind her this first introduction to "American" food—tins from corporate canneries and fruit transported far from its tropical origins—Antin's mother again took charge of the family kitchen. The family soon returned to fare she adapted from their Russian homeland: potatoes, onions, cabbage, dark bread, and salted fish. Tin cans and bananas, readily available in 1900, would not become prominent on the Antins' shelves. The Antins seemed determined to have the familiar; at least in this episode of their family life, they represent millions of cultural conservatives, firmly ensconced in isolated eating communities into which corporate producers and a national food marketplace rarely reached.

Throughout the nineteenth and into the early twentieth centuries, culinary conservatives in ethnic and regional enclaves seemed capable of halting, or even reversing, the experimentation, borrowing, and exchanges characteristic of the colonial era. Antin's father's choice of American foods reminds us that immigrants of the late nineteenth century, along with the peoples of the conquered South, Southwest, West, and Hawaii, became incorporated into a country that was undergoing a fundamental reorganization of its food supply. New systems of transport, distribution, and corporate organization increasingly linked the country's many regions into a single national marketplace. New corporate food producers had strong incentives to convince all Americans to like the standardized foods they could produce or distribute en masse—Gold Medal flour, Coca-Cola, Van Camp's canned beans. But they could also introduce and circulate new and exotic foods from obscure or far-off places, as evidenced by the bananas from Central America, which are frequently mentioned in immigrants' descriptions of their first encounters with American food at Ellis Island.

As cultural conservatives, the Antins had plenty of company. Despite impressive changes in the food supply, large numbers of potential consumers—perhaps even the majority of Americans—seemed unwilling or unable to participate in the national food marketplace on a regular basis. Few ate much of the foods that corporations could produce in vast quantities. Conservatism, rather than novelty and diversity, seemed to define pleasure for many eating communities of Americans in the nineteenth century. Still, just beyond the boundaries of their communities, new producers and retailers of food beckoned from far-off canneries and slaughterhouses. Ultimately, they would entice ever more consumers. In retrospect, the culinary conservatism of the nineteenth century appears to be a temporary pause on a quick road to new exchanges and new creole dishes.

P eoples who had been incorporated into the American nation through force and conquest—notably white rural southerners after the Civil War, Indian tribes throughout the country, African-American slaves, and Hispanics of the West and Southwest—were often too poor to enjoy canned or imported foods, and often too suspicious of outsiders to want to try. In the American South, for example, the food of the upland Carolinas throughout much of the century remained frontier food, dominated by hog meat and hoe cake. If anything, the Civil War, Reconstruction, and the rise of sharecropping diminished the quantity and quality of diets in this region. The historian Joe Gray Taylor is convinced that "on the average the slaves of the Old South had more and better food to eat than the sharecroppers, black and white, of the post-Civil War Era."[2] As pointed out by an ex-slave who had enjoyed eating "collards, turnips and other good vegetables wid cornbread. Chunks of meat . . . wid de greens, too, and . . . lots of buttermilk," "Marse know'd if dey worked dey had to eat."[3] On the other hand, another former slave remembered, "De slaves didn't git no flour bread, not even seconds; dey had to eat de grudgin's."

After the Civil War, sharecroppers, black and white, found it hard to provide even the basics of their simple antebellum diet. Trying to subsist on small parcels of land, and often without any cash income for much of the year, they easily became indebted to the landowner's store or commissary even for locally raised items—beans, molasses, corn—as well as for processed foods from farther afield, like salt pork or wheat flour. Observers noted the monotony of sharecroppers' diets: "At home wives sliced off thick pieces of the Iowa meat and fried it for breakfast, boiled hunks of it for dinner and fried more of it for supper. They thickened the gravy with flour and served it and molasses as sop for corn bread and biscuit. Three times a day and fifty-two weeks a year, many ate meat, corn bread, biscuit, gravy and molasses."[4] Holidays brought a fried chicken, for even very poor sharecroppers could keep a few fowl, which they devoured completely after slaughter—an important plus in the withering heat and humidity of a Carolina summer. By the early years of the twentieth century, however, the poorest upland whites, and most African-Americans, ate even less meat and more meal. "We do not know what we would do in the South, white folks or black folks, if there were no hominy grits."[5] A poor woman told an interviewer, "Landlord's got a store on de place, en he 'low [allow] you so much a week on de books . . . He didn' 'low us but a twenty-four-poun' sack of flouah, en a twenty-four poun' sack of meal, en eight pound's of lard, en maybe a bar of soap. Ef you got molasse you didn' git no sugah . . . Meat? Whooo! We didn' git no meat, but we'd ketch a mess of fish now en den."[6] Clearly, the intense poverty of sharecroppers left little money for pleasure. The monotony of their diets reflects the limits on their lives as much as any culinary conservatism. It also shows that corporate mass producers could serve even very poor consumers once they dominated the production of staple, familiar items.

Work in Piedmont textile mills brought a slight improvement in diet, largely because it guaranteed a steady, if small, cash income with which occasional new foods could be purchased. Carl Voegtlin, a pharmacologist in Spartanburg, visited a family that in one month in the spring of 1911 "bought a hundred pounds of flour, a half bushel of meal, some lard, salt pork, and 'preparation,' the name given alum baking powder. The only variety the diet afforded was one can of peaches, one of salmon, a nickel's worth of crackers, and a jar of pickles."[7] There were three cases of pellagra in the family. These poor consumers bought the products of the modern food industry, but again they bought staples, not novelties.

While noting in the 1930s that "nearly every day I cook Irish potatoes and pintos . . . We don't care much fer meat and I reckin it's a good thing we don't," the poor millworker Kate Brumby also took pride in her simple cooking. "No rollin' pin and fancy cut-out biscuit fer me, I cook thick . . . so's they'll be a heap of crumb. Little thin biscuits wa'n't meant fer gummin'."[8] Working with extremely limited ingredients, southern women nevertheless took considerable pride in developing new cooking skills in the nineteenth century, notably making biscuits and cakes from purchased white flour and, by late in the century, home canning to supplement more traditional techniques of pickling and preserving.

In addition to their cooking skills, the female descendants of slaves seemed to have learned and retained a knowledge of healing that originated with Native Americans' use of local herbs and plants. As Nellie Boyd of Murrell's Inlet, South Carolina, remembered, "When anybody got sick, de old folks made hot teas from herbs dat dey got out of de woods."[9] Both "boughten" foods and local products, in other words, provided ample room for the development of a satisfying sense of expertise and culinary competence.

For southern rural men, pleasure in the familiar came from their subsistence skills—curing and barbecuing hog meat, and hunting for small game, especially rabbit and squirrel. The Carolinas boasted not one but two styles of barbecue: Up Country barbecue and Low Country barbecue—the former with a rich tomato-based marinade and the latter with pepper and vinegar tastes predominating. Maintaining a modest smoke house—and in some cases a secret still to produce "moonshine"—gave men a source of culinary pride, and was a sign of their independence, even when they worked in the mills. Recipes for Brunswick stew varied from place to place but almost always included freshly hunted small game. African-American men specialized in catching and roasting 'possums, served up with sweet potatoes, and in transforming the humblest of offal—notably chitlins (or chitterlins)—into a delicacy.[10]

For white, upland Carolinians with secure tenure to their own land, the economic hardships of the Civil War and Reconstruction passed rather quickly, and subsistence farming provided a bountiful diet, marking their superior status. Holiday tables, in particular, mimicked the variety and bounty, if not the sophistication, of the "groaning" tables of the South's former plantation elite. Like that elite, prosperous upland farmers depended on black cooks and hands to prepare, set, and serve these tables.[11] During the Great Depression, Max Revelise enjoyed a South Carolina Country Christmas Dinner, sampling homemade corn liquor, blackberry and scuppernong wines, eggnog; turkey stuffed with cornbread dressing, chickens stuffed with plain white bread dressing; baked ham spiced with cloves; country sausage; liver pudding; and hogshead cheese. He was surprised to find no fresh greens or salads on the table, only coleslaw and a single purchased luxury—celery from a nearby city market. Other vegetables appeared only as ingredients in chicken salad and potato salad. Side dishes included buttermilk biscuits and purchased ingredients in a macaroni pie (with cheese), canned peas, canned corn, candied sweet potatoes, and a wide variety of condiments. For desserts, guests could choose from ten to fifteen types of cakes, plus three kinds of pies, and ambrosia.[12]

Revelise also noted that "large quantities of food are sent to the colored folk in the kitchen and on the back porch" because the white guests had made "scarcely a dent" in most of the platters of his holiday feast.[13] Men, too, often abandoned the holiday "groaning" table rather quickly. Although by the turn of the century many southerners, especially women, had become tee-totalers—based on religious convictions that had been awakened by the evangelical movements that swept the South beginning in the 1830s—tradition demanded "a swig of cawn behind the barn" as part of men's homemade holiday traditions.[14] Indeed, almost everywhere in the upcountry, "Christmas was a day of powerful liquoring."[15]

The nineteenth century saw little change in the eating habits of Carolina's coastal elite, who had always supplemented local foods with imports. Antebellum rice planters near Charleston continued to eat and drink bounteously, as they had in the colonial period. A comparison of Sarah Rutledge's *The Carolina Housewife* from the 1840s to Harriott Horry's eighteenth-century collection of recipes (published only much later as the *Colonial Plantation Cookbook*) reveals a more extensive, but otherwise quite similar, collection of recipes.[16]

Culinary change, when it came, followed the decline of rice production more than the growing popularity of foods grown or processed far away. After its zenith in the 1850s, Carolina rice production dropped precipitously, and cultivation gradually shifted to Louisiana and the American West. The end of slavery, followed by decades of bad weather and several disastrous hurricanes in the years around 1900, hastened the abandonment of rice cultivation. By 1906 a frustrated but determined woman planter wrote in her end-of-year diary, "It almost seems as though I was meant to give it up. The rice-planting, which for years gave me the exhilaration of making a good income myself, is a thing of the past now—the banks and trunks have been washed away, and there is no money to replace them."[17] Her sense of loss was palpable, though, as her diary records, she continued to eat very well from the game, meat, and gardens of her plantations.

African-Americans in the coastal Carolinas also ate local foods, with little recourse to mass-produced and packaged foods. It is likely that they ate better after emancipation than before. Under slavery, they had eaten much corn meal and corn bread, but also the cracked rice they raised for sale, cooked slowly over an open fire in the form of porridge, gruel, or hoppin' john. Slave rations, distributed each Saturday, typically included 10 quarts of (cracked) rice or 8 quarts of field peas or cowpeas, a bushel of sweet potatoes, a pint of molasses in some weeks; two to three pounds of salt fish in the winter or two pounds of salt pork, bacon, or occasionally beef during the summer. Of these rations, only the salt pork may have been purchased. A plantation slave cook prepared meals for as many as two hundred adult workers, often cooking in the fields or carrying meals there so as not to interrupt the pace of work. A second cook prepared a special diet for the children, with buttermilk or clabber added to generous, if bland and monotonous, rations of corn meal and pone. Holidays meant extra meat rations, molasses, good quality rice, and—however strictly prohibited by law—a ration of whiskey or wine.

Since coastal overseers organized slave work by the "task system," many slaves had additional time for gardening (sometimes worked by moonlight), fishing, and hunting. Slaves supplemented their own diet and sold surplus vegetables and fresh meats to their masters. They raised corn, sweet and Irish potatoes, peas, beans, eggplant, okra, peanuts, turnips, collards, melons, and tomatoes in their own gardens. Slaves on rice plantations gathered much seafood—oysters, crabs, turtle eggs, and eel—and they hunted for wild game and birds. Some raised pigs, poultry, and even cows for their own use, although they most frequently sold all of their eggs to whites. Familiar foods like these, concluded one historian, were the main source of pleasure for slaves; the foods they produced required extra work but provided mastery, mobility, and a sense of autonomy as well. With relatively secure access to land, and with the rich wild reserves of coastal wildlife, former slaves extended these activities after freedom.

With their agricultural know-how, African-Americans continued to cultivate small plots of rice in the Carolinas on a subsistence basis into the 1930s. As coastal dwellers, they also continued to exploit the natural bounty of their region. A student of black life on St. Helena noted that "the tidal rivers are alive with crabs and oysters, and in midsummer shrimp are plentiful. Shark, catfish, black fish, whiting and sheepshead are caught with hand lines in quantities."[18] Bubberson Brown, born on Edisto Island in the early twentieth century, noted, "They used to go into the creek every week, the last of the week, pick oysters, get clams and crabs . . . My old grandmother raise many a children on them oyster."[19] Remembering her very poor childhood, an elderly African-American woman nevertheless concluded, "When we were children, being black and being poor, we thought we ate that way because we were poor, but we were eating the best of food, nothing but natural food." Her friend continued, "We had all fresh vegetables, everything out of the garden. And we had seafood. My daddy was a fisherman . . . He used to catch shrimps, oysters, clams, crabs . . . We ate rice at every meal."[20]

In the conquered and still agricultural Southwest, too, Mexicans had little incentive, and little cash, with which to enter the national marketplace or to enjoy the products of corporate food producers. Mexicans who migrated to the American Southwest came to work in first carting, then commercial agriculture, construction, industry, and domestic service. Their diet blended native ingredients like corn, beans, squash, and chiles with the rice, flour, and fruit introduced by the Spanish and the meat of the animals they often herded in northern Mexico (pigs, steers, goats, and sheep, often grilled or barbecued). An early Anglo report on rural Tejanos in the 1820s reported them eating "tortillas [corn cakes], beef, venison, chickens, eggs, cheese, and milk; and sometimes bread, chocolate, coffee, tea, and sugar may be secured."[21] New arrivals from Mexico ate much the same. Ernesto Galarzo described a common breakfast for barrio boys like himself: tortillas "warming on the comal [earthenware griddle], the beans coming to a boil in one pot, the coffee in another." The boys in the family waited until the men had eaten to enjoy "a bowl of coffee, a tortilla with beans and pepper, and a few sucks on a chunk of brown sugar, the panocha that was kept in a clay pot on a shelf out of our reach. The women always ate last." Lunch was a repeat of breakfast, or—for men traveling to work— tacos rolled in cornhusks. Supper meant "freshly made tortillas, wrapped in a double jacket of napkins and stacked in the cream-colored basket . . . the chiquilhuite," accompanied by "frijoles do la olla sprinkled with browned rice and washed down with coffee, but no pepper."

In San Antonio, Tejanos and new arrivals from Mexico lived in neighborhoods and cooked and ate foods that marked them as different from German immigrants and Anglos. San Antonio's Mexican women prepared tortillas with the metate (grinding stone) and the comal. They cooked and often ate on the ground or casually seated on beds or chairs. The corn or flour tortilla, dipped into a common pot, served—Galarzo remembered— as "fork, plate and napkin." The making of tortillas fascinated Anglo observers and fed pleasant memories of skilled and powerful mothers and aunts, working together. Galarzo prized his mother's skill: "She plucked small lumps, one by one, from the heap of corn dough she kept in a deep clay pot. She gave the lump a few squeezes to make a thick round biscuit which she patted and pulled and clapped into a thin disk . . . On each twist the tortilla seemed to slip loose but she would clamp it gently for another tat-tat."[22]

Special meals were as simple as panocha-flavored corn gruel on Sunday evening or as elaborate as the tamaladas that celebrated major religious holidays and community get-togethers. Sarah Deutsch has described the raising of food and provisioning of families as a female responsibility throughout the Hispanic Southwest. Wherever Mexicans settled in the United States, the tamalada continued to assert women's obligation—and power—to feed their families. In San Antonio, the making of tamales by groups of Mexican-American women kin came to be associated with Christmas celebrations. A group of sisters and their daughters might prepare as many as fifty dozen of the corn-husk-wrapped steamed masa for one holiday season. There was no question of switching to simpler methods using prepared foods; it was a given that the work took all day: washing the corn husks without cracking them, grinding corn for masa, boiling meat (chicken or pork), smearing the husks with cornmeal, adding a bit of the meat, folding the corn wrappers properly, binding each with a strip of corn husk, and steaming in a pot properly prepared with water, rocks, banana leaves, or napkins.

Menudo too became an equally labor-intensive meal prepared for family celebrations. After finding the required tripe (in this case beef), the women of the Arizona Grijalva family washed it many times, soaked it in salt water, then boiled the tripe for four hours, adding hominy, pepper and salt, herbs and chili. Visitors to the family party drank wine, tequila, and brandy and ate bread to accompany the "mealy and brothy" menudo, noting that "the soup glistened with globules of fat and substance boiled out of the tripe." Desserts and coffee followed. The menudo was hot and spicy as a result of the liberal use of chili in its preparation.[23]

Familiar foods also helped migrants from Mexico maintain their health, for they believed that some foods were hot and others cold, and that lactating women and the sick in particular needed to avoid certain foods in order to maintain health and "balance." Women after childbirth, for example, sought hot foods—meat, toasted tortilla, broth, and milk—but avoided cold foods like pork, fruit or fruit juices, beans and fresh vegetables. Special drugstores also offered herbal medicines in Mexican neighborhoods.

Even more than in Mexico, however, Tejanos new and old—like eaters throughout the American Southwest and Mexico's El Norte—made flour, rather than corn, tortillas an important staple. Some even ate flour tortillas with butter, as Anglos did their bread. They also ate homemade dishes like atole, homilade (hominy with cheese and chili), pozole (pork and bones with corn, condiments). And they continued, along with Anglos of the Southwest and Mexicans of El Norte, to take special pleasure in grilled meats and barbecue—a product of the long ranching and herding traditions of the region. Over time, the Mexicans who settled in San Antonio increasingly ate the snacklike market foods of central Mexican cities, and these they did purchase from local dealers. Mexican vendors sold tamales and enchiladas, carrying them through town in two buckets—one on each hand. Their tamales were hot in temperature only, not spiciness, for they were sold mainly on crisp fall and winter days.[24]

Popular market snacks included tacos of bean or beef, quesadillas, chalupas, enchiladas, empanadas, corn on the cob, sweets-bunuelos, pan dulce, fruits in dozens of forms—and menudo. Vendors also sold coffee, frothy chocolate, and a wide variety of sweet breads and candies.

Far more than their poor neighbors in the Southeast, Mexican-Americans' recourse to the market was to local, small-scale producers; few purchased the salted meat or processed flour mass-produced in the upper Midwest. Subsistence farming and local trade continued to reinforce localism and conservatism in both regions.

Similar in some ways to the conquered peoples of America, immigrants like the Antins, though they voluntarily chose life in the United States, had equally compelling motives for maintaining their own customs and for limiting their use of processed and mass-produced "American" foods. Religion imposed special demands on the Antins and other Orthodox Jews of Eastern Europe. There, the elaborate rules of kashruth had long separated Jew from Gentile. Jewish boys learned the biblical laws which permitted the eating of some animals but not others; they understood why special Jewish slaughtering practices had evolved, and the blemishes ritual slaughters looked for when they examined slaughtered animals. They learned also why women could on occasion slaughter and examine poultry. Religious instruction taught them why some parts (such as the hind quarters) of permitted animals were nevertheless prohibited, and why meat dishes (fleischig) had to be separated from milk dishes (milchig). With considerably less formal instruction than the menfolk, however, Jewish women ensured that healthful, clean, kosher food actually arrived at the family table.

Women's vigilance sent them regularly to consult with local rabbis about cooking problems, for kashruth regulations had many fine points. Thus, as a manual explained, "If milk boils over and flows under a meaty pot standing next to a milky pot on a cold or luke-warm base and the meaty pot and its contents are also cold, or at the utmost luke-warm, then everything remains usable provided that there has never been a direct contact between the meaty and the milky pot by the overflowing milk. In other words, the overflowing milk must have been entirely disconnected from the milky pot at the moment it touched the meaty pot; otherwise the meaty pot is unusable but its contents may be eaten."[25]

With the move to the United States, Jewish eating became complicated by uncertainty about the purity of foods which originated outside the community. Jews well knew that Americans preferred meats and lard from the prohibited, dirty or "treyf" pig. Jewish peddlers traveling the rural roads of the United States rarely ate more than bread and eggs when away from home. In American cities, Jewish housewives struggled to provide pure foods, shaped by the regional Jewish cuisines of Eastern Europe. Jews from the Ukraine ate many cheese dishes, while those from Hungary ate spicier concoctions with paprika and peppers, but no pork. Sephardic Jews brought with them cuisines influenced by long years in diasporas in Latin, Ottoman, and North African regions.

Eastern European Jews generally enjoyed hot and scalding foods, often soups with potatoes and onions, dark—even black—rye breads, sometimes smeared with chicken fat ("That was a meal"), soft, tender, and fatty meat and fishes, and spicy and salty foods. They ate few vegetables, and then mainly carrots, dried legumes, and beets.[26] Salty herring and pickles emerge repeatedly in the memories of Jewish New Yorkers growing up on the Lower East Side. Herring "was very popular. It was very cheap . . . It stimulated your appetite." It could also be had in endless variety—schmaltz herring, pickled herring, tomato herring. And, recalled Sol Kaplan, "That time, every corner had a pickle store."[27]

When very poor, however, Jewish mothers might serve "potatoes, potatoes, potatoes," or as one Yiddish speaker remembered, "Zuntag, bulbeh, Muntag, bulbeh, Dietstag und Mitvach, bulbeh, Donnerstag und Freitag, bulbeh, Shabos delebt min a bulbeh, kugel" ("Sunday, potatoes, Monday, potatoes, Tuesday and Wednesday, potatoes, Thursday and Friday, potatoes, and on the Sabbath you get a potato kugel").[28] In other families, the staple of poverty was instead krupnick, "a cereal soup made from oatmeal, or sometimes barley, potatoes, and fat," sometimes with milk.[29]

Kosher rules dictated special cooking customs as part of Judaism's many domestic religious rituals, from the lighting of Sabbath candles and the challah at the end of the Sabbath meal, to the third and sometimes fourth set of special dishes (in addition to the separate sets for milchig and fleishig meals) used only for the preparation and service of Passover holiday meals. Feasting and fasting accompanied a yearly cycle of religious events. For a Sabbath an immigrant child remembered eating "Friday evening, stuffed fish, noodle soup and meat; for Saturday morning, radish garnished with fat, cholet" (a ragout made of meat stewed with vegetables and prunes), pudding, usually of noodles, and stewed fruit. The third Sabbath meal before sunset on Saturday consisted of "white bread and a piece of fish."[30]

For Passover, families searched the house to remove any remnants of leavened bread, which was forbidden in remembrance of the Jews' hurried escape from Egypt. A separate set of Passover dishes served the seder meal marking the beginning of the celebration. It included symbolic foods as part of the required religious ceremony: four cups of wine, bitter herbs, haroset (a sweet mix of fruits, nuts, spices, and wine), salt water, and springtime herbs, a plate with three matzos. Along with these symbolic foods came special delicacies, whether matzah balls and gefilte fish, chicken soup or borscht, with baked and fried pastries made from matzah meal. Sweet foods accompanied Rosh Hoshanah (new year), after fasting and atonement on Yom Kippur. And all year round, hospitality was simple but offered to all comers as women called to their neighbors, "Come in, come in, sit down, have a glass of tea." For Jews, welcoming a poor guest for the Sabbath meal was not only a act of sociability but of faith as well.[31]

Immigrant Catholics and Orthodox Christians also had their own special rules for eating, which distinguished them sharply from the vast majority of Americans who were Protestants. Most urban Catholics ate fish on Friday and other fast days of the year (notably Christmas Eve, Lent, and Holy Saturday). Catholic Germans prepared for their meatless Lenten fast with a celebration of pancake-eating and baked goods. Mexicans' Lenten fasts coincided with the flowering and fruiting of cactus, and both cactus fruits and nopalito paddles appeared in meatless dishes. Greek and Eastern Orthodox faithful eliminated meat, fish, dairy products, and their derivatives, and even oil, not only during Lent but during some fast days before Christmas and Easter.[32] And Russian Molokans followed Mosaic laws much like those of the Jews' kashruth. Tied to deep religious beliefs, food customs like these encouraged a particularly intense culinary conservatism among recent immigrants.

Most immigrants did not bring with them strict religious rules dictating their diet. Their initial culinary conservatism in the United States originated elsewhere. New immigrants faced many changes over which they had relatively little control—where they would live, what kind of work they would do, which language they would be required to learn to speak. At least they could exercise control over their meals. This feeling of mastery may have initially overwhelmed any normal, counterbalancing interest in the varied foods of their new homeland.

Immigrant farmers probably had the greatest opportunity to continue Old World habits, since they could, within limits, raise their own food. Northern Europeans' efforts to raise barley, rye, and buckwheat sometimes foundered, especially in the warm climate of Texas. Fruit trees, and the sour fruits used in northern European soups and in Czech baked goods, could not prosper on the driest expanses of the Great Plains. Overall, however, most immigrant farmers quickly agreed with what one German told a friend: "Even though I'm still not rich, I always have enough to eat, I slaughtered 3 head of hogs and a cow . . . I have more potatoes than I need, a whole barrel full of sauerkraut and so you can see that I don't go hungry. I now weigh 241 and my wife 104."[33]

For the Bohemians (later called Czechs) living in their rural "Pragues" in Minnesota, Texas, Oklahoma, and Nebraska, customary eating meant one-pot dishes, like soups and stewed meats (thickened with a flour roux), dumplings, and elaborate yeast breads and strudel pastries. More than Americans, Bohemians struggled to raise oats, rye, barley, and poppy, alongside the ever-present American potatoes, wheat, and corn. Bohemians at home ate potato pancakes, buttermilk, and fermented cottage cheese; many attempted to make their own wines with local berries or grapes.[34] Home brewing of beer—"piva"—flourished wherever Bohemians settled. In some families, women served a "sweet dinner" of fruit dumplings or jam omelette on Friday, in order to respect their Catholic faith's prohibition of eating meat on that day. Fish was rarely available on the Great Plains.

Special meals symbolized the Bohemian way of rural life. Bohemian women prepared roasted ducks and geese, accompanied by mushrooms and mushroom sauces. (Local morels replaced the "stone" mushrooms of their homelands.) Accompanying the poultry were cabbage and sauerkraut dishes, dumplings, and freshly baked desserts. For Christmas, women baked still more cookies and especially coffee cakes, like houska (a braided bread with almonds, raisins, and candied fruits, with powdered sugar on top). On Christmas Eve, families ate lentils, dumplings, and fish with potatoes, along with a variety of desserts. Christmas dinner usually meant roast goose, dumplings, and sauerkraut. Easter foods carried special symbolic meaning—the bacon symbolizing God's mercy to mankind, the bread representing the body of Christ, the butter molded into the shape of the paschal lamb, the eggs signifying the new life that starts in Christ, the ham standing for joy and abundance, the horseradish for the suffering of Christ, the wine evoking the Last Supper.[35]

A student of Czech foods noted that the earliest settlers "ate what they had on hand, and memories attached to those foods are . . . embodied in memories of the 'lean years.'"[36] But for most of their children, different and more bountiful food memories prevailed. For Frantiska Brzon Palecek, who grew up on a farm, the foods that evoked the particularities of Bohemian eating were holiday foods. Palecek remembered her mother as a fine cook and a keeper of a large vegetable garden. She prepared duck, sauerkraut, dumplings, vdolky (a flat bread with butter and apple butter), skubanky (mashed potatoes with butter and homemade cottage cheese), roliky, kolacky, houska (this time with poppy seed topping), and limburger cheese (which only her mother liked). Palecek especially remembered Sunday meals, which included homemade noodles and freshly slaughtered hen cooked into a rich soup. Other special food events looming large in her memories were the yearly slaughtering of the hog in the fall and the making of jaternice, a sausage with everything in it "except the pig's eyes."[37]

Among Czech farmers, who lived scattered in the countryside, communities came together to celebrate their Catholicism or their shared Bohemian origins by partaking of their Old World foods. At parishes with names like St. Wenceslaus, St. Ludmila, and St. John Nepomuk and in the Czech Halls, which became the meeting places of Czech associations like the Sokols, shared meals assumed mammoth proportions. At a 25-cent church dinner in the 1930s, a visitor reported eating kolace ("a kind of biscuit dough pressed down in the center with prunes or apricots and sprinkled with poppy seed and baked"), rohliky (kolace dough twisted into various shapes), rye bread with caraway, potato dumplings with sauerkraut, roast chicken, gravy, baked pork, peas, corn, baked beans, and coleslaw with cucumbers and cream.[38]

For the Japanese who became the fifth largest group of immigrant farmers on the Pacific coast, eating well also meant eating largely what one raised, supplemented by familiar foods imported from the homeland. Starting as farm laborers, many Japanese after 1900 became farm tenants, and then—carefully circumventing discriminatory laws—landowners. Born in California in 1919, Hiroshi Shikuma grew up on a strawberry farm in the Pajaro Valley, together with six brothers and sisters. His father eventually purchased land in the name of his citizen son. The family ate Japanese food exclusively—Japanese style rice, which they purchased from a Japanese importer in town, and fish purchased from Japanese and Italian fish peddlers who stopped weekly at their farm. The family raised all the rest of their food. Shikuma's mother prepared a wide range of familiar American vegetables Japanese style; the family also raised diakon and napa cabbage, which they viewed as "Japanese vegetables." Like most Japanese, this family used no dairy products. Their food revealed a concern with simplicity, purity, beauty, and lightness. They favored pickled vegetables and fish, miso, and soy products.[39]

Growing up in a family of six daughters (the first also born in 1919), Chiyo Mitori Shimamoto remembered the foods associated with holidays and the community meals in summer, when Japanese farm families gathered to eat from lacquered picnic baskets. But the real culinary high point of the year for Japanese families in the Stockton area was the communal making of mochi cakes for Japanese New Year. These were rice cakes prepared with a special variety of rice and steamed in a metal washtub kept specially for the purpose. First the men gathered to pound and knead the steamed rice, then the women gathered it into mounds, rolled handfuls of dough, sprinkled them with potato starch, and pinched and flattened the cakes into the appropriate shape. The families preparing the mochi cakes divided them for home use. Prior to cooking, they were stored in a crock of fresh water that required changing every day, and when the family was ready to eat them, they were toasted on the stove. Shimamoto's family preferred mochi softened with water, heaped on a plate, and seasoned with soy flour and sugar. Their supply—made with fifty pounds of rice—lasted a month.

They ate mochi on New Year's Eve accompanied by buckwheat noodles with a sauce of grated mountain potato roots. New Year's foods had special symbolic meaning for the Japanese: eggs for life, fish roe for fertility, black beans for health, mochi for strength, lobster for longevity, and red fish for happiness. Shimamoto's mother offered guests a fish platter surrounded by plates of other delicacies; visiting and celebrations occupied an entire week.[40] In other communities, women contributed traditional dishes—chicken teriyaki, ozoni (a soup with rice cakes), mame (beans), and sushi—to a potluck community celebration at a Gakuen, or Educational Society Building.

As these examples suggest, immigrants sought to maintain their familiar foodways because food initiated and maintained traditional relationships, expressed the extent of social distance between people, demonstrated status and prestige, rewarded and punished children's behavior, and treated illness. Thus in the late nineteenth and early twentieth centuries, even immigrants settling in urban areas tended to eat differently from native-born Americans or immigrants from other backgrounds, and with only limited recourse to processed foods. Greenbush, a ten-block triangle in Madison, Wisconsin—an enclave of Lombard, Sicilian, and Sicilian-Albanian artisans and common laborers at the turn of the century—provides an excellent example of one urban eating community. As a small town it offered Italians a better chance to combine industrial life with subsistence gardening than New York or Philadelphia, but the lives of Italians in "the Bush" surprisingly resembled Italians in those bigger cities.

Generally of peasant background, Italians in Italy had already struggled to produce food on limited lands while living in densely settled villages. They knew the ostentatious eating habits of their better-off urban neighbors but poverty usually forced them to eat simply—a staple grain (corn cooked as polenta; chestnut or wheat bread), vegetable minestras (thick soups), a little cheese, and wild greens. Few rural Italians ate much muscle meat, and on special occasions they appreciated seafood and organ meats more than Americans or landlocked Europeans did. Eel or dried codfish, lamb or goat, testicles, lungs, and brains all figured in Italian festival meals.

In the Bush, Italians found fresh foods and wine either not readily available or very expensive; low incomes and tradition encouraged them to grow or produce their own. Sarah Brashi Jones remembered, "My mother loved to pick cicoria (dandelion) in the area where the medical building now stands . . . She would carry them back to her kitchen, wash and boil them and season the greens with onions and garlic." "Gathering" and theft overlapped. One boy remembered carrying "little packets of salt in our pockets. While walking by the prolific neighborhood gardens of late summer, one never knew when a bunch of celery or a ripe tomato or two might jump out of the garden and into your hand."[41]

Even in New York, Italian immigrants kept chickens, goats, and an occasional pig in tenement kitchens and basements. In Brooklyn, large backyard gardens were the norm. One boy felt gardens marked Italians as strangers. "There was another difference between us and them. We had gardens, not just flower gardens, but huge gardens where we grew tomatoes, tomatoes, and more tomatoes. Of course, we also grew peppers, basil, lettuce and squash. Everybody had a grapevine and a fig tree."[42] Men in Greenbush did much of the kitchen gardening, their children remembered, but as a strenuous "hobby, a means of providing for their families and a labor of love." Women processed vegetables. Josie Magnasco Schuepback recalled women in the Bush preparing "conserva" Sicilian-style: "Fresh tomatoes were strained and cooked until all the water had disappeared. They were set on wide tables and sun-dried until thick and only small amounts remained." One daughter complained of the hard work: "Tomato board time wasn't our favorite . . . My four sisters and I were expected to stand in the heat, shoo the flies and support the boards on our shoulders that were resting at an angle off the backyard fence." Men were responsible for wine-making. According to Vito Paratore, "Italian men just loved to brag about their homemade wine. It could taste like vinegar, but they were so convinced that it was the best in the neighborhood, this 'Marsala' of theirs."[43] Wine was so much a part of an Italian meal that children could not recall when they started drinking; Robert Mondavi claimed, "I had it from the beginning, even with a teaspoon."[44]

Italians in the Bush could easily store their harvest bounty. In Grace Bonanno's home, "The part of our basement that wasn't heated was where my father kept his wine. It was ideal for storing other items, too. Flour was purchased by the sack, so that stayed downstairs with barrels of 'snowapples,' shelves of canned tomatoes, peaches, pears, capunatina and crocks of firm, crisp peppers, olives and tomato paste. We used to dry tomato halves . . . All that hard work paid off when the snow fell."[45] In bigger cities, by contrast, women more often complained of difficulties in preparing and storing large quantities of food, and they purchased food daily.

Special and especially abundant foods accompanied celebrations of rites of passage. In the Bush, Christmas in one family meant "Braciuolini, a thin piece of beef that was seasoned, filled and rolled, then tied. It would simmer in sauce and was served with pasta. There were home baked breads, an oil and vinegar salad, a relish dish of olives and finocchio, the anise flavored Italian celery and dessert always made with ricotta cheese . . . we would roast chestnuts." Families celebrated Shrove Tuesday with Mardi Gras parties and sfinge (puffs of dough with a sweet filling). Ending Lent, in another family, "A baby lamb was our annual Easter fare. Two aunts lived next door so the roasting in the backyard was always a family affair." The lamb was basted with parsley, garlic, black pepper, lemon juice, and oil before and during grilling. A third woman made a special engagement party of Sicilian-inspired "cassata" (a pound cake decorated with candied fruits and nuts and chocolate with pudding between the layers). Women of the family provisioned even the elaborate wedding ceremonies that Italians enjoyed in the Bush. One recalled that "few of us had wedding cakes. Instead, Italian cookies were baked in the amounts of bushel baskets-full by the Italian women." Women of the church served a breakfast immediately following the wedding, and in the evening a reception dinner of soup, chicken, potatoes, a tossed salad, and bread. Wedding feasts concluded with confetti (almond candies in tiny net bundles) and large platters of cookies.[46]

Food celebrated Italians' connections to friends, neighbors, and kin. Indeed, offering hospitality began at home: A social worker in New York reported that "the coffee pot is constantly at hand, and if any one should drop in between meals it is expected that he or she will accept a cup of coffee."[47] In the Bush, larger gatherings included summer weekend picnics. Everyone brought food, but the club or organization that sponsored the outing supplied watermelon, beer, and wine. On St. Joseph's Day, the Sicilians of the Bush opened their homes to friends and neighbors in celebration of friendship: "La tavola di san Giuseppe" on March 19 required meatless dishes, but in great abundance. In the Bonanno family, the altar-like table contained out-of-season fresh fruits, vegetables, fish dishes, rosolio (liqueur), fig and other cookies, biscotti, vegetable omelets, and a Sicilian specialty (ironically called pasta Milanese), which was pasta with sardines and fennel, topped with the toasted bread crumbs characteristic of Sicilian cuisine.[48]

Bountiful food like this symbolized Italians' satisfaction with American life. In New York, one immigrant elaborated her memories into images of mountains of food consumed, and equal quantities carelessly discarded out the window.[49] In Chicago, Sophonisba Breckinridge concurred; at picnics, she observed, "the housewife who has packed the most food gets the most attention, and they all gorge themselves."[50] Yet Italians also remained fond of their vegetable diets. When the descendants of Madison's Bush community shared their mothers' recipes, vegetable-based dishes made up one-third of the total recipes in Volume One of their cookbook.

Eating bountifully did not mean eating like Americans. To abandon immigrant food traditions for the foods of Americans was to abandon community, family, and religion, at least in the minds of many immigrants. One Italian boy pitied "Med-e-gons" (Americans) who ate only turkey on Thanksgiving, noting "there was no animosity involved in that distinction [between Italians and "Med-e-gons"], no prejudice, no hard feelings, just—well—we were sure ours was the better way." Reflecting on the relationship between ethnic and American foods and nationality, he concluded,

"It never occurred to me that just being a citizen of the United States meant that I was an 'American.' 'Americans' were people who ate peanut butter and jelly on mushy white bread that came out of a plastic package."[51]

A mericans," in other words, ate processed food, produced in faraway corporate factories. Viewed from the perspective of southern, Tejano, and immigrant eating communities, one could not have guessed that white bread or factory-canned jellies even existed in 1900, since they did not eat them. Yet the nineteenth century also saw the creation of food corporations of national dimensions, and their ability to ship food everywhere in large quantities increasingly linked a nation of many regions into a single national food marketplace. While sturdy, the cultural conservatism of isolated eating communities depended on their continued isolation. And isolation was clearly diminishing by century's end, as the national marketplace and the mass-produced goods of the modern food industry increasingly entered enclave communities across the country.

Students of American history are accustomed to thinking of an American industrial revolution built on railroads, steel, oil, and automobiles. Yet in many ways food was the leading manufacturing sector of the nineteenth century—expanding fifteenfold from 1859 to 1899, while general manufacturing increased only sixfold. If industrialization did not automatically transform American eaters into a homogeneous people of nationally uniform tastes, it certainly created the material conditions for a marketplace that was national in its geographic dimensions and corporate organization. The mechanization of food production perhaps failed to take immediate command of consumers' imaginations, but it became an increasingly visible fact of economic life in the United States, and it had already affected how "Med-e-gons" ate.

It is understandably difficult to imagine an industrial revolution spearheaded by food production, for we usually contrast "industrial" with "agricultural" worlds, and we know that our food supply begins with agriculture. We do not usually think of food as a manufactured product because we associate it instead with raw materials—more a natural resource than an industrial commodity. Yet the history of agribusiness shares much, organizationally, with industrial corporations. And few eaters, even in the nine-teenth century, ate their foods in an unprocessed or raw state. Transform-ing food from an agricultural resource to an edible dish is a type of manu-facturing. As food processing increasingly moved from farm to factory, it became an important industry—generating fully 20 percent of the nation's manufacturing product in 1900.

In addition, by 1920 the first conglomerate food companies (General Foods, Standard Brands) began to set new standards for corporate, central-ized organization in food processing. Food retailing followed somewhat later—first chains of grocery stores, then supermarkets and chains of super-markets, then restaurants, and finally chains of eateries. All substituted their goods and services for the work of millions of housewives in their kitchens.

As Thomas Jefferson had feared, the decline of the yeoman farmer (not to mention his wife, with her canning jars and home-baked bread) accom-panied the triumph of corporate production. Jefferson's rival, Alexander Hamilton, had not envisioned the development of what we call agribusi-ness, but the term aptly describes the farms that a later observer called "factories in the fields." Pioneered by wheat and cattle raisers on the Great Plains and the "bonanza farms" of California's central valley in the 1870s–1890s and by produce farmers in New Jersey and Florida around 1900, large-scale farming was risky business. This was especially true in the Far West, precisely because producers had to struggle to reach large markets of consumers interested in their products, who were mainly in eastern cities.

Corporate processing of the yearly harvest, in tandem with agribusi-ness, created the first of many layers of middlemen between corporate growers and urban consumers. The principle of canning fruits, meats, and vegetables had developed in France during the Napoleonic wars, but a long century of technical tinkering—with temperatures, baths, and the production of cans—preceded its boom toward the end of the century. In Pittsburgh, the rapid growth of canning giants like H. J. Heinz emerged through much the same dynamic of corporate competition, concentration, and vertical and horizontal expansion evidenced in Heinz's better known (and far better studied) neighbor, Andrew Carnegie, with his massive steel works.

In the 1830s and 1840s almost every little farm center in the United

States had a small mill for processing corn and wheat. Many milled so slowly and inefficiently that one farmer joked, "I could eat that meal faster than you can grind it."[52] The outpouring of grain from newly settled farms on the Great Plains in the years 1850–1890 encouraged the concentration of milling in nearby towns like Minneapolis and St. Paul. Only after mechanics had solved major technical problems for storing, cleaning, and transporting large quantities of wheat did profits become secure. The result was the same as in canning: decades of experimentation with milling equipment accompanied the emergence of corporate milling giants like St. Paul's General Mills and Pillsbury and Minneapolis's Washburn and Crosby mills with their Gold Medal brand flour. Large-scale milling lay the technical foundation for large-scale production of key wheat products like crackers and bread. By 1900 corporate factories baked almost all American crackers, while small-scale hand-baking of bread persisted for another twenty years or so. After 1920 even this succumbed to the marketing onslaught of mass producers like the Taggart Company (later called Continental Baking), whose Wonder Bread—the first bread available ready-sliced as well as uniformly white and spongelike—rapidly became the national standard.

In many respects, the story of meat packing best demonstrates the main themes of the economic history of American food industries in the nineteenth century. With access only to small, local markets, farmers had little incentive to produce a surplus of meat for sale; as one frontier farmer noted, "There was no market place, no demand and no price."[53] With improved transport, however, first the old Northwest (in the Ohio Valley), then California, then the vast southern ranges of the Great Plains became centers of specialized cattle-rearing. Yearly drives from rural New England to Boston and New York gave way to drives from western Pennsylvania and the Ohio Valley to New York. The large-scale driving, salting, pickling, and packing of hog meat for flat-boat transport to southern eaters also became a specialty of Cincinnati.

Before the 1870s most butchering and preparation of meat occurred not far from its urban consumers, creating the stench and chaos always associated with meat processing. After 1870 cattle drives from Texas ranches went first to regional butchering centers like Wichita, Kansas City, and Omaha, and then—with improved rail connections—directly from fattening stations in these provincial centers to Chicago, which became the main meat packer and processor for most of the eastern United States.

The stockyards of Chicago perfected the "disassembly" line that had been developed by butchers of pigs long before Henry Ford dreamed of his automotive assembly line. Indeed, contemporary descriptions of Chicago's slaughterhouse districts closely resemble those of England's dark, satanic industrial mills. In Sinclair Lewis's *The Jungle*, dehumanizing and penny-counting corporate bureaucracy prevailed—as did hard labor and long hours, noise, and rapidly moving, sharp machinery that could sever human fingers as easily as sausage casings. Whole animals entered from the nearby stockyards into the top floors of Swift and Armour factories; rivers of blood, tons of guts and bones, and neatly packaged or canned pieces of flesh emerged from the bottom floor, along with thousands of exhausted, often blood-drenched, workers at the end of the day. Lewis's images, even if exaggerated, are apt reminders of just how industrialized food manufacturing was becoming.

The mass production and marketing of food in this period depended on transportation networks of canals, railroads, and highways, and the new technology of steam engines, ice boxes, mechanical refrigeration, and aluminum cans. By the twentieth century, scientific research on plant and animal life, on the chemical composition of food and how it is digested and used by the human body, and on the purity and safety of processed and manufactured foods began to generate close ties between university and corporate communities. With governmental support, major agricultural industries like citrus, wine, and produce financially supported the creation of academic departments of agriculture, food chemistry, and, at the University of California, enology (the study of wine). The breeding of new varieties of plants and animals and experiments with new means of processing—notably freezing—were all well under way by 1940.

With technical innovations, cooking too moved into the factory. The manufacture of ready-to-eat cold cereals in the nineteenth century ultimately changed what most Americans ate for breakfast. One of the best examples of this coupling of science and food manufacturing from the later nineteenth century comes from the life of Dr. John Thompson Dorrance. An MIT-trained chemist, Dorrance created condensed soups for the

Joseph Campbell Company, a business that had previously specialized in canning mince meats, jams, and "beef-steak ketchup."

The same processes of centralization and corporation building changed food retailing, too. Until 1920, the country store served most rural Americans, while municipally owned markets struggled to provide rapidly expanding cities with locally produced meat, grain, milk, and vegetables. The managers of country stores still accepted maple sugar, eggs, and grain in exchange for sugar, coffee, candies, or imported foods. The store owner in turn sold this local produce to city merchants in exchange for products from city markets. The casual nature of the trade is captured by J. M. D. Burrows' writing of his early days in Iowa: "I bought that wheat, and I bought those hogs; and this was the commencement of the produce trade of Davenport."[54] In cities, municipal markets provided stalls for butchers and farmers coming to town to market their fresh products. Outside these centralized markets, small grocery stores specialized in the sale of dry, bulk, and imported items like flour, beans, and bottled, canned, or preserved goods—items that traveled longer distances. In urban areas in the South, local farmers also peddled their products door to door, transported in a horse-drawn wagon.

The expansion of long-distance trade and the rapid growth of commercial and industrial cities initially strained existing means of urban provisioning, resulting in irregular and spoiled supplies, especially of meat and produce. Again, the butcher J. M. D. Burrows expressed the problem from the merchant's point of view: "We had no railroads. Everything had to be moved by water, and, of course, had to be held all winter [when rivers and canals froze]."[55] In New York around 1800, visitors to working-class neighborhoods noted that "shoppers in the public markets passed among carts of putrid vegetables and week-old fish and stepped carefully around the heads of sheep, lambs &c., the hoofs of Cattle, blood, and offal strewed in the gutters and sometimes on the pavement, dead dogs, cats, rats, and hogs."[56] Sixty years later, with improved refrigeration, New York's markets were only modestly cleaner. While Thomas De Voe was excited by their "endless variety and vast amounts of meat, poultry, fish, vegetables and fruits," he noted also that they had "not room enough to receive and properly display them for sale, much less room enough to accommodate the thousands who purchase," and he saw also "the great mass of confusion and corruption, the crowded state, and especially the want of system" in markets as an ongoing disgrace.[57]

By 1900 large-scale farmers and processors began to organize their own routes to tantalizing mass markets of urban consumers. Burrows became a large-scale packer of pork, then a miller of corn and wheat for sale to distant markets, usually through a series of middlemen traders. In 1854, on a trip through Albany, New York, he was surprised to discover Albion Flour from his own midwestern mill, and he asked the owner to tell him how he had acquired it (through commission houses in New York and Chicago).[58] Growers' and ranchers' associations hired agents, or contracted with processors or city commission dealers, who began to function as wholesalers at auctions and exchanges near rail terminals, bypassing municipal markets. Sears and Roebuck experimented with food delivery to rural purchasers, while grocers like the sons of George Huntington Hartford of the Atlantic and Pacific Tea Company opened "economy" stores that purchased and sold small quantities of packaged, and usually branded, foods at low prices. By the 1920s, A&P and scores of smaller, regionally based competitors had established chains of retail stores, with their own complex network of connections to producers. Some, in fact, became producers of their own bread and canned goods and owned their own brand lines. By the 1930s the most innovative grocers were expanding their wares beyond the traditional dry and processed staple goods to include produce, dairy, and meat, thus becoming supermarkets.

In nineteenth-century cities—where workplaces were located ever farther from home—more Americans also became willing to pay for and eat food prepared outside their families. First boarding houses, and later residential hotels, catered to single migrants, providing them, along with growing numbers of travelers, with the "American" plan of eating. It provided three fixed meals a day, served at a common table, but without the drink that accompanied tavern meals in the colonial era. By the 1830s, when cities grew larger and distinctive residential and commercial areas first emerged, new drinking places—often called grog shops—were clearly separated from "eateries," although both beckoned businessmen and clerks who no longer traveled the long distance home for their noonday meal. Grog shops evolved into saloons, and later bars. Eateries, too, evolved into a wide variety of businesses catering to particular groups of eaters—from the child on the way home from school, to the businessman looking to bolt a quick, self-served meal, to the society lady seeking a dignified light repast while shopping, to convivial and sophisticated dining and recreation among one's peers, whether among New York's "500" or among the "Bowery B'hoys."

Precisely because few immigrant, rural, and poor Americans at first visited these new sites of food retailing, few of the processed foods of America's food industries appeared on their tables. Many Americans' culinary conservatism around 1900 reflected their continued economic isolation from the new national marketplace.

Viewed from the perspectives of immigrant and ethnic minorities in the years around 1900, it appeared that a combination of poverty, isolation, and cultural conservatism allowed many Americans to avoid confronting fully the homogenizing effects of industrialized canning, milling, and meat packing and the long-distance transport of meat, fruits, and vegetables. If anything, many American eaters seemed somewhat reluctant to enter that marketplace, and preferred—even in urban settings—to grow at least some of their own food, bake their own bread, and—generally—to allow women's domestic labor to produce what might already be bought for cash at the grocery store. Their choice reflected much about themselves: their preference for familiar foods, their deeply rooted traditions of family solidarity, their poverty, their desire to avoid the wage-labor that generated cash for consumer purchases. In some cases it also reflected their century-long experiences with precarious and limited food supplies in their homeland; peasant economies with their cultures of "limited good" made acquisition of any new goods a possible provocation to jealousy, competition, and disruption of the communal group.

At the same time, mass production seemed well organized to deliver the very staples on which deeply rooted regional diets depended. Under its influence, regional eating habits in the nineteenth century did evolve toward greater homogeneity. Wheat, beef, and sugar became more plentiful everywhere, while corn, cider, whiskey, rum, and game declined in importance. Prepackaged beef and white, manufactured "American" bread—"the world's worst" according to some—symbolized American eating among an expanding mass market of native-born and middle-class Americans.[59] Many Americans of the era also saw beef and white bread as symbols of their country's bounty and its technical progress (even though pork consumption continued to surpass that of beef until 1960). Dieticians, too, described a generic American diet in the years around 1900 as "meat in relatively large quantities, with beef predominating and pork second in popularity; potatoes, cabbage, onions, and other fresh vegetables in season and moderate amounts; a variety of fresh fruits in summer but chiefly apples in winter; white bread and rolls, cakes and pies; butter, eggs, milk for baking and relatively moderate or small amounts for drinking."[60]

But even if most Americans ate a diet high in meats, sweets, and white flour foods—and many did—the eating habits of northern and southern European immigrants, Asian immigrants, native southerners, and Texans remained distinct, with different meats, different sweets, and different flours and flour-based dishes preferred in each community. Culinarily, regional and ethnic cuisines, as the historian Harvey Levenstein argues, had not yet "merged almost invisibly into those of the dominant culture."[61]

Yet increasing numbers of Americans could no longer raise their own food by 1900, and even Japanese farmers like the Shimamoto and Shikuma families bought rice, soy sauce, and flour. Thus, balanced against foreigners' obvious predilection for self-sufficiency and culinary conservatism was a growing conviction that the United States was a place where the limits of the Old World had been transcended. Many rural peoples around the world had believed in an alternative world like the Italians' "la cuccagna"—an era or a place where bountiful food, feasting, and even gluttony symbolized the social and economic equality missing in their own lives.[62] Immigrants quickly recognized that there were no "streets of gold" in America, but the bounty and ready accessibility of the food marketplace did evoke visions of la cuccagna for many, allowing them to indulge and enjoy a sense of equality and well-being as food consumers. Even when they lived—as most did—on low incomes, isolated from the national marketplace, the pleasures of culinary consumer choice were already within reach.

When they did go to market, foreign-born consumers preferred buying from businessmen of their own kind. Corporations operating through a nationwide rail network were not yet the country's main provisioners. In part that was because corporations did not yet know what America's many eating communities wanted. It was entrepreneurs sharing the tastes of their customers who knew best the tastes of enclave consumers and could dominate enclave economies. And it was through enclave businessmen that immigrants and other culturally conservative eaters would first sample the products of other groups and corporations. Together they would begin to revise the regional creole dishes of the colonial era.

CHAPTER THREE

Ethnic Entrepreneurs

In 1915 the small Chinese community in Locke, California, supported 6 restaurants, 9 grocery stores (two with their own slaughterhouses), a flour mill, and numerous boarding houses—all run by Chinese businessmen selling to Chinese consumers.[1] In 1899 the much larger Jewish Lower East Side in New York City boasted 140 groceries, 131 kosher butchers, 36 bakeries, 9 bread stands, 14 butter and egg stores, 24 candy stores, 7 coffee shops, 10 delicatessens, 9 fish stores, 7 fruit stands, 2 meat markets, 10 sausage stores, 20 soda water stands, 5 tea shops, 11 vegetable stores, 13 wine shops, 15 grape wine shops, and 10 confectioners. Here, too, Jewish businesses produced and sold to Jewish customers.[2] Descriptions like these suggest how important consumption was becoming, even among cultural conservatives like new immigrants and the rural eaters of the South and Southwest. The desire for the familiar provided the foundation for businesses in these enclaves, and those businesses in turn made culinary conservatism possible. Women like Mary Antin's mother turned to them in large numbers for the familiar ingredients which enclave businessmen, not distant corporations, best understood.

As impressive, extensive, and complete as these lists of ethnic businesses seem, their self-sufficiency and economic isolation nevertheless proved transitory. Already in 1890, Antin's father had probably bought the "little tins that had printing all over them," as well as the queer, slippery bananas, from the very same stores. The businessmen of enclave communities soon brought the products of mass manufacturers in far-off locations to Locke and to the Lower East Side. Eventually, too, they would deliver foods of Chinese and Jewish eaters to consumers of other cultural backgrounds.

The relationship of enclave businessmen and ethnic consumers was usually a close one, and it supported a culture of business quite unlike that of America's growing corporations. But conflict abounded. Ethnic enclave businesses competed intensely among themselves, as driven by profit motives as any other businesses in the United States and as vulnerable to the fickleness of their customers. Enclave consumers provided a rather fragile financial foundation for ethnic businessmen, who, like many other Americans, desired security and upward mobility. The unpredictability inherent in enclave markets repeatedly encouraged small businesses to look farther afield, beyond the boundaries of ethnic communities, for a wider market of more diverse consumers.

Few saw this fragility in 1900. Lacking cosmopolitan palates, American consumers at the turn of the century bought much of their food from entrepreneurs "of their own kind." Ethnic and regional food cultures created quasi-monopoly markets for cultural insiders. In these markets, businessmen needed a secure and loyal clientele more than large amounts of capital. While it was hard to succeed for long in the business of food purveyor, it was not at all difficult to get started. Thousands of humble immigrant and minority entrepreneurs did so.

At the beginning of the chain were immigrant farmers. Often, they had introduced crops new to the United States in order to eat, and to sell, foods familiar in far-off homelands. When Elise Waerenskold arrived in Texas in the 1850s, for example, she reported unhappily that she had been unable to buy seed for "any kind of cabbage or cauliflower, kohlrabi, Swedish turnips, or French turnips (botfeldtske)." She advised prospective Norwegian immigrants to bring seeds with them. In a later letter she asked a friend to send fruit pits, and in 1870 she instructed another to bring trees along for her. She requested empress, bergamot, and gray pear trees; glass and pigeon apple trees; green and St. Catherine's plum trees; and cherry trees. She promised to pay for the transportation of Norwegian gooseberry and currant bushes. By then, Warenskold was already successfully raising the cabbage and cauliflower absent in her early days in Texas.[3]

Agricultural innovation by immigrant eaters was even more pronounced in the West, which by the end of the nineteenth century had become the center of American agriculture. In Hawaii, Chinese rice growers imported familiar fish varieties from Asia in order to stock local streams and irrigation ditches. One farmer—Look Sing—introduced an Asian shellfish that was popularly used in important festival dishes in China and was not available in the New World. In California, Japanese farmers introduced Napa cabbage and the radishes of their homeland. Felix Gillet introduced soft-shelled walnuts, and Louis Pellier imported prune plum cuttings, both from their native France. Italians in the Santa Clara valley continued to cultivate prickly pears (popular with Sicilians) until the 1940s; Sal Lo Bue believed his grandfather had first introduced them. Not far from Lo Bue's farm, Santo Ortolano claimed to have introduced broccoli, an Italian favorite, in 1902. "No one liked broccoli for a long time," Ortolano noted. Ortolano also grew the long, giant squashes known in Sicily as "guguzz"; these were candied by immigrants for incorporation in festival pastries.[4]

Everywhere, too, immigrant farmers sold surpluses of these culinary oddities, thus becoming truck gardeners for their urban countrymen. Italians in the Greenbush section of Madison remembered ordering tomatoes from two old Sicilian truck farmers, who "delivered to our backyard, usually in quantities of five to ten bushels every day."[5] More often, truck farmers organized urban markets to sell their wares. Mexican farmers near San Antonio set up their market in the Military Plaza, where a visitor in 1897 described how "the green of the big stacks of watermelons foils the yellow of carrots, and is shaded off by the paler green of the cabbage mountains . . . The dull red and clear white onions, the pink radishes, pale cantaloupes, carmine tomatoes and brown potatoes."[6] In Denver, Italian truck farmers peddled their produce door to door, while in San Francisco, Italian commission agents organized Colombo Market in 1874 to connect the many Italian farmers and consumers of this growing city.

What could not be grown locally could be imported—albeit at a price.

In California alone, Chinese immigrants created a market for almost 35 million pounds of imported rice: 32 million pounds came from China, the remainder from Hawaii. As late as 1932, Japanese in Hawaii still purchased 158,800 pounds of umeboshi (red-pickled plums) valued at $5,460 and 98,623 pounds of fu (gluten cakes) for $17,259.[7] Italians in California created a strong market for Mediterranean products: in 1879 the state imported 4 million gallons of wine; 140,000 cases of sparkling wine; 500,000 gallons of brandy; 1,500 tons of figs; and 300,000 gallons of olive oil.[8] By 1930, importers of green chile from Mexico included the Arthur Commission Company in Milwaukee; Albuquerque's Mercantile Company; the Gebhart Chili Powder Company in San Antonio; the Rutherford Chile Company in Kansas City; La Mexicana in San Francisco; McCormicks' Spice Company in Baltimore; and Jose La Llomera of New York.[9]

Not surprisingly, this sector of American food trade was dominated by ethnic businessmen, who best knew consumer tastes and the place to purchase the desired products. As early as the 1880s, Chinese importers in San Francisco organized a Chinese Chamber of Commerce to keep abreast of customs and tariff regulations affecting their trade; they incorporated in 1909. During the same years, grocers and wholesale groceries operated by Germans and other Central Europeans dominated food importing from Europe.[10] The 27 importers listed in the 1906 San Francisco Directory reflected the range of the town's eating communities by that time: German, German Jewish, Italian, French, Japanese, and Slavic importers outnumbered those with English-origin or ethnically unclear surnames.

Even relatively small grocers often used personal connections to import and then sell small quantities of local homeland specialties. These ventures did not always work out for the best. In Brooklyn, one small-scale importer and grocer accidentally split open a barrel of olive oil during its transport from basement storage to the family's flat; his daughter recalled seeing "a great oil river . . . run down the stairs and spread in a vast oily smear across the linoleum of the lower floor." This unfortunate incident quickly terminated the family import business.[11]

San Francisco's Domingo Ghirardelli had better luck. He began life in a Genovese family of pastry makers and spice importers, and first practiced his importing and candy-manufacturing skills in Peru. Around the middle of the nineteenth century, after moving to San Francisco, Ghirardelli continued to import spices, while beginning to grind spices and chocolate in a local factory. Ghirardelli's sons then made the family's cocoa and chocolate products popular in San Francisco and beyond.[12]

Even the humblest of urban immigrants could parlay production for family consumption into small businesses, often organized and initially run from a hard-working woman's kitchen. Over time, these small producers provided domestic alternatives to imports. In New York and other cities, Italian immigrants' taste for pasta and flavored ice desserts turned hundreds of homes and grocery stores into small-time factories. Visitors to New York's Little Italies at the turn of the century found macaroni under production on every block—sometimes in cellar bakeries, sometimes in homes, sometimes in shop stores attached to tenement apartments. Pasta was hung up to dry on frames in windows, cellars, and tenement roofs. Until World War I most Italians made their pasta, whether for home consumption or sale, from imported Russian durum wheat. After World War I, when it was temporarily unavailable, they turned to American durum wheat flour; this change finally sparked a few investors in large-scale manufacturing of pasta.

The La Rosa Company, founded in 1914 by a Sicilian who had imported olive oil from his native Sicily beginning in 1907, expanded only after World War I. By 1930 the company had 300 (Italian) workers and sales of $3–5 million a year. Still, as late as 1937, a WPA investigator declared the macaroni industry "more or less at the stage of transition from home industry to the modern factories of mass production"; he found 8 major plants operating in Brooklyn and Queens, among them La Rosa and Ronzoni.[13] The transition from small-scale domestic to factory production took even longer for Italian ices, beginning in 1930 with New York's Marchioni Spumoni Company.

Local farmers and domestic producers sometimes competed directly with importers of foreign goods; in other cases, however, importers themselves provided the capital for mass cultivation of a desired product. In the 1930s a Brooklyn Jewish woman who had noted the popularity of imported plum tomatoes with her Italian customers found an Italian partner to import plum tomato seeds. Together they began raising and eventually canning this popular variety of tomatoes in California, shipping to eastern consumers. In Hawaii, large numbers of Japanese and Chinese immigrants encouraged local production of Asian staples like rice, tofu, miso, and koji. Indeed, Hawaii soon grew so much rice that it exported it, temporarily, to the mainland.

The Second World War, like the first, provoked a crisis for immigrants accustomed to importing key food items and for the ethnic businessmen who handled the trade. In San Francisco in the 1930s, C. Granucci and Sons had imported Italian cheeses; Italian and French dried mushrooms; tomato paste; Norwegian, French, Italian, Spanish, and Portuguese sardines and other canned fish; and their own Granucci brand olive oil from Lucca, in Tuscany.[14] But after World War II broke out, Italians had to switch to California olive oil—which they found "only fair"—and to Spanish olive oil. When the price of imported parmigiana cheese soared from 80 cents to $1.60 a pound, putting it beyond the reach of ordinary eaters, consumers began to accept comparable cheeses manufactured in Argentina and Wisconsin.[15]

Kosher eaters could not easily depend on imports, so the arrival of Eastern European Jews led to the rapid growth of a variety of food industries in America. Kosher butchering attracted particular attention. During the first decades of the twentieth century there were more than 10,000 kosher butcher shops in the United States, as many as 9,000 in New York alone. By 1917, at the height of Orthodoxy in America, a million Jews ate 156 million pounds of kosher meat each year.[16] Because the rules of kashruth required meat to be soaked and salted (to remove blood) within 72 hours of an animal's slaughter, kosher meat generally sold for four or five cents more per pound than other beef. (And if prices increased, Jewish women took to the streets, boycotting and even destroying shops that sold meat at inflated prices.) With high prices as an incentive, meat packers in Chicago, though far away from the center of Jewish life in New York City, attempted to provide kosher meat, hiring a Jewish "shochet" (butcher) and shipping the koshered meat back East via refrigerated train cars. But Jewish consumers remained skeptical. A 1925 New York State study claimed that 40 percent of the meat sold as kosher in the city was actually ritually unclean. And as late as 1929 one, third of New York's beef was still slaughtered locally for Jewish customers so concerned with purity that only local meat could serve.

Efforts to satisfy Orthodox consumers' concerns and certify meat as kosher even if it traveled long distances recurred periodically. In 1887 eighteen Orthodox synagogues in New York, Philadelphia, and Baltimore united and called for Jacob Joseph, the chief rabbi of Vilna, to come serve as their head. Among his duties, he was to organize the kosher meat business. Lacking financial backing and facing opposition from beef and poultry butchers and from other rabbis, Joseph's efforts foundered. In 1909 the Kehillah (community association) of New York attempted again, without much success, to unite all branches of Judaism around a program of certification. In 1923 the Union of Orthodox Jewish Congregations started an official kashruth supervision and certification program, but limited its attention to processed foods, thus avoiding clashes with the large numbers of rabbis already engaged in certifying the city's many butchers. Encouraged by mayors Walker and La Guardia in the 1930s, the Kashruth Association focused on certifying the kosher poultry market, but the purity of meat remained a matter of uncertainty for Orthodox consumers, even after New York State passed a Kosher Law enforced by a Bureau of Kosher Law in its Department of Agriculture in 1934.[17]

Just as important to Orthodox Jews was the purity of Passover matzos, and their production, too, became big business quite quickly. For example a baker from Hungary, Jacob Horowitz, founded Horowitz Brothers and Magareten Company in 1883; his Hungarian-born countrymen had asked him to produce Passover matzos, since they did not trust non-Hungarian bakers to do it properly. Horowitz and Magareten soon faced competition in the sale of Passover matzos from Ruach and Strumpf and other bakers. Meanwhile, Goodman and Son, Gottfried and Steckler, and Nathan Messing began to specialize in producing other baked goods—bagels, challah, cookies, and strudels—in forms and tastes familiar to the Jews of Eastern Europe.

Jews from that region had also long eaten kosher sausages, which could not be imported under U.S. import laws in the twentieth century. While delicatessen owners sometimes produced their own, most eventually purchased from sizeable sausage factories, like the Hebrew National Kosher Sausage Factory and the Williamsburg Genuine Kosher Meat Products Company in New York. Kosher butchers also offered sausages they called kosher "hot dogs," modeled on the German sausages that were marketed at American fairs and sporting events, following their introduction at the St. Louis world's fair in 1904. Disagreements quickly arose over who produced the best of this kosher New York specialty. Was it Nathan's? Was it Hebrew National? Lee Silver of New York insisted that the true Hot Dog King was Abe Gellis of Isaac Gellis Delicatessen. Gellis, defending the superiority of his kosher hot dog, which he made in his own delicatessen, complained that "Hebrew National uses hydrolyzed plant protein, which is an additive, and to me that's not kosher."[18]

In the Southwest, a burgeoning population of Mexican immigrants created demand for their own culturally unique products. In San Antonio, Bartolo Martinez opened a mill in 1896, believed to be the first masa mill in the country. His Molino Para Nixtamal company prepared dough for tortillas; Martinez then delivered the mixture about town in a wagon. By the 1920s Francisco Garcia, a Basque immigrant who came to San Antonio via Mexico, had opened San Antonio's first tortilla factory, competing with many other smaller producers and with housewives working in their own kitchens.

Farther west in California in the last years of the nineteenth century, a young and struggling wine industry revived with the arrival of millions of new immigrant wine drinkers to eastern cities. Whatever the popularity of wine in Charleston in the colonial era, the United States had not become a nation of wine drinkers, and efforts to produce a palatable wine from local grapes repeatedly foundered as they had in the colonial era. In the 1840s Elise Waerenskold's Norwegian neighbors in Texas successfully brewed mead and beer at home, but she lamented that she "had not tasted a glass of wine" in four years.[19] Wherever immigrant wine drinkers settled—Germans in Cincinnati, Missouri, and California in the 1850s, and Italians in New York after 1880—commercial efforts to produce wine followed, often undertaken by immigrant farmers and vintners. Still, it took almost one hundred years to produce a palatable American wine. The problem was not lack of expertise about the making of wine—immigrants had brought that with them since colonial days. As one historian of American wine explained, "The problem [was] to find a grape that would, first of all, survive, and second, yield a juice worth converting into wine."[20] Until the 1960s, those few natives who cared about wine generally drank expensive imports. A British observer claimed that "the others ('winos' apart . . .) drank hard liquor, or Coke, or beer by the can, unless they were first-generation Americans or recent immigrants of Italian or . . . Mediterranean stock."[21] Immigrants provided the necessary consumers to spark new investment in California vineyards.

Before 1860, California wine-making flourished on a small scale around the sites of the former Spanish Missions in the south, especially around Los Angeles. Two San Francisco musicians and wine importers, the Germans Charles Kohler and John Frohling, began a trend, however, when they purchased a northern vineyard in order to produce wine for their wine shop and importing business. With California's incorporation into the United States, the development of the transcontinental railroad in 1869, and the arrival of millions of wine-drinking Germans and Italians, growers in California's northern counties extended grape production and tried new wine-making techniques. Strong demand provided a strong incentive: 7,000 Italians in Trenton, New Jersey, alone supported 51 sellers of wines and liquors.

Before the 1860s, family-based vineyards and wine-making prevailed, and East Coast wine markets were controlled by Ohio and New York producers. In the 1850s Kohler began efforts to market his wines in the East. Large-scale production of European rather than mission grapes was then introduced by the Hungarian revolutionary count Agoston Haraszthy, who imported over 100,000 cuttings of European vines in the 1860s. Haraszthy hoped to get state support to create a 6,000-acre vineyard, with marketing offices in New York, San Francisco, Chicago, Philadelphia, and London. Failing to get legislative support for his enterprise, he purchased Buena Vista vineyards with private backing but quickly began randomly selling his European vines to pay off his debts. Lands devoted to grapes expanded after the introduction of these new vines, but the origins of the root stocks were often lost in the process, discouraging European vintners from experimenting with Old World techniques like vintaging. In 1855 there were 1 million vines in California; in 1860, 8 million; in 1870, 28 million. The 1876 Philadelphia Centennial Exposition gave good advertising to California wines, whose acceptance by the public was aided by the collapse of French and Italian wine exports owing to phylloxera devastation.[22]

After 1860 the founders of northern and southern California vineyards producing for eastern immigrant consumers were almost all foreigners: the French Pierre Pellier and Pierre Mirassou in San Jose; Etienne Thee and Charles Lefranc (founders of Almaden) at Los Gatos; the German Carl Wente and the Irishman James Concannon in Livermore Valley; the German Charles Krug and the Finnish Gustav Niebaum (founder of Inglenook) in Napa; the Italian-Swiss Agricultural Colony in Cloverdale. After 1880 Italians began to buy older vineyards from these pioneers and to start new ones.

California vineyards soon specialized in producing either red wines, called Chianti by their Italian vintners and "dago red" by their consumers, or sweet white dessert wines, some of them carbonated. They sold these blended, bulk wines in barrels to wholesale grocers and importers in New York and other eastern cities. The years before 1900 saw recurring boom and bust, and intensive competition. In an effort to regulate competition and to market their wines more effectively, two groups of grape growers formed marketing cooperatives in the 1890s: a multi-ethnic group of mainly second-generation Americans (the sons of German and other Central European wine makers) founded the California Wine Association in 1894; it competed with the California Wine Makers' Corporation composed largely of Italian growers. With 60,000 people employed in the industry in 1910, and a yearly production of 50 million gallons of wine, production for eastern immigrant markets had become very big business.[23]

Closer than producers to conservative enclave consumers, and far more numerous, were local immigrant retailers. Among these, the humblest were pushcart street vendors. One Italian immigrant son believed that purchasing from the street itself distinguished immigrants from native-born Americans, since "we had a bread man . . . and a fruit and vegetable man, a watermelon man and a fish man . . . Americans went to the stores for most of their food—what a waste."[24] In New York, immigrant vendors pioneered in decentralizing market sites, bringing foods to consumers and relocating sales in residential neighborhoods, usually in the form of impromptu pushcart markets set up adjacent to Jewish, Italian, and, later, Spanish tenement buildings. While most of the immigrant pushcart traders were men, in the Jewish community women too joined the crowded markets along Hester and Broome Streets. One, Annie Jacobs of the Blake Street Market in Brooklyn, refused her grown-up children's offer to pay her twenty-five dollars to stay home. "While I've got my health, I'll earn my own living."[25]

In a city like New York, where huge public markets like Fulton received 50 million tons of fish each year, and where six billion pounds of fruit arrived to be processed and sold annually, immigrant pushcart operators speeded the path from producer to final consumer. To established, native-born Americans, these peddlers symbolized the chaos and dangers of the food marketplace (Was the food tainted? old? rotten?) but also the ambition and verve of "penny capitalists." What could seem more "American" than a hard-working, striving immigrant small businessman? Pushcart vendors helped make the prices for groceries lower on the Lower East Side than anywhere else in New York, or indeed in the nation. A sympathetic historian even termed the pushcarts "social democracy in the marketplace."[26]

One did not have to be foreign-born, however, to understand the effectiveness of marketing to consumer housewives in their homes. In the southern city of Charleston, slaves had dominated huckstering as they had hunting, gathering, and gardening in the years before the Civil War. After freedom, African-American hucksters, selling watermelons, seed cakes, and street snacks like "monkey brains," "bennies," and groundnuts, gave Charleston's streets a unique look—and sound—into the twentieth century. African-Americans bought and sold all kinds of fruits and vegetables, flowers, berries, baskets, seafoods, and poultry. On a typical day, crowds of hucksters, with their wagons and carts, arrived at sunrise at markets where customers shopped on a daily basis. The hucksters, they told a local writer, came "from up de road," or "across from Jeems Island" or "ober de new bridge." Charleston's African-American fishing boats, which, the same writer noted, were "manned by intrepid sailors known far and wide for skill and daring," also supplied the city's famed seafood.[27] Several hundred small creaky boats entered the harbor like a swarm of mosquitoes, giving them their name—the mosquito fleet.

Natives and visitors alike noted the haunting calls with which black street vendors announced their wares in the marketplace. Joe Cole had a small shop, called Joe Cole and Wife, but he walked the streets with a limp, yelling

> Old Joe Cole—Good Old Soul
> Porgy in the Summer-time and Whiting in the Spring
> 8 upon a string.
> Don't be late, I'm sattin' [sitting] at de gate
> Don't be mad—Here's your shad
> Old Joe Cole—Good Old Soul.

The same writer described hucksters who called themselves "vegetubble Maumas"; she described them as "wonderful, wide-chested, big-hipped specimens of womanhood that balance a fifty pound basket of vegetables on their heads and ever and anon cry their goods," including one who called out her yams as "Swete Pete Ate Her."[28]

A short step above the street huckster in the hierarchy of enclave retailers, and even more ubiquitous in American cities, was the small grocer serving an ethnic clientele. Mary Antin's father made this crucial transition: he began by selling cold lemonade, hot peanuts, and pink popcorn at a beach-side stand, and then graduated to a small store in a Jewish neighborhood.[29] Thousands of men and women followed the same path. In New York in 1938, almost 10,000 groceries still catered exclusively to Italians and an equal number to Jews. In Chicago, in a 25-block immigrant area with 113 retail stores, 44 sold food of some sort. Needless to say, fierce competition marked the trade. One needed only a few hundred dollars to purchase the necessary stock, often from a failed grocer eager to sell out. In the 1930s the smallest Jewish grocers in New York averaged only about $175 weekly in gross income.[30]

In larger communities, the most successful grocers specialized. Delicatessens offered kosher meats, while New York's Jewish entrepreneurs also opened the unique, and mysteriously named, "appetizing stores" that offered fine, flavorful products like smoked fish and luxury canned goods, both American and imported. In the 1930s there were about 500 appetizing stores in New York City, and their owners had formed a trade association. There were, however, no appetizing stores in Jewish communities in other cities.[31] Italian neighborhoods, too, had their pork stores and salumerie, their bakeries and confectioneries. And in a New York Hungarian neighborhood, a resident remembered finding on one block a bakery, pork store, grocery store, ice cream parlor, laundry, candy store, and beer parlor.

In large communities, successful retailers also expanded to become wholesalers. One was the grocer Andrew Schoch, born in Württemberg, Germany, in 1850. Schoch arrived in the United States in 1866, worked on a farm in Minnesota, learned English, then clerked in a German grocery story in St. Paul. Together with a cousin, he opened his own store in 1874 with a $3,000 investment. As late as the 1890s, when the grocery first began advertising, it did so in German, claiming itself to be "St. Paul's bedeutendster [leading, or best-known] Grocerladen."[32] By 1914 Schoch's was incorporated and occupied an entire city block in downtown St. Paul. It employed 150 people. Having done $15,000 in sales in its first year, Schoch's expanded to a $2 million business by the 1920s. Besides the retail grocery, which had been its first department, it operated a large wholesale department selling to hotels, restaurants, and dining cars of railroads; it roasted its own coffee, baked its own bread, and ran its own meat market.

Other successful grocers like New York's Jewish Krasne family and Boston's Armenian Mugar family (founders of Star Markets) started out with small chains of groceries serving their ethnic communities. Immigrant wholesalers and commission agents linked them to far-off corporate producers. In New York, produce agents bought from the city's large auctions that brought fruit and vegetables from all over the East Coast and from California. These agents were as divided by ethnicity as the eating communities they provisioned. While three (presumably Jewish) commission agents—Breslauer & Fliegler, Nathan Lieblich, and Sam Berger—dealt only in fruits and vegetables, Italian dealers listed specialties with great precision. Angelo Fruit Distributors at Washington Market handled tomatoes, apples, string beans, berries, and peppers, while Tony Annunziato (who worked out of the Bronx Terminal Market) sold grapes and apples. A few Jewish commission agents' listings hinted at the preferences of their eating communities. Kornblum and Company on Warren Street listed potatoes, onions, cabbage, turnips, carrots, and cucumbers—a very different range of vegetables from those handled by their Italian counterparts.[33]

While ties to a specific eating community were important to dealers like Schoch, Annunziato, or Kornblum and Company, they were of greatest significance to the smaller retailers. More than capital, enclave retailers needed a dependable clientele. In Boston's Italian North End, for example, according to one resident, "People would go to a particular store because it carried their favorite brand of sausage, or something special from the paese [hometown] in the old country . . . No grocery store would ever attract Avellinese customers if it did not carry soprasatta (a sausage made from pig's head) at Eastertime." A fellow North Ender concurred: "Italians do not go to the nearest store for groceries but went to the store they knew carried their favorite regional foods."[34] The shelves of any small grocery store closely reflected the peculiar eating customs of its customers: Greek stores offered lamb, pastries, imported olives, flat breads; the Jewish store offered tea, pickles, and herring.

If a grocer had too few customers, he attracted new ones with a common ploy—credit. In doing so, of course, he also attracted the poorest consumers, increasing the risk of his business operations. When clients lost work, or when unemployment soared, or when quarrels and disagreements shattered friendly community relations, grocers lost their stores. A Bulgarian woman described how she and her husband lost their business after extending credit to fellow countrymen, who then deserted them during the Great Depression, leaving them with no cash to purchase goods. The woman was bitter about how clients treated her after she had extended them credit: "I went around to collect some money and people would pretend they didn't know me and would close their doors." The truly bitter end was that she and her husband were forced back into the mill jobs they had temporarily escaped.[35] Mary Antin's father, too, was either unlucky or incompetent enough that all his businesses failed. When Mary became sick, the family found itself in debt to another grocer, just as families had once been in debt to them.

Mary Antin nevertheless reached positive conclusions about the fraught relationship between humble ethnic grocer and humble ethnic consumer. "The poor grocer helped to keep me in school for I do not know how many years."[36] Another immigrant noted, "We had an angel of a man whose name was Herman . . . He would trust most of the neighbors. He had a little mahogany-colored book, and he would put down all the things he would trust you with, expecting to be paid either Friday night or Saturday morning."[37] Even in enclave businesses, however, caveat emptor reigned. The daughter of a German farmer remembered her father staying up all night to check the figures in their "store book." His effort paid off, when he found that the grocer, as he suspected, had overcharged him a few dollars.[38] Thus, consumers, too, had mixed feelings about credit. But those who needed it avoided chain stores (which operated on a cash-only basis) well into the 1920s and 1930s.

Given the close ties between ethnic retailers and their clientele, it is scarcely surprising that food businesses functioned as informal community centers. Serving drinks transformed any business into a center of community life. In San Francisco, German and Irish grocers installed small tables where drinks could be dispensed, and a school boy writing on temperance at school protested, "If it wasn't for our pap's selling beer and whiskey along with OTHER GROCERIES, quite a number of us boys couldn't dress as well as we do."[39] Beyond the grocery, Germans had their "lokale" and their saloons, where beer was the main beverage; Irish and British immigrants had their bars and public rooms for consuming ale and whiskey; Italians had cafes for drinking beer, wine, and coffee; Greeks had their Kafenion (coffee shops); Jews enjoyed their tea rooms. Ethnic drinking habits showed visibly on urban streets. In New York, one investigator for *The New York Times* found only 321 saloons on 170 Jewish blocks on the Lower East Side but 256 saloons on 70 Italian blocks just west of the Bowery.[40]

Particularly among Germans, beer drinking and social life went hand in hand. Beer was an essential food for Germans and several other northern European immigrant groups. Bohemians on the Great Plains and Norwegians in Texas brewed at home, and a Swiss migrant in Minnesota wrote home, "So little by little, we expect to become . . . well off . . . with our own wine, sugar, coffee (made from wheat!), beer [and] fruits of all kinds."[41] Children in these groups began drinking early; a German woman from New York's Yorkville German neighborhood recalled, "I drank beer from little up. Anything my father had at the table for supper, we could have. He always had his beer, so we all had our little glass."[42] A Chicagoan explained, "You can depend on the beer, but you can't tell about the milk you get down here."[43]

In cities throughout the United States, ethnocentric bars catered exclusively to one group of consumers.[44] Swedish saloons served Swedish punch and provided meeting rooms for labor unions and singing societies. For Italians, the saloon was a gathering place for men during the long idle periods between construction seasons; padroni might recruit workers there. Polish bars provided a place for dancing.

In San Antonio, the German community's Alamo Street saloons were more civilized than most. Writing about "Glamourous Days in San Antonio," Frank Bushick insisted, "There were no six-shooter brawls or glass throwing, no vulgarity or vice, in the German saloons of this type."[45] Germans found "American" (by which they often meant Irish) bars and their drinking customs both peculiar and unhealthy. Speaking of an American bar in New York, one German observed, "The saloonkeeper stands behind the counter, like in the shops in Germany," and the men there drink "everything standing up, all in one gulp, you can imagine how that hits the head." Germans preferred to drink slowly and leisurely in groups seated in a cheerful or "gemütlich" (comfortable, intimate, homelike) atmosphere.[46] Another German complained of American drinking, "You can't stand around, you get neither a bench nor chair, just drink your schnapps and then go."[47] Germans equally disapproved of the Yankee habit of treating, which put pressure on slow drinkers; they preferred "Dutch treat," with each paying for his own drink. The German lokal and beer garden were extensions of home, where, according to New Yorker Junius Browne, wives, children, and sweethearts "are a check to any excesses or impropriety, and with whom they depart at a seemly hour, overflowing with beer and bonhomie, possessed of those two indispensables of peace—an easy mind and a perfect digestion."[48] The presence of German women and children in drinking establishments, even on Sundays, shocked American Protestants and prohibitionists, however.

Immigrant neighborhoods often had more bars, tea rooms, or coffee shops than they could sensibly support, so for these businessmen, too, competition was intense and business risk high. Saloons in particular were practically on every corner. The small mining town of Hibbings, Minnesota, housed 70 saloons in the early twentieth century.[49] Beginning in the

1880s, when brewers financed 70 percent of them, opening a saloon became very inexpensive. One Chicago barkeeper remembered, "All you need, you might say, is the key to the place, and you can get that by paying the first month's rent."[50] Tied to their community, barkeepers, like grocers, extended credit. The Irish butcher and meat packer Patrick Cudahy saw men throwing stone dust on themselves so they could appear to be employed stone cutters and could go into the stone cutters' preferred saloon "to get a few drinks 'on trust.'"[51] Like ethnic grocery stores, most saloons failed, usually during economic recessions with high unemployment.

For some groups, retailers of food were almost as important as the purveyors of beverages in providing opportunities for sociability. The numerous men without women in communities of immigrant sojourners especially needed prepared meals. Italian, Chinese, and Japanese gang laborers working under a boss or padrone often hired their own cook as they traveled to railroad sites or California harvests. Finnish, Albanian, and Greek men housed together in cities in cooperative boarding houses, called poikatalo in Finnish.

More commonly, however, groups of men found meals in boarding houses operated by women, who provided bedding, laundry, and meals for a fixed weekly payment—equal to about half of what an entry-level female worker earned in a garment factory or cannery. At any given time, between one-quarter and one-third of immigrant families kept boarders, allowing women to operate small businesses from their own homes, based on their traditional cooking and cleaning skills. A German described the food he received in 1855 at a German boarding house as soup, vegetables, and meat at noon and in the morning and evening meat, cheese, and butter.[52] Women cooked for an average of eight boarders, baking bread and often preparing eight separate meals at eight separate times: one reported cooking different meats in one pan, "each with a tag of some sort."[53]

Rosa Mondavi, who lived in a Minnesota mining town, kept 16 male boarders by the time she reached age 19. Her day began at 4:30 A.M. and ended at 11:30 P.M.; after dinner, she packed lunches for the following day. The largest and most successful boarding houses eventually functioned much like hotels. Women rarely operated these, but ethnic ties remained strong in defining the clientele. Minneapolis city directories in 1880–1881 listed 60 boarding-house hotels, including a Hibernia House and "The

Scandinavian." Twenty-five years later there were 130, with German, Polish, and Scandinavian names, owners, and residents.

Competing with boarding houses to feed unattached men were small restaurants, which also sometimes evolved from grocer, delicatessen, or boarding family businesses. New York claimed roughly 10,000 Italian restaurants in the 1930s, and according to a survey, "Every district, city and province of Italy is represented in New York by its restaurant, which serves as a meeting place for fellow townsmen." Most of these restaurants were extremely simple and undecorated, with sawdust on the floor and dirty windows.[54] Restaurants catering to the city's Jews were not much different. Their suppliers reckoned that lunch rooms and restaurants, mainly kosher and catering to the Jewish trade, did about $292 million in annual trade in the 1930s.[55] Still, the Egyptian Rose, a Jewish Aleppan restaurant opened in 1919 by Rose Rissry, seemed to its client like "more than a restaurant . . . It was a social plaza for the Syrian Jews to play backgammon, have Turkish coffee, and talk to each other."[56]

For Jewish and Italian New Yorkers, the boarding house or restaurant, like the small grocery, provided an important route for an ambitious immigrant to escape wage work. When, for example, Malka Grossinger—reportedly a brilliant cook, and the daughter of a tavern-keeper—tired of working in the garment industry, she opened a restaurant. By working 18 hours daily, she and her husband, Selig, soon made a small profit, but after two years the work broke her husband's health, so the family transferred to the country to open a boarding house in the Catskills.

As Malka Grossinger eventually would, too, a wide variety of enclave businesses expanded by catering to ethnic and family celebrations. In Trenton, merchants at the annual Italian festa honoring a favored patron saint offered shelled filbert nuts on a string, torrone, anise cookies, zeppole, clams on the half shell, and Italian pastries. By the 1930s Italian caterers replaced the women who had provided food for the banquets of ethnic fraternal organizations, for weddings, and for other rites of passage. In Jewish communities, caterers took on the additional function as "ritual specialists," providing food for bar mitzvah celebrations, confirmations, graduations, engagements, sweet-sixteen parties, and the circumcision celebration, the bris. Caterers modeled their food on what people ate at home, but provided it on a more lavish scale. For Jews in 1940 this might mean a meal of a grapefruit half, gefilte fish, mandl (egg drops), half a chicken, peas and carrots, kugl, candied sweet potatoes, ice, and apple strudel.[57]

Catering family celebrations became big business, particularly as immigrants attained a modicum of economic security and could enjoy spending surplus cash on important rituals. In Jacksonville's Greek St. John's Orthodox Church in the 1930s, all the Greek restaurants in town collaborated to cater a huge wedding with 400 guests. The meal was a banquet of cold roasted lamb, roasted beef, lettuce and tomato salad, celery, stuffed ripe olives, roquefort cheese, sherry, and muscatel. The wedding cake had been purchased from a local bakery.[58] In New York, the Irish-run Dublin House specialized in banquets for ethnic societies and the Knights of Columbus. Some ethnic societies themselves went into the catering business or operated restaurants for community celebrations: the Germania Hall had its own restaurant in the nineteenth century, as did the Polish National Home in the twentieth.

Kosher-eating Orthodox Jews demanded increasingly sophisticated food service, not only because of their special dietary rules but because of their increasing economic prosperity. Grossinger's boarding house in the Catskills became a successful summer resort hotel by keeping a strictly kosher kitchen. The Grossingers were by no means pioneers in this. Beginning in 1899, Jews had bought about a thousand farms near Ellenville, New York, and many ran small-scale boarding houses for the tired, overheated, yet more prosperous workers of New York—small businessmen in the cigar, leather, and garment industries, clothiers, furriers, jewelers, and professionals.

Respecting sabbath laws was difficult in the countryside. Malka Grossinger explained, "Before sundown on Friday it is necessary to cook and store the bulk of Saturday's food, which can reach huge proportions in a busy resort. Hence the ice Harry got on Fridays. Hence, water all over the kitchen and the place too crowded to move on the busiest day of the week." Despite ceaseless efforts, Grossinger's hotel suffered a temporary financial crisis when malicious gossip spread that it was not "really strictly kosher": guests reported drinking milk in the barn fewer than six hours after eating a "fleishig" meal at noon. Who but an entrepreneur of the same eating community could have responded as skillfully as Selig

Grossinger did? Familiar with the questioning spirit of rabbinical reasoning, Selig reminded his critics, "Don't you know . . . that it says in the Talmud that the six-hour rule doesn't have to be observed if it's a question of health? Why do people come here from the city? For their health. And why do they have milk in the barn at five o'clock? For their health." With their reputation secure, the Grossingers eventually even hired non-Jews, but taught them the laws of kosher. One—a German chef named Fritz Vaihinger—boasted that he had become "perhaps the world's leading exponent of kosher cookery, an acknowledged authority on all questions of Jewish dietary law."

Promotionals for Grossinger's resort also consciously linked Jewish traditions of matchmaking with the resort's continually evolving kosher cuisine. Under their guidance, food not only provided an opportunity for sociability but the means to endogamous marriage and reproduction within American Judaism. According to Grossinger's historian, "First they get the young couple to sit together, then they keep bringing additional foods: first waffles; then Danish pastries hot from the oven. They agreed to another cup of coffee and a nibble of pastry. Only who can stop at a nibble of Grossinger's hot Danish pastries?" When a couple became engaged, Grossinger's got an advertising gimmick, and the couple got a free honeymoon at Grossinger's.[59]

Grossinger's provided for community sociability on a grand scale, refreshing the connections of food with culture. Locally, saloons, restaurants, and groceries served the same function of cultural preservation. Thus, when the Yiddish writer Reuben Iceland, a factory worker in New York and part of a group of younger writers who called themselves Di Yunge, sought the company of his peers, they abandoned Sholom's coffee house of the "elders" on Division Street and began gathering in the basement restaurant of Goodman and Levine's, with its "smell of roast herring and cooked fish, sour borst, fried pancakes, bad coffee, scalded milk." Why did they meet there? "Not because, God forbid, they had such a fondness for dairy dishes, but because it was the center of Di Yunge." When Iceland forgot himself, and a family engagement he had planned with his wife and young child, he was met late at night by the grocer in his building, already open for business at 3 A.M., who greeted him with the bad news, "Young man, wasn't it your wife who ran to the police to look for you?"[60]

Proprietors of groceries and eating establishments could easily develop reputations as wise men for solving small disputes or introducing new-comers to local politics. To maintain an hospitable atmosphere and the clear head wisdom required, saloonkeepers limited their own drinking. One reported to an oral historian, "As a restaurant man, a saloonkeeper, I don't get intoxicated. I don't drink before five o'clock, and then at five o'clock, I drink maybe three highballs. After that, I don't drink no more."[61] This was good business sense, of course, but even more it was a sensible strategy for community leadership.

Enclave economies fostered a distinctive business culture which com-bined profit-making, family labor, high business risks, and communalism. This was neither the guiding culture nor the organizational structure of the modern food corporations that were evolving simultaneously with enclave businesses. In the new food industries, wage-earners replaced family labor, hierarchy replaced communalism, and bureaucracy replaced personal ties between owners and employers and between retailers and consumers. In all these respects, enclave business—while equally motivated by profit-seek-ing—seemed out of step with the values and structures of the national food marketplace and its expanding corporations.

Perhaps the most striking feature of enclave businesses was the predomi-nance of family labor at every link in the food chain, from farmers to retailers. German and Central European farmers, for example, brought with them to the United States a long tradition of women and children performing heavy field work, including plowing, haying, and harvesting alongside the men of the family. A German woman like Katharina Wolf Langendorf Tiek of Madison County, Illinois, recognized the hardships that such traditions of family work imposed on her. In 1869, while plowing a potato field with an incompletely tamed horse, the horse "knocked me over and struck me in the back with its hooves and the plow caught in my skirt and took me along . . . You can imagine what pain I suffered. Four days later I had a little girl."[62] Immigrant women's work in the fields was interpreted as a shocking rejection of the norms of domesticity that na-tive-born American women had adopted by the turn of the century.

The commercialization of farming and food production did not end but merely altered immigrant women's labors. While immigrant men were raising a staple crop for market, immigrant women often became the family "breadgivers," responsible (with the help of the youngest children) for huge gardens, pig pens, and poultry yards, and for preserving, canning, and drying foods for wintertime consumption. Linda Schelbitzki Pickle found evidence in her German-American grandfather's account books that his only contribution to household food was to purchase four bags of flour a year; her Nebraska grandmother "produced everything else that the family needed."[63] To the north, in Minnesota, men sought wages in lumbering and mining, while women and children fed families on marginal farms in a harsh climate and marketed their small surpluses locally. Finnish children recalled mothers who canned for several months of the year—fish, rhubarb sauce, and jam in the spring; blueberries, blackberries, and strawberries in the summer; vegetables as they ripened, especially pickles; wild game and meat in the fall. They also sometimes complained of "endless berry picking" and of bounteous but monotonous meals of bread, potatoes, root vegetables, milk, butter, and meats. Immigrant women's food processing also provided the basis for small businesses. As late as the 1920s, Finnish women traded their excess butter instead of using scarce cash for groceries. One family's monthly purchases were limited to coffee, sugar, yeast, spaghetti, graham flour, and baking powder.[64]

In the city, too, food businesses linked home and workplace, facilitating family labor. Grocers set up housekeeping behind their store, so that in Mary Antin's Arlington Street, "customers were used to waiting while the storekeeper salted the soup or rescued a loaf from the oven."[65] A Swedish girl growing up in her father's grocery store in the Midwest carried with her into later life vivid memories of wandering back and forth between kitchen and storefront, where, as the storekeeper's daughter, she sampled many kinds of candies. Her grandmother and her aunt also ran small stores in the mining town where she was born.[66] The semifictional Umbertina (based on the Italian-American grandmother of novelist Helen Barolini) began selling sandwiches to the men who worked with her husband, then expanded into the grocery trade in an upstate New York community. Experimenting with "vertical expansion," she leased a farm where her children raised produce for the store. Her much older husband became her assistant, purchasing at the farmers' market or entertaining customers with stories and roasted chestnuts. With the help of her sons, Umbertina became an importer, too.[67]

Immigrant drinking establishments depended as much on family labor as any other business. In Chicago, wives of saloonkeepers worked hard to keep bars well stocked with food; they also tended the bar. Laws in Massachusetts and Illinois prevented the hiring of children from outside the family, but saloonkeepers' children generally worked with their parents. In San Antonio Frank Bushick reported that "patrons dropping in" to the German bars of the city "would be waited on by a barmaid, possibly the 'mama,' a large, round-waisted house frau in a comfortable house wrapper, knitting or sewing in the family quarters where she could watch the bar and attend to the business."[68] Native-born Americans were as horrified to find German women working in saloons as they were to find women customers there.

Sharply different in their labor regimes from modern corporations, small family businesses nevertheless remained the dominant form of business in the United States until the 1930s. Two thirds of American retail businesses in 1923 were still mom-and-pop stores.[69] And family management survived considerable expansion, even in enclave businesses. Nine of Andrew Schoch's eleven children worked together into the 1940s to run their father's business. In the case of the Ghirardelli family of San Francisco, one son became president of the incorporated family business in 1895, and he and his siblings owned a majority of company shares. Ghirardelli's grandchildren continued to run the company—albeit with decreasing effectiveness—in the years after World War II.

Grossinger's, too, long remained a family-run enterprise. In its early years daughter Jennie's "rich husband" (her cousin Harry Grossman) provided a cash income for the two-generation family by working in the city while other family members ran the boarding house in the country. In 1919 the Grossinger family debated how to use the money they had saved: father Selig wanted an automobile, mother Malka thought it sensible to use savings to buy truckloads of chickens and gefilte fish. Jennie argued for becoming a real hotel, and she got her way. Different responsibilities fell to each member: Selig raised much of the hotel's food; Malka ran the kitchen, assisted by a deaf son; Jennie became bookkeeper and gradually assumed control of all business details; Harry drummed up business and developed the idea of the free promotional weekend.

Students of small business observe that family businesses survive because—like the Grossingers—they use unpaid family labor to save and expand rather than purchasing consumer goods and a higher standard of living. Even then, many do not prosper, and their survival depends exclusively on the often back-breaking labor of the family, including women and children. Indeed, women like Florence Hoy—who opened a Chinese grocery store with her husband in the early 1930s—worked 12-hour days, from 7 A.M. to 7 P.M., six and a half days a week with no vacations.[70] As Mary Antin's father or Jennie Grossinger's mother might have countered, however, exploitation within the family allowed men and women alike to avoid the wage dependency, industrial discipline, supervision, and bureaucracy of the corporate workplace. Family businesses were a better route to autonomy than they were to making a fortune.

Even the bigger and more successful businesses of enclave economies depended on communal cooperation among producers and consumers rather than upon incorporation and bureaucratization. Cooperative rotating credit associations in some groups allowed Japanese wage-earners to save money, and to become tenant farmers and to open small stores; the same form of self-help organization gave West Indian immigrants in New York the cash they needed to open small groceries. In German-settled Anaheim and later in the Italian-Swiss Colony of northern California, immigrants experimented (unsuccessfully) with cooperative wine-making. Across the country in New York, Jewish workers and consumers experimented, considerably more successfully, with cooperative bakeries.

The Jewish Workmen's Circle opened its first cooperative bakery in Paterson, New Jersey, in 1902. Over the next twenty years, six Jewish and four Italian and Finnish cooperatives opened in the Northeast. The largest was the Brownsville bakery opened by two branches of the Workmen's Circle in 1918; it operated its own stores, and in the 1920s had ten trucks delivering $400,000 worth of bread. Its success rested on the active participation of bakers' unions and the absence of conflict in workplaces where workers were also owners.[71]

Grocery (or consumer) cooperatives were even more widespread. Often they developed from lineage, kin, hometown, or fraternal associations among immigrant consumers. In Locke, California, Chinese immigrants organized a "shares" grocery store and communal gardens, while Italians in Madera, California, founded a Consumers' Cooperative with its own newsletter: it welcomed Italians, native-born Americans, and Mexicans as members.[72]

Cooperation among food buyers became an especially important alternative to private business and family enterprise in the grocery trade of the upper Midwest. Even more than producer cooperatives of butter, cream, or cheese—which functioned essentially like business partnerships—consumer cooperatives in this region fostered a genuine critique of corporate and capitalist American food businesses. Immigrant cooperators had European intellectual roots; with few exceptions, their cooperatives followed principles first outlined in England's Rochdale Cooperative—open membership, democratic control, and the return of surplus earnings to consumers in proportion to the amount they spent on purchases. These were "cooperative commonwealths" in the marketplace.

Consumer cooperators par excellence were Finnish immigrants in rural areas of Minnesota and Michigan, with their many co-op groceries. Their historian concludes that "no other group, immigrant or otherwise, succeeded in establishing such a large number of consumers' cooperatives that have existed over such a long period of time."[73] For many Finns, cooperation was an integral part of working-class struggle. Preceded by Finnish experiments with mutual aid insurance companies (a common expression of fraternalism in other immigrant communities too) and by cooperative boarding houses, the main expression of Finnish consumer cooperation was retail distribution.

In the years between 1904 and 1907 Finnish buying clubs evolved into small cooperative grocery stores; by 1913 eleven "Finn stores" operated in Wisconsin, Michigan, and Minnesota, in both mining towns and isolated rural communities. After the Finnish Socialist Federation and its newspapers spread the word of their success, a boom in cooperative store openings occurred in the period 1913–1917. Federation, first proposed in 1914, became a reality in 1917 with the foundation of the Cooperative Central Exchange (CCE); it changed its name in 1931 to Cooperative Central Wholesale (CCW). Federated cooperatives survived postwar inflation, and the cooperative movement expanded rapidly for the next twenty years.

Politics more than business pressure was the main threat to stability and growth in the CCE/CCW. Many radical Finns believed their stores were not essentially business institutions but rather weapons in a working-class struggle against capital. Workers on strike, angered by unsympathetic local storekeepers or faced with a mining town company store, often united themselves into cooperative buying clubs. By the 1920s about 10 percent of Finnish cooperators attempted to link their consumer cooperatives directly to the Communist Party, transforming them into political organizations. Eventually defeated within their local cooperatives, Communist cooperators then withdrew from CCW to form their own, short-lived, alliance. After their withdrawal, more non-Finns joined cooperative stores, apparently more willing to cooperate once economic interests prevailed over left-wing politics. The CCW at that time replaced its red star label—a design featuring a red star and hammer and sickle, which appeared on coffee and canned goods—with the less controversial, but still glowingly red, "cooperative" label.

For almost twenty more years, retail cooperatives performed well as businesses and as forms of community activism. In 1919 the CCE had opened a bakery; and eventually a clothing department, coffee roasting plant, feed mill, and cooperative publishing office followed, along with a federation of women's guilds and a newspaper for cooperators. Its success reflected in part the CCE's one-week course in bookkeeping—introduced along with a simple system of bookkeeping devised by manager N. V. Nurmi.[74] V. S. Alanne, head of the education department, also developed a curriculum that taught managers and employees about the principles of both business and cooperation.

According to the archivist who arranged the extensive papers of the CCW, the co-op became the main institution for many rural Finnish communities. It was, he reported, "more than merely a retail business that they considered their own. The cooperative movement represented a way of life, providing not only for their material, but social and cultural needs as well."[75] The survival of cooperatives as a form of business thus also required the reproduction of an entire way of life. Training began with managers, who studied cooperative philosophy, beginning with Rochdale, and the history of cooperative movements in Europe and the United States. Alanne believed that Americans had made an important addition to cooperative philosophy, for in this country, "when they become successful in any particular line of business, and their membership increases, they begin to EXPAND into new lines of goods or services," typically through federation.[76] As late as the 1940s, long after Communist cooperators had withdrawn, part of the training course for cooperative managers required them to tackle fundamental economic issues by answering essay questions like, "Name the advantages and disadvantages of the capitalistic system."

In midwestern towns, it was women who taught cooperative consumerism to the children and grandchildren of Finns, and to some of their non-Finnish neighbors as well. By the 1940s, with an English-speaking second generation coming of age, women's auxiliaries in the Central Cooperative Wholesale developed a wide range of social and educational activities to promote the cooperative philosophy among the newer generation: they sponsored summer camps, fair booths, and Saturday schools and circulated newsletters in order to "broaden and develop understanding of the cooperative movement as a way of life as well as a way of business."[77] Such women believed they were "the bosses' real bosses," since their "buying dictates what goods shall be handled."[78]

Despite efforts to pass along the cooperative way of life, cooperative grocery and retail stores fell into decline after World War II. Their decline reflects the passing of the Finnish immigrant generation, the collapse of their radical labor movement, and the purchase of cars, which made corporate grocery chains accessible to rural consumers. Even convinced cooperators noted that the philosophy of cooperation became increasingly incompatible with good business practice during this period. A 1953 evaluator for the CCW noted that cooperative managers saw their positions as "just a job and not a very good one at that" and that the cooperative stores themselves "have only fair to poor (some VERY sad looking) produce displays."[79] Fewer and fewer managers matched the cooperative zeal of one Mr. Thornton, whom a visitor from the CCW found to be a "very pleasing personality." The inspector "enjoyed observing the way he was serving his customers, carrying groceries into the cars, opening the doors for incoming patrons, etc., it was certainly a pleasure, compared with some of the rude service we get in most of our cooperative societies."[80]

Lacking sufficient numbers of personable, and servile, managers like Mr. Thornton, small cooperatives found they could not compete with corporate groceries.

When one compares enclave businesses to the rapid growth of modern food corporations in the nineteenth and early twentieth centuries, it is easy to emphasize their fragility, failures, and backwardness. In a sense, however, enclave businessmen were also ahead of their time: they sought to make profits by effectively serving relatively small market niches, long before this became a popular corporate strategy after World War II. Enclave businessmen serviced market segments that were as yet unrecognized, and untapped, by bigger businesses. Only Sicilians knew that Sicilians would eat and buy guguzz. In enclave business, it was not money but cultural capital that underwrote profits, as small, family-based enterprises offered their friends and neighbors what large corporations could not.

The importance of cultural capital highlights striking differences between native-born African-Americans and immigrants from Europe and Asia. The African-American entrepreneurs of Charleston's food industries marketed not to other African-Americans but to their biracial southern community. Emancipated slaves did not have eating traditions distinctive enough to generate an enclave market where blacks enjoyed special knowledge.[81] While cooperating as consumers or producers seemed relatively unproblematic to Finns or Italians or Japanese, W. E. B. Du Bois's advocacy of Negro cooperation in the 1930s struck his colleagues in the NAACP as a dangerous rejection of their goal of equality through integration. The NAACP eventually ousted Du Bois for such nationalist radicalism, which seemed to support the separation of blacks from white society, in order to create an enclave economy of their own—much as the Nation of Islam does today.

Enclave businesses also regularly revealed the limits of familism and cooperation as alternatives to corporate forms of business enterprise. Even in New York's Jewish community, with its long European ghetto-based tradition of communal organization (kehillah), communal efforts to guarantee the ritual purity of slaughtered meat and poultry repeatedly foundered. Enclave conflicts were more the product of tensions between brother and brother, between family butcher and his suspicious neighbor/consumer, and between family and community interests, than they were a fight-to-the-death between small, anticorporate immigrant businesses and modern, corporate American food industries. As the case of kosher meat reveals, the sources of failure came from inside ethnic communities—from competing ethnic provisioners, family feuds, and shrewd ethnic consumers, not from the ruthless capitalists of America's industrializing food corporations.

Even as enclave businesses flourished and the cultural conservatism of their consumers seemed invincible, savvy but financially insecure ethnic businessmen looked for less volatile markets. They began to deliver the products of the national marketplace to enclave consumers. At the same time, they also learned to lure new customers to cross ethnic boundaries and purchase dishes of ethnic roots and inspiration different from their own. A second round of multi-ethnic borrowing and blending was soon under way.

CHAPTER FOUR

Crossing the Boundaries of Taste

In the 1920s, a Texan concerned that visitors to New York might "run along home with the idea that New York . . . is simply a collection of B&G Sandwich Shops [and] Thompson One-Arm Cafeterias" surveyed the fuller culinary scene in his guide to *Dining in New York*. He recommended Sardi's as "an Italian-American restaurant [that] quietly specializes in the three sea-food dishes that made the fame of Prunier's of Paris." He sent visitors uptown to Arnold Reuben's for a pastrami sandwich and downtown to the Lower East Side to Perlman's, where "insolent, lackadaisical waiters talk back to you, bawl you out, bang your order down in front of you, bring you tall, blue siphons of seltzer wherewith to wash down the amazing rich food." He recommended Moneta's on Mulberry Street, "ruled over by the watery gray eye of Papa Moneta himself," and also the low-priced Barbetta's, with its artistic clientele. He suggested a visit to The Bamboo Forest/Young China and the Chili Villa—one operated by Mr. Williams, a former student in China, and the other by a New Englander who supplemented her "hot tamales" with Cape Cod clam chowder on Friday night.

A trip to Harlem, he warned, promised danger, along with glimpses of "black folks who behave" and "white folks who don't," and the opportunity to enjoy "barbecue restaurants, coffee-pots, quick-lunches, fish-and-chips places" and the "best fried chicken, sweet potato pie, and bacon and eggs in all New York." For the visitor seeking American food, the author suggested the Yoshida Room, "owned by Japanese . . . run by Japanese . . . manned by Japanese," but serving American blue plate specials that included pork chops and apple sauce, and minute steak, without so much as "a water-chestnut, a leek, or a bamboo shoot on the premises."[1]

Rian James, the guidebook's author, believed that what made New York unique, and intriguing, was not its corporate chain cafeterias and sandwich shops but its ethnic diversity. Already in 1930, New York's multi-ethnic population had become an essential part of the city's appeal to visitors and tourists. Ethnicity and cultural diversity were necessary ingredients—along with skyscrapers and vast museums—in what made New York the city it was. James seemed to think that Americans might feel some anxiety about visiting Italian, Chinese, or African-American restaurants, so his guide offered them necessary help in identifying and enjoying them. At the same time, James obviously believed that many Americans, regardless of background, could also find pleasure and novelty in the food and atmosphere of ethnic restaurants, at least once they knew what to expect and how to get there.

The boundaries around ethnic enclaves in the United States have never been firm or impermeable. National corporations, ethnic businessmen and clients, and consumers from a wide variety of backgrounds all have had their own motives for "crossing over." Transgressing the cultural borders of America's many eating communities proceeded in a series of overlapping phases from the mid-nineteenth to the early twentieth centuries, but the years between 1900 and 1940 represented a particularly intensive phase of cross-cultural borrowing.

During these years, ambitious businessmen in ethnic communities, eager to escape the fragile and changing personal loyalties of their enclave clientele, sought new consumers in their multi-ethnic urban and regional markets. As they moved out, however, they did not leave their cultural origins behind them. On the contrary, they frequently created a variety of market niches where businessmen like themselves dominated particular types of food trade. These niches included marketing ethnic foods adapted for multi-ethnic eaters and selling new snacks or "street foods" of wide appeal to a national market. In some areas, immigrant retailers also dominated the grocery or restaurant trade, while not selling foods of any particular ethnic origin.

Neither crossing over nor ethnic niches were unique to the twentieth century. An earlier generation of immigrants had made foods as diverse as French sauces and German beer popular with American eaters. In the nineteenth century, America's newly wealthy industrial "robber barons" discovered cosmopolitan, French-inspired food and made it a culinary symbol of their newly elevated status. Immigrant restaurateurs, chefs, and hoteliers educated America's nouveaux riches in how to eat and behave like aristocracy, and were also the main purveyors of their extravagant French meals.

A modest cafe founded in 1828 by the seaman and Italian Swiss immigrant Giovanni Del-Monico and his confectioner brother became the favored eating place of the wealthy. From a simple coffee house with pastries and a European clientele, the Delmonico family business expanded after changing its name to sell "macaroni and filets" to New York's middling classes in the 1830s. After a fire—and the arrival of several more members of their family—they moved and opened a larger restaurant. Lorenzo Delmonico—nephew of the founders and the restaurant's actively involved manager and urbane host until his death in 1881—made French cooking the center of Delmonico's menu, initiating what became a decades-long fad among wealthy American eaters. Delmonico's interpretation of French cuisine was defined by offering choice and excess: there were 346 entrees, some incorrectly translated, on his bilingual menu; these included 11 soups and 27 veal dishes. None of the Delmonico family had formal training in cooking, whether French or any other cuisine, but they quickly hired French and German chefs, educated at fine European restaurants. Other immigrants with experience in fine restaurants created Delmonico's signature deferential service, which contrasted sharply with the slapdash, noisy atmosphere of the beefsteak, ale, and pie eateries of antebellum New York. Deferential staff, as much as its vaguely French cuisine and fine imported wines and liqueurs, defined Delmonico's fare as "high class."

On the other hand, middle-class Americans who tried the cuisine at Delmonico's during its early days often lacked enthusiasm for these new, continental tastes. One visitor thought the servings much too small and complained that "we satisfied our curiosity but not our appetites." Another found olive oil about as palatable as lamp oil. But wealthy Americans learned to love the restaurant. During the 1860s and 1870s, under Chef Charles Ranhofer, Delmonico's catered the most conspicuously expensive and extravagant dinners of the era, aping the grandeur of France's Second Empire. A visiting Englishman entertained his clients—American coffee and tea merchants—by spending $20,000 for music, trees, and a gold-leaf menu of ten courses, with two to six dishes in each course. Wines, champagnes, and liqueurs accompanied each course.[2]

Everywhere in the United States, wealthy investors in the 1870s constructed grand hotels and French-inspired restaurants to feed and accommodate newly status-conscious travelers. Just as the Delmonicos had done in New York, restaurateurs in towns like Dubuque or Chicago hired European staffs to introduce cosmopolitanism to their own nouveaux riches. In Chicago, the German father of memoirist Elsa Proehl Blum prided himself on teaching wealthy Americans how to eat and how to live well. Paul Proehl had been born in 1858 in Dresden, where his parents owned a fine hotel. After an apprenticeship in German cooking, Proehl trained further at Maxim's in Paris. Then he immigrated to New Orleans to manage a recently opened "Paris-style" hotel. After marrying a musician, he became maître d'hôtel at the Congress and Auditorium Hotel in Chicago, "centers for much gay social life" with a daily round of "swell luncheons" and "brilliant dinners." The hotel had a French restaurant, a palm garden, and huge banquet rooms. Aware of the parties and glitter of a grand hotel, Elsa Proehl Blum grew up thinking that "Chicago was in those days the Paris of the U.S.A."[3]

Even San Antonio, still almost a frontier town in the 1870s and 1880s, had its own grand hotel, built by the German brewer William Menger to provide first-class accommodations. Menger continued to lager his beer in the hotel's basement, but upstairs he offered elegant reception rooms and restaurants, where traveling cattlemen enjoyed banquets that included French wines and local meats like buffalo hump, wild turkey, deer, and turtle, cooked and sauced in the French manner.

The appeal of foreign food and drink was not limited to the wealthy. While robber barons savored French food in fine restaurants, humbler Americans developed a taste for German lager beer. Before 1840 Americans had drunk the dark ales and porters of the British Isles or high-alcohol drinks distilled from sugar and corn. Lager beer was a lighter, more effervescent drink than ale and porter, manufactured with yeast that fermented to the bottom of a vat; it required cool storage (in a lager) over the winter. Lager beer had developed in Central Europe and probably was introduced in the United States by Philadelphia brewer John Wagner, who brought the necessary yeast when he left his position as a Bavarian braumeister. In 1844 Fortmann and Company introduced lager production to Cincinnati, and the brewery that would grow into the gigantic Pabst Brewing Company began operating in Milwaukee. Boston got its first German lager brewery in 1846, Chicago in 1847, San Francisco in 1849, St. Louis in 1852, and San Antonio—where one-third of the population was German—in 1855. In the Midwest, especially within the triangle of German settlement bounded by Cincinnati, St. Louis, and Milwaukee, every little town had its own brewery. Indeed, according to one historian, "breweries were as much a part of many Wisconsin communities as churches, schools and flour mills."[4]

Most brewers were Germans, as were their earliest customers. The names of Brooklyn's early brewers make the origins of lager in the German community there very clear: Meltzer, Liebman, Seiz, Worthschaft, Wundchenmeyer, Bull, and Gottschalk. Initially, all produced on a small scale: in New York, Ruppert's in its early days sold beer from house to house.[5] But these businessmen did not limit their markets to Germans for long. From a modest production of only 750,000 barrels in 1850, total barrelage rose to 3.8 million in 1860, 6.5 million in 1870, 39.5 million in 1900, and 59.5 million in 1910.[6] A historian of beer has called this the "German engulfment of the American brewing industry,"[7] while a historian of the prohibition movement noted, "In just a few decades, the amount of alcohol that a statistically average American consumed in hard liquor was replaced by the equivalent amount carried in brewed drinks."[8] In 1850 that statistically average American consumed 1.5 gallons of beer annually; fifteen years later his consumption had doubled to 3 gallons.

Beer became popular with new immigrants and old Americans alike. For some immigrants it was a familiar drink; the south Chinese had brewed it at home (calling it wine), and Jewish men had learned to drink it from their Christian neighbors in Eastern Europe. By 1900, however, Mexicans and Cajuns also drank beer, as did Basques. So did southern blacks and poor whites. Some Irish immigrants held to their ale and porter, but their children joined the multi-ethnic crowd of lager fans. Italian men stopped in saloons to talk to comrades and drink a glass of beer, or they sat in their kitchens drinking beer and eating roasted garbanzos. Italian women drank it, too: Rosa, who worked at Hull House, remembered that "in the summer when it was so hot you couldn't stay in those buildings, the women and the boys and girls and babies were sitting down in the street and alley. All the women would bring down their chairs and sit on the sidewalk. Then somebody would say, 'All the women put two cents and we'll get the beer.' So everybody did and the children would run by the saloon and get the can of beer. That's all the please we had—the cool from the beer in summer."[9]

The operators of German saloons and beer gardens seemed uninterested in maintaining the cultural boundaries around Klein Deutschland. In the years just before World War I, 40 percent of San Francisco saloonkeepers had German names, and Chicago Germans dominated not just their own ethnocentric lokale but also the saloons that catered to a multi-ethnic crowd.[10] It seems likely that consumers preferred German to other saloonkeepers because of the special pleasures they offered alongside the lager beer. No one knows who invented the "free lunch," although saloons in both New York and San Francisco claimed to have done so. Whatever its origins, it quickly became popular with workers and businessmen in most American cities. Gertrude Berg's Jewish grandfather described how pleased he was to eat at a free lunch counter "for the price of a glass of beer—five cents."[11] In San Francisco, visitors found that "no formality, whatever is observed at eating . . . All eat standing, and it is not a rare occurrence to see millionaires walking about the room, or leaning against the bar in eager converse—each with a chicken drumstick or wing in one hand, a slice of bread and cheese in the other, like country school-boys at noon-time." The cheapest saloons served "a few chips of 'bologna,' . . . a plate of cheese, some dried beef, crackers, pickles, mustard and sausage," all for 5 cents. Two-bit saloons offered a full meal.[12]

German brewers also attracted new pleasure-seeking customers by attaching beer gardens to their breweries. These were large, tree-lined out-door spaces or cavernous, parklike interior halls: "Immense buildings," according to one observer, that "will accommodate from four hundred to twelve hundred guests."[13] Junius Browne reported that New York's Atlantic Beer Garden was "the most cosmopolitan place of entertainment in the city; for, though the greater part of its patrons are Germans, every other nationality is represented there, French, Irish, Spaniards, Italians, Portuguese, even Chinamen and Indians."[14] On the other side of the country in California, too, according to the nineteenth-century chronicler B. E. Lloyd, "Beer gardens became rivals of Babel. Not only the German population centers there on Sundays, but foreigners of different nationalities, and many Americans, join in the eating, drinking, and merry-making."[15]

Saloons and beer gardens provided more than a beer; they sold entertainment and recreation—theater, song, and games—even charging admission. In San Francisco, Lloyd found "dancing, swinging, bowling, jumping, running, and singing constitute a part of the amusements." The result was that a "free and easy feeling pervades the whole throng."[16] In New York in the 1850s and 1860s, lager beer became a fad among urban youths "on the town." A contemporary noted, "New Yorkers ran mad after it, and nothing was spoken of or drunk but LAGER." The same man noted a popular English-language celebration of this new habit of "stepping out":

> Twas drank in 'fader land' first,
> But now we drink it here,
> Then drink it boys! Drink freely!
> Three rounds of lager bier!

Besides drink, one could enjoy billiards, shuffle boards, and bowling in many saloons.[17] New York's Jewel City Cafe had a beer garden downstairs, and immigrant Gustav Mann praised a "high-class restaurant, cafe, and nightclub with dancing" upstairs.[18]

W hat America's wealthy had done earlier for French cuisine and elite cosmopolitanism, its artists and intellectuals accomplished for the Italian food of newer immigrants during the Progressive Era, associating it with cultural rebellion and adventure. On both coasts, Italian restaurants attracted urban "bohemians" who had settled in nearby neighborhoods. In New York, the memoir of Maria Sermolino describes one such "table d'hôte" managed by her father in New York's Greenwich Village.

Gonfarone's Restaurant got its start as a hotel for Italian migrants; at first it offered an inexpensive fixed menu for residents in a dining room of "about fifteen tables with fifty to sixty cane-seated wooden chairs," sawdust on the floor, and the "smells, noises, and commotion of the kitchen" in the dining room. As it attracted consumers from outside the Italian community, the restaurant eventually grew to five buildings along Macdougal and Eighth Streets. It served businessmen at lunchtime, and in the evening its clientele ranged from college students and clerks to lawyers and other professionals.

Author Sermolino insisted that Gonfarone's was "not essentially an artists' and writers' hang-out. It had none of the trappings of pseudo-bohemian retreats and was completely devoid of all artistic trappings." But she also describes Greenwich Village bohemians—those "impecunious American artists and writers in the neighborhood"—as frequent customers in the restaurant.[19]

What attracted bohemians to Gonfarone's? Sermolino did not believe the restaurant's appeal lay exclusively in its food. A typical menu in the first decade of the century included a pint of California red wine, assorted antipasto, minestrone or spaghetti with meat or tomato sauce, a choice of main dishes (boiled salmon with caper sauce; sweetbread with mushroom gravy; broiled spring chicken or roast prime ribs of beef), vegetables and salads (spinach, potatoes, green salad), a dessert (biscuit tortoni or spumoni), fresh fruit, assorted cheeses, and "demi-tasse." At 50 cents, the menu was far more expensive than a typical workingman's dinner but well below the prices of a restaurant like Delmonico's.

Sermolino suggested in her memoir that Gonfarone's special atmosphere was as important to cross-over consumers as its food or moderate price. Gonfarone's offered entertainments with its meals, including a knife-brandishing chef, a juggling waiter, and a bus boy who played harmonica. Of even greater importance, Sermolino believed, was the fact that her "papa, and Madama Gonfarone, his partner (who was the head chef), and the waiters and bus boys and cooks, and the bartender and the dish-

washers and musicians, spoke and thought and acted 'Italian.' This little
Italian world was friendly, pleasant and gay." And that was what bohemian
guests craved, even more than spaghetti bolognese. According to Sermolino, guests ate at Gonfarone's to learn and to practice new values. Her
father "helped propagate among Americans a simple, Latin variety of hedonism. They opened up new approaches to sensory and spiritual pleasures
. . . They brought new tastes, new sounds, new scents, new form, new
colors, but above all, new feelings to America." They taught that "life was
not all hard and earnest" but "an adventure to be enjoyed."[20]

These were precisely the values that appealed to bohemian eaters, in
their rebellion against the self-restraint and moral probities of Victorian-
ism. The case of San Francisco's Italian restaurants makes the linkage
between food, Latin hedonism, and bohemianism even clearer. There,
too, the Italian restaurant Sanguinettis had offered a table d'hôte with
"dago red" for local factory workers before the 1906 fire; thereafter, bohemians and other travelers directed there by hotel guides dominated among
its clientele.[21] San Francisco's Bohemian Club was supposedly founded
around the Italian table of another restaurant nearby, operated by Joseph
Coppa. Coppa had come to San Francisco from Turin via Paris and Guate-
mala, and his restaurant—known before the fire for a large mural—became
the meeting place of Coppa's School of Literature, a group described as
"hard-drinking high rollers" who took inspiration from Coppa's "Table
Red" wine.[22] San Francisco guidebooks pointed tourists to restaurants
with "bohemian atmosphere"—including sawdust on the floor, an informal, talkative chef or owners, singing bartenders, and a clientele of intellectuals, artists, or patricians cultivating an anti-Victorian rebellious flair
in their dress and leisure-time pursuits.[23] It was an atmosphere that quickly
generated competition from non-Italian entrepreneurs. Even New Orleans
boasted its bohemian hang-out: Cafe Lafitte, described by an urban guidebook writer, "Scoop" Kennedy, as a place "complete with wagon wheels,
sputtering candles and colorful characters."[24]

While New York uptowners flocked downtown to Greenwich Village,
uptown restaurants in the theater district, such as Rectors, soon also promised "bohemian" atmosphere, complete with Italian or other foreign foods
prepared for a fast, theatrical crowd of bachelors hoping to meet actresses.
A historian of New York night life describes the appeal of such places to

New York's middle classes, who "in leisure desired the same lack of responsibility" but who "in everyday life" remained "committed to the world of
respectability."[25] Not surprisingly, immigrant restaurateurs (first Rumanian
Jews, and later Greeks and Russians) also developed the food and entertainment emporiums that came to be called nightclubs.[26]

By the 1930s, Italian restaurateurs consciously marketed a dining "experience," not just ethnic food. A 1927 brochure of San Francisco's Italian
Chamber of Commerce advertised that "the Italian Food Shops and Delicatessen Stores of San Francisco's Latin Quarter are the Meeting Places of
the Bohemians and of those who Love 'La Cucina Italiana.'"[27] In New
York, guidebooks for out-of-towners distinguished between the unacceptable dimly-lit restaurants of Little Italy, located in cellars with "their windows always covered with steam," and the midtown Italian restaurants,
whose newly altered menu and ambiance attracted a multi-ethnic crowd.[28]

Guides to San Francisco's restaurants agreed with Maria Sermolino in
New York: eating in their city was much like travel, only much easier
because in San Francisco "it is but a step across a street from America into
Japan, then another step into China. Cross another street and you are
in Mexico, close neighbor to France. Around the corner lies Italy and
from Italy you pass to Lombardy, and on to Greece."[29] Gertrude Berg knew
her father's Samovar restaurant in New York's Spencer Arms Hotel "had
to make believe," so that people could forget they were on West 69th
Street.[30]

No enclave businessmen enjoyed greater success attracting culinary
tourists in search of inexpensive exoticism than Chinese restaurateurs in
the Chinatowns of New York and San Francisco. Even more than Italians,
however, they had to modify their offerings to accommodate American
tastes. Beginning with the Gold Rush, the Chinese of San Francisco had
gained considerable cross-cultural experience serving up all manner of
"English" dishes in cheap restaurants and cafes for miners. Later, Chinese
chefs often managed the kitchens of prestigious San Francisco French
restaurants as well. They also busied themselves trying to sell Americans
variations of their own homeland dishes.

Fried rice and chow mein originated among Chinese immigrants cooking for non-Chinese eaters. While the exact origins of these and other

dishes may never be known (Was chop suey left-overs cooked for drunken American miners or a special dish prepared for a Chinese visitor?), by the 1850s miners had already ventured into Chinese kitchens willing to try something other than fried eggs and beans. Many viewed Chinese "Hangtown" fry (a relative of what we know today as Egg Foo Yung) as a cheap alternative to American meals, dished up by Chinese cooks.

Still, Chinese food seemed too adventurous for Americans more sedate than miners. B. E. Lloyd's 1876 guide to the "lights and shades" of San Francisco scarcely mentioned Chinese food as a viable option for visitors. It noted instead that the Chinese—while usually penurious eaters—often staged great banquets where exotic and rare, but sometimes also disgusting, foods were consumed.[31] At this date, Chinese food was mentioned as a curiosity but not yet recommended for consumption by tourists. Even in the 1930s, the San Franciscan Clarence Edwords hesitated to recommend many Chinese restaurants to middle-class eaters because of what he called Chinese chefs' disregard for sanitation and "the usual niceties of food preparation." He suggested that visitors to San Francisco try an "artistic Japanese meal" instead. Edwords was even more squeamish about Mexican restaurants, however, with their "usual disregard for dirt"; he reported monkeys, cockroaches, and parrots at Felipe and Maria's, despite its "truly Mexican" food.[32]

After the 1906 San Francisco fire, "Chinatown" relocated to a quarter envisioned by city fathers as a potential tourist attraction. One Chinese restaurateur succeeded in attracting cross-over tourist consumers by dressing a Chinese woman in European style and having her serve drinks, while Chinese musicians entertained eaters with music.[33] Chinese restaurants that catered to tourists moved upstairs, to differentiate themselves from the simple shops serving Chinese food to Chinese bachelor workers at street level. As early as 1883, a guide for strangers in San Francisco urged tourists to hire a guide to take them to Chinatown, but also recommended four restaurants where they could safely eat—all above street level, of course.[34]

Thereafter, guides to tourists regularly emphasized the exotic "dangers" and mysteries that could surround their search for a meal in Chinatown. Guides sometimes conceded that readers might be "timid travellers," and recommended they not ask too much about the ingredients.[35] They often described a restaurant's exotic or luxurious decor—balconies with carvings of twining vines, red upholstery, and dark booths—in greater detail than its menu. Two Polish Americans claimed that eating food in Chinatown restaurants was akin to consuming "a plate of cooked grass and noodles" but they—along with others apparently—nevertheless saw a meal in Chinatown as a necessary, if slightly anxiety-producing, part of an urban holiday.[36]

By the 1920s and 1930s San Francisco guides described Chinese food more sophisticated than chop suey and chow mein. A whole range of eateries now beckoned from the city's Chinese district: simple rice shops, noodle shops, chop suey and chow mein shops, along with night clubs, and finer restaurants, all competing for the tourist trade. Guides for New York and San Francisco suggested that tourists allow waiters to recommend shark fins or other new dishes, and to let themselves be guided to new tastes.[37] Some even emphasized the healthfulness of Chinese food, insisting that the "Chinese cook is really a Chinese doctor," and listing the wide variety of "interesting foods"—ginger, bitter squash or melon, sea worms, birds' nests—used in their cooking.[38]

In New York, the most avid cross-over consumers of Chinese food were Jews. Some Jewish New Yorkers remember eating Chinese food as a regular end-of-sabbath meal, and some Chinese restaurateurs even noted "kosher" dishes on their menus.[39] Years later, Jews, remembering this practice, would wonder whether kosher chow mein, if eaten regularly on Saturday night, and sometimes even prepared at home by their Jewish mothers, might not be considered an authentically Jewish dish.[40] Most of the food consumed by Jewish diners in Chinese restaurants was probably not strictly kosher. But since Chinese chefs chopped the forbidden pork and shellfish very finely, offered a wide range of poultry dishes, never used milk (which kashruth laws forbade in meat dishes), and served tea (also popular with Russian Jews), a Chinese meal offered Jewish New Yorkers what one called "safe treyf"—a combination of the familiar and the forbidden. Reported one older Jewish man, "I felt about Chinese restaurants the same way I did about the Metropolitan Museum of Art—they were the two most strange and fascinating places my parents took me to, and I loved them both."[41] Here, then, was cosmopolitan urbanity for the Jewish middle classes, a more day-to-day confrontation with the cultural diversity that other tourists sought intermittently as excitement and adventure.

Novelty, entertainment, and a sense of partaking in the excitement of big city life were the same cultural bridges across which immigrant entrepreneurs marketed inexpensive snack foods, sometimes of ethnic inspiration, to the masses of low-income consumers. Some of their inventions—the urban creoles of their age—became new culinary symbols of their home regions, in the same way that rye'n'injun, flour tortillas, and hoppin' john symbolized the regional cuisines of the colonial era.

New York street snacks included frankfurters, hot corn, sweet potatoes, pretzels, ices, ice cream, chewing gum, knishes, arbis, and sweets. (Arbis were cooked yellow peas, reported Federal Writers' Project employee Benjamin Simms, "served to the buyer in a glassine or white paper bag with salt and pepper.") Jewish carts offered baked apples and retchinicks—a soft cake made from buckwheat.[42] Areas around garment shops swarmed with "glib-tongued salesmen" of bagels and knishes, warmed "in an erstwhile baby carriage that now bears a portable hot oven."[43] Dining at the pushcart was not as elegant as a meal at Delmonico's or even Gonfarone's. But street foods offered low-income consumers from a wide variety of backgrounds an inexpensive way to purchase new and novel foods and to experience their own version of multi-ethnic cosmopolitanism.

Greek entrepreneurs were particularly visible in the street-snack trade, creating a distinctive retail niche with the confections of many nations, from peppermints to Turkish taffy. Around 1900 Greeks took over the manufacture and sale of candy and sodas from German and French confectioners like Sebastian Chauveau of Philadelphia, who had first manufactured and popularized gum drops, jujube paste, and marshmallows. Two pioneers in this Greek niche were Eleutherios Pelalas of Sparta and Panagiotis Hatzideris of Smyrna, who had opened their Chicago sweet shop in 1869. Chicago quickly became the "Acropolis" of the Greek-American candy business. Practically every busy corner in the city was occupied by a Greek candy store. From store-front candy, successful Greek retailers moved on to ice cream and soda, but then they had to work night and day "to pay for marble soda fountains and expensive furniture."[44] Still,

Theodore Saloutos, the first historian of America's Greeks, believed that generally confectioners catering to the multi-ethnic crowd enjoyed more success and higher status in the Greek community than the owners of a shoeshine parlor or enclave coffee shop. Greeks flocked into the ice cream trade, and came to dominate it, much as German saloonkeepers of an earlier generation had dominated the beer trade.

Other street vendors adapted immigrant eating habits to invent new novelties for multi-ethnic consumers. Vendors at the 1904 St. Louis Exposition (popularly known today as the St. Louis World's Fair) adapted the wafer-like cookies popular with Swedish and German immigrants into cone-shaped containers for ice cream. Italian vendors in California found a healthy market for a Mexican specialty they popularized as "hot tamales." Throughout the Southwest, Mexican-American market stands like the one described by Richard Vasquez offered "burritos de huevos, chorizo, frijoles, tamales, tortillas, both the flour and corn types, and a few other things, such as hot dogs and hamburgers."[45] Most of the purchasers were not Mexican-Americans, although many of the vendors were.

Popular street snacks, whether invented, blended, or ethnic specialties, soon came to symbolize their cities, just as the creole blends of the colonial era had symbolized their regions. The muffulettos of New Orleans originated with the sesame-studded rolls on which the Sicilian grocer Sal Lupo, circa 1900, had layered meats, cheeses, and the olive fragments he could not sell from the bottom of the olive barrels. Elsewhere, urban eaters called somewhat similar sandwiches hoagies, poorboys, grinders, and heroes.

Unique to Fall River, Massachusetts, and a few nearby Rhode Island towns was a creole that Octavio Paz almost certainly would reject as an abomination of the melting pot: the chow mein sandwich. In this popular dish invented in the 1920s, chefs ladled chopped meat, celery, onions, and bean sprouts in gravy onto a hamburger bun or Portuguese bread along with chow mein noodles. Both Chinese and non-Chinese lunch counters served the sandwiches, even offering meatless versions on Fridays for Catholic customers. For the Depression-era youth of Fall River, "the chow mein sandwich was a real treat," cheaper even than a Chinese meal, costing only 30 or 40 cents.[46]

In the Southwest, Ignacio (Nacho) Ahaya gave Tex-Mex cuisine a new culinary symbol when he invented and named a snack after himself. Work-

ing one day at a border club in Piedras Negras, Ahaya was asked to prepare
a snack for Anglo officers' wives while the cook was out. A local described
how he "grabbed a whole bunch of fried tortillas, put some yellow cheese
on top, let it heat a little bit, then put some sliced jalapenos on it."[47]
Apparently the officers' wives enjoyed their "nachoes," and the popularity
of the dish spread.

In New York, Louis Auster carefully guarded the secret to his "egg
creams," a mixture of soda water, cocoa, and sugar that he created in the
1920s. His grandson reported that "people came from miles and miles . . .
egg cream was tantalizing. It was like marijuana. They needed it." Only
when he was approaching death did Auster teach his sons and grandsons
the secret formula of his egg creams. It was a day, his grandson recalled,
"like my bar mitzvah," when a boy realizes, "Today I am a man."[48]

That "deli" would triumph over egg creams as a nationally recognized
symbol of New York eating was not obvious at the time. Germans had
opened the first delicatessens in New York without making New York a
"deli" town (although Richard Hellmann, a German operating a deli on
Columbus Avenue, did succeed in marketing his mayonnaise widely by
1915). During the Depression, delicatessen owners had to work hard to
market their relatively expensive cold cuts (for "feinschmecker") to a
wider, multi-ethnic public. The Mogen Dovid Delicatessen Corporation, a
trade association of Jewish deli owners, wanted to change that, by altering
consumers' assumption that the delicatessen store was "only for Jews" or
"only a luxury."

In its monthly publication for members, Mogen Dovid editors noted
that "the choicest delicacies can become necessities if the people get used
to them and can get them at ordinary prices." A later article by a member
of the association noted that "the Jews, because of their more delicate
taste, have taken to delicatessens more readily than others, and they are
the ones who contribute most to the spread of the article among the
general population," but a third author nevertheless hoped to spread the
word with "a lot of advertising." A fourth author agreed: in the midst of
the Depression, "Our trade still has large markets to capture or to develop."
Delicatessen owners reported progress attracting more customers, and of
diverse backgrounds, when they offered sandwiches with exotic names.
The most successful deli food of the Depression was the Reuben sandwich,

popularized by Arnold Reuben from his own tiny delicatessen. Reuben subsequently named sandwiches for any actor who visited his store—allowing him eventually to leave the deli trade and open a real restaurant.[49]

One deli founded during this period symbolized the final transformation of delicatessen food from a Jewish to a New York specialty. Lillian and Louis Zabar founded their delicatessen in Brooklyn in 1934: Mr. Zabar ran the smoked-fish section; Mrs. Zabar cooked the prepared dishes. Their sons, who remain involved in what became a deli famous throughout the world, described their mother as the company's first maker of blintzes, potato salad, stuffed cabbage, and coleslaw. After it moved to the Upper West Side, Zabar's accomplished what the deli owners of an earlier era had only dreamed of: it became a market where multi-ethnic consumers crowded its narrow passageways to sample not only pastrami, kosher sausages, and smoked fish but also pasta salad and feta cheese.

In Michigan, the pasty became a simple but satisfying symbol of Great Lakes eating. A turnover of pie-like crust with filling, the pasty originated in Cornwall, England. Cornish miners then brought it with them to Michigan's Upper Peninsula, where Finns (who believed it to be an American dish, since Cornish miners, after all, spoke English) adapted it to their own tastes. The Finnish pasty of the Upper Peninsula contained beef, potatoes, onions, and carrots or rutabagas. Church women sold the first pasties as fundraisers, and the first commercially produced pasties appeared after World War II as bar food. Today pasties are widely available in specialty shops, bakeries, restaurants, bars, and grocery stores across northern Michigan, the Upper Peninsula, and upper Minnesota. It is as commonly eaten as the hamburger; a frozen version is even marketed to Michiganders who have retired to California and Florida.[50]

In the Southwest, it was chili that came to define a new regional and creole Tex-Mex cuisine. Early Anglo visitors to San Antonio reported eating "hashes" and stews of meat and peppers dipped up by a spoon as early as 1828. Their meals came from Mexican cottages off the Military Plaza, where a visitor, Edward King, in 1874 assured readers that a "fat, swarthy Mexican mater-familias will place before you various savory compounds, swimming in fiery pepper, which biteth like a serpent; and the tortilla, a smoking hot cake, thin as a shaving, and about as eatable, is the substitute for bread. This meal, with the bitterest of coffee to wash it down

. . . will be an event in your gastronomic experience." Experts south of the border steadfastly denied that chili was a Mexican dish. But by the end of the 1870s and in the 1880s, entrepreneurial Mexican "chili queens" were selling the dish to miners, traders, soldiers, and market patrons from stands and long tables on the Military Plaza. In 1893 the World's Fair in Chicago introduced the meal to the nation, by hosting a booth that called itself the San Antonio Chili Stand. Chili quickly became a prime attraction for tourists to San Antonio and other Texas towns.[51] When San Antonian Atlee B. Ayres visited New York, he learned that people there "remember our city because of the Chili Stands, the Menger Hotel and the Alamo."[52] Chili was declared the state food of Texas in 1977. In the 1980s, *Favorite Recipes of Famous Texans*—a great favorite of Anglos—passed along chili recipes from Texans such as Lady Bird Johnson, Frank Tolbert, Bill Clements, and Ron Bird.

Consumers in German-dominated Cincinnati also made a chili concoction its new creole culinary symbol. Completely unrelated to the chili of San Antonio, Cincinnati chili is a meat sauce flavored with chili pepper, cinnamon, and all-spice. When served with spaghetti, it is called "two-way chili," but a hungry consumer can also have it three-way (with cheese), four-way (with onions added), or five-way (topped with beans). An immigrant from Macedonia, Tom Kiradjieff, invented the dish. Kiradjieff migrated to New York in the 1920s, where he first sold Coney Island hot dogs topped with Tex-Mex chili. When he moved to Cincinnati in 1922, he developed Cincinnati chili to attract new customers to his lunch stand. His chili had a flavor reminiscent of Balkan and eastern Mediterranean cooking (notably its combination of tomato, cinnamon, and all-spice). But no one in Cincinnati thought of Cincinnati chili as a Macedonian dish, nor did Kiradjieff market it as such.

The dish evolved as Kiradjieff worked with his multi-ethnic customers. The original decision to mix the sauce with spaghetti, and to make beans optional, was Kiradjieff's. In the 1930s his customers requested it be served more like the Italian spaghetti they knew, that is, with its sauce on top of the spaghetti, and with additional accompaniments as layers of topping.

By the 1940s, Kiradjieff and his family marketed Cincinnati chili from their chain of Empress Restaurants. In the 1950s, five brothers from Greece who had worked and trained in Kiradjieff's restaurants altered the recipe somewhat and opened competing restaurants—the Skyline chain. Skyline then brought chili to the Kentucky suburbs of Cincinnati. Like pasties, frozen and packaged versions of Cincinnati chili sell to native Ohioans retired to Florida.[53]

Thus, wherever large numbers of immigrants settled, cross-over buying and selling transformed regional creoles into twentieth-century forms. New Yorkers now ate "deli," Jewish rye, and spaghetti, while Californians more often experimented with soy and dago red. New migrations added the "Mex" to Tex-Mex and other southwestern cuisines. In the Midwest, the modified central and northern European foodways of Germans, Bohemians, Finns, and Scandinavians defined a new regional cuisine based on pot roasts and casseroles, with their European "roux" (butter and flour) thickeners replaced by mushroom soup, and on yeast-risen baked goods like coffee breads and kolache.

The popular ethnic foods of the 1920s and 1930s were not those we know today. Ethnic food meant chow mein, not dim sum; spaghetti, not pizza; pastrami, not bagels; tamales, not fajitas. Restaurant and eating guides of the 1930s still misunderstood pizza (a toothsome "inch-thick, potato pan-cake, sprinkled with Parmesan cheese and stewed tomatoes") and "beigels" ("hard-crust doughnuts") but recommended both to prospective buyers.[54] Some enclave foods still remained in their enclaves, not having attracted cross-over consumers.

Recently arrived immigrants also developed cross-over economic niches by dominating the production, processing, or sale of foods unmarked by any obvious ethnic labels. Almost everywhere, for example, immigrants pioneered and dominated truck gardening of vegetables for multi-ethnic regional markets. As early as the 1720s, Germans specialized in providing New Orleans with cabbage, fruit, salads, greens, beans and peas, and fish. In Texas in the 1840s and 1850s, they developed truck gardening around port cities like Galveston and Indianola. In the 1890s Belgian farmers became truck specialists in San Antonio, and by 1910 they were able to sponsor the Famous Belgium Gardeners' vegetable float in the annual Battle of the Flowers Parade.

In California, Chinese immigrants made up between half and three-quarters of the cultivators of specialized vegetable crops in the early 1880s. Many had turned full-time to provisioning other miners, to escape hostility in the minefields. Men like Tu Charley of the Yban River basin in the 1890s peddled over a 100-mile territory the cucumbers, tomatoes, beans, melons, and produce he had raised. Others traveled smaller distances with baskets of produce on a bamboo pole balanced across their shoulders. In 1870 San Francisco had over a hundred Chinese truck gardeners; by 1880 Chinese truck gardeners were also prominent in Los Angeles and in the upper Sacramento Valley. Polly Lawrence, of the Italian Ghirardelli family, remembered that during her childhood a Chinese man came daily to the family home with his fresh produce.[55]

Fishing often became an important niche, too, with immigrant fishermen marketing to a multi-ethnic urban market. In Tampa, Florida, Giovanni Savarese began a fishing fleet in 1885 that grew to 15 vessels and 150 smaller "smacks." As the Italian population of Tampa increased (attracted to jobs in the cigar industry), Italian fishermen and fish markets proliferated; by 1920 there were 20 fish markets, directly marketing the fish of Tampa Bay. In San Francisco, the Chinese developed shrimp fishing and drying in several colonies around San Rafael, San Bruno, and San Mateo. They introduced the use of funnel-shaped traps for shrimping and fishing. At first, their market was their own countrymen in California and China. Once established, they also delivered fresh bay shrimp to San Francisco restaurants. In 1880 half of all California fishermen were Chinese; thereafter Italians (who made up 40 percent in 1880) increasingly replaced them. Most Italian fishermen were from Genoa and Sicily; Sicilians specialized in squid fishing.

In Texas and Minnesota, dairying became an important economic niche for northern Europeans. On the Great Plains, even in the midst of severe droughts, Swedish farmers raised more dairy cows and produced more milk than their American neighbors. Scandinavian and German farmers disparaged Americans for their neglect of haying and their willingness to go without milk while their dairy animals foraged for themselves in the winter. Dairying was a challenge to Europeans accustomed to more temperate climes, especially during the extreme heat and cold of Great Plains summers and winters. An English woman complained that "for two or three months the milk, freezing as soon as it is taken from the cows, affords no cream, consequently no butter. It is nevertheless possible to obtain butter, by keeping the churn near the fire and churning cream and milk together," a method she found "exceedingly troublesome."[56] The child of a German noted that "on some hot days Mother sat down cellar with her churn which was barrel-shaped . . . During the summer months we'd have to keep the churn in a cool, dark place or it would dry out and leak."[57] In Minnesota, a Finnish child reported how she "packed butter in clean crocks, covering them with waxed paper which we secured with string. We poured rich cream into pint and quart bottles, separating the stacks of cardboard bottle caps that had to be pried apart and firmly pressed on."[58] In Fresno, California, Danes developed dairy farming and buttering; in Marin county, it was Swiss "milkers." None of these dairy experts marketed exclusively to their own kind, or to ethnic enclaves. Their dairying expertise allowed them to provision other milk-drinkers, too.

Similarly, in many American cities, Germans dominated baking. In Manhattan, between half and two-thirds of the city's bakers were Germans in the years between 1870 and 1890, and the same was true in San Francisco, where Marguerite Clausen's father had arrived from Germany at age 14. Throughout Clausen's childhood, family life revolved around his bakery, first in San Francisco, then, after the earthquake and fire, in multi-ethnic Sausalito, Fairfield, and Richmond. Of her father the baker, Clausen reported, "We didn't see much of him," for he got up early to bake, then delivered his goods, then went to sleep very early in order to rise again at an early hour. Her father used no machinery in his bakery until near the end of his career, in 1933, when he had begun using a mechanical mixer to prepare cakes.[59] Clausen's clients were not Germans: throughout the United States around 1900, Austrians, Alsatians, and Germans sold not their dark breads but the fine, white "Vienna bread" Americans preferred. With time and the mechanization of baking, Germans also formed an important contingent of workers in bread factories.

Unlike the German bakers, an even larger niche for cross-over immigrant workers failed to appear as food processors in census figures. These were domestic servants and cooks—fixtures of life in northern middle-class American families. In the South, domestics and cooks were African-American women. Elsewhere, immigrant women of many backgrounds, along with some Chinese and Japanese men, struggled to cook meals daily for families who wanted familiar food, not the foods of the enclaves from which their workers had emerged.

Foreign-born domestics had to learn how to prepare American food—and often rather quickly, as their employers showed limited interests in the foods they already knew how to cook from home. One Mexican girl reported home, "You should see the way the americanos eat. They have a machine that makes ice cream and they eat it every night, after they have chicken or steaks . . . And they have an icebox . . . La señora is teaching me how to cook all the foods."[60]

Special cookbooks prepared literate Chinese men and Finnish women for the challenge. The *Ch'u shu ta ch'uan Chinese and English Cookbook* also offered aid to the employer "who desires good things to eat" but suffers frustration because he is unable to talk "to the Chinese cook or because his Chinese cook does not know the methods of preparation." The cookbook provided bilingual recipes for 41 American puddings, 35 cakes, 25 soups, 60 meats, and 40 vegetables.[61] There was not a single recipe for Chinese food among them.

In *Kokki-Kirja (Complete Directions for the Preparation of American Foods)*, Finnish domestics received directions in Finnish for 588 American-style recipes, listed by their English names; the cookbook also included a glossary of household terms.[62] Again, no Finnish recipes appeared among the American ones.

Far from vast immigrant settlements and their enclave markets, and far from the kitchens of urban middle-class America, astonishingly small groups of immigrant businessmen in the American South established a visible niche as grocers and restaurateurs to native-born blacks and whites. In Mississippi, Chinese men fleeing West Coast discrimination against Asian laborers began selling groceries to poor blacks and whites in rural towns in the 1870s. They sold not dried squid or soy sauce but the staples of southern cuisines—cornmeal, fatback, crackers, beans. The same was true even in Charleston, with its African-American fishermen and street traders. In 1824 a German Lutheran church, a German "friendly society," and an Irish "Hibernian society" had joined Charleston's synagogue as symbols of the city's (limited) ethnic diversity. Charleston's first city directory, published that year, lists grocers and sellers of grog with Swedish, French, Scottish, Irish, and German names, scattered widely throughout the city. By 1850 Germans (the largest group) almost completely dominated the import, wholesale, and retail grocery trade, and many of them sold to black customers. In a society where ownership of plantations defined wealth and status, immigrants instead pursued entrepreneurial paths to prosperity in food business. Apparently they encountered little competition from native whites, and the competition from slaves was not sufficient to prevent the creation of their own niche.

Charleston business directories after the Civil War reveal the tenacity of this ethnic niche. Germans still dominated bread and cake baking, candy and confection making, and the wholesale and retail grocery trades. Germans and Irish were well represented as butchers and (along with Italian- and Spanish-surnamed businessmen) as retailers of tropical fruits. Germans outnumbered others as importers of liquors and wines, while men with Irish names more often sold the beverages. Of the 13 restaurants in Charleston in 1869, Germans operated at least 8.

Typical of immigrants in the Charleston grocery trade was Otto Tieneman, who arrived in South Carolina in 1839 and went into business in 1841. By the 1880s Tieneman and his sons employed ten workers and did $600,000 worth of business as provision dealers. At that time, an Irishman, James Cosgrove, together with his son, supplied the city's retailers with soda water, ginger ale, lager beer, ales, porters, mineral waters, and fine cigars; Cosgrove had arrived in 1852. A Charleston business booster during these years felt he had to single out two American grocers as "among the few native born Charlestonians engaged in any branch of the grocery or provision business in this city."

Even smaller groups of newly arriving immigrants challenged German and Irish dominance in the grocery and liquor trades after 1880. The Italian A. Canale, "Importer of foreign fruits and wholesale dealer in apples, potatoes, onions, lemons and nuts"—a native of Genoa—employed ten assistants in his $100,000 business in 1884.[63] By 1910, fruit dealers in the city's directory were 10 percent Italian and Greek. Greeks quickly established retail groceries and restaurants as their preferred business niche. The first Greek opened a restaurant in Charleston around 1900. By 1910 Nick Stratakos and George A. Panuchopoulo operated Charleston's Academy Inn, which they advertised as "the best restaurant in Dixie."

They offered standard southern fare, while the nearby Globe Restaurant operated by "Geuiseppe" Savarese offered the "Italian Plan . . . Spaghetti a Specialty." In 1910 Greeks ran 17, and Italians 5, of Charleston's 60 restaurants. During the 1920s Greeks began opening groceries, and by the 1950s, they operated 10 percent of the city's groceries and roughly a third of the city's restaurants, cafes, and lunchrooms.[64] Their customers included both black and white Charlestonians.

In this respect, Charleston was quite typical for much of the American South, where Greek immigrants began as hucksters of home-manufactured candies and then operated what might be the only ice cream parlors, candy stores, lunchrooms, and restaurants in small and medium-sized southern towns. Typical was Garifolos Zenos, who came to the United States in 1909 to work in his brother's candy store in the oil boom town of Sour Lake, Texas, and then opened his own ice cream and candy store in Port Arthur. Zenos's Confectionery Store became famous for its huge, decorative mirrors and its 24-foot onyx soda fountain. The path of the Greek immigrant Tom Anthony was not totally different: it first took him to Chicago to work in a factory and then to Atlanta, where he operated a fruit stand. After returning home to fight in Macedonia, Anthony settled in 1912 in San Antonio and opened the Manhattan Restaurant. Similarly, two brothers-in-law, George Petheriotes and Angelo Mytelen, first peddled fruit in St. Louis and sauerkraut in New Orleans, then operated a series of cafes in Hattiesburg, Gulfport, and Houston. In Houston, they then expanded into the wholesale coffee business with their sons.

In Alabama, Greek immigrants owned 90 percent of the state's restaurants. The Birmingham candy-seller Nicholas Christu, like many immigrant food retailers, had consciously settled where "there were no [other] Greeks," so as to avoid business competition.[65] But this of course meant that there were no Greek consumers either, and little familiarity with Greek food among native southerners. As a result, only a few of the many Greek restaurants in the American South offered Greek cuisine. Greek restaurants generally sold inexpensive, southern home-style cooking: Beef stew, dumplings, vegetables, macaroni and cheese, with an occasional gyros "sandwich" or Greek salad. In Charlotte, North Carolina, Greek restaurateurs sold lots of grits, but they eventually removed moussaka from the menu, since few customers were interested. In nearby Monroe, a Greek owner reported, "Customers like Greek salad and baklava . . . but the best sellers are chicken tenders, beef and Italian food."[66] Greek businessmen prepared skordalia (olive oil and garlic) only for Greek kitchen workers and countermen.

Even in cities with substantial immigrant populations, like New York and Chicago, the sale of "American" foods from lunchstands and diners became a Greek niche. Diners had begun as wagons and carts that purveyed "chewed sandwiches" and other cheap meals round the clock in New England's factory districts in the 1870s and 1880s. After 1900, Greek immigrants helped transform them from streetcars into small trolley-like but permanent buildings that offered quick counter service at all hours of the day and night. In New York the only way to identify a Greek-owned diner or lunchstand might be the little blue paper cups decorated with the Parthenon and a frieze. Even today in diners, "You have to satisfy everyone," according to Charles Savva who came from Cyprus in 1973. A *New York Times* reporter found that his Harvest Diner in Westbury, Long Island, served everything from "pancakes to lobster tails, omelettes to spaghetti, moussaka to matzoh ball soup." Most of New York's 1,000 Greek-owned coffee shops and diners today still offer encyclopedia-sized menus and a gargantuan array of multi-ethnic desserts.[67] But most of their offerings are not Greek foods.

Greeks selling regional, or multi-ethnic, foods to multi-ethnic customers provide the most puzzling example of an ethnic niche in twentieth-century food markets. Why, after all, should 85 percent of Chicago's Loop restaurants be Greek-owned, as the historian Theodore Saloutos reported them to be in the 1950s? These were not men who had learned the restaurant trade in Greece. It seems equally inexplicable that among 956 Greek men surveyed in Chicago in the early twentieth century, mostly of peasant origin, 105 were waiters and cooks, 83 were operators of ice cream parlors, 55 were operators of restaurants, 24 were proprietors of fruit stores, 15 owned saloons, and 13 owned candy stores.[68] Consumers and other restaurateurs alike seemed very aware of the existence of this Greek economic niche. Thus, in the 1940s the German Catholic and Polish Jewish purchasers of Minneapolis's popular Schiek's Cafe worried over their prospects: "What do we know about the restaurant business?" they asked themselves, and their public. "We are not Greek or Chinese so how can we be successful?"[69]

One explanation for the development of ethnic niches outside enclave economies points to their origins in the business practices of immigrant entrepreneurs. Although ethnic family ownership and cooperation remained common in niche businesses, as they had been in enclave businesses, the real key to creating and expanding ethnic niches was wage labor recruited through ethnic channels. Wage labor in a niche restaurant or grocery store provided a cheap source of help for the proprietor, while providing a kind of apprenticeship for wage-earners eager to open their own businesses eventually.

Like enclave businesses, cross-over businesses generally began as family-based enterprises. In the restaurant partnership of Maria Sermolino's father with an older Italian woman chef, Sermolino's mother ran the cash register, and she and her sister helped bartenders make drinks and glued labels on wine bottles. On the other side of the country, in California, Chinese shrimp men called their businesses the "four family association," while an Italian described fishermen as "a lot of fish people together, all Italians, like a family."[70] Fishermen in San Francisco learned their trade—weaving nets, sailing, fishing—from their fathers, often beginning work at age 7 or 8. When fathers died, a partnership of brothers often carried on the family business.[71]

As family businesses grew, cross-over entrepreneurs eschewed bureaucratic and corporate hierarchy and sought to continue their personal contacts with their customers, usually on a cash basis. In San Francisco, Achille Paladini, a fisherman, had pants made with special pockets "that extended to his knees" in order to carry enough cash for a day's business. Although Paladini eventually operated a string of fish trucks, he worked alongside his children and employees until his death.[72] German brewers, even the most wildly successful and wealthy, built "dynasties," not corporations. In St. Louis, Adolphus Busch got his start in large-scale brewing when he married Lilly, the daughter of Eberhard Anheuser. His son August

A. ran the family business after his father's death. August A. Busch's sons Adolphus III and Gussie (August, Jr.) headed Anheuser Busch through the 1930s and 1940s. In 1975, Gussie's son August III took over.[73]

Not surprisingly, the intense cooperation among family members and co-ethnics brought criticism from American businessmen unable to enter an economic niche. In Minnesota, the Chippewa/Ojibway peoples had sold wild rice since their first encounters with European fur traders in the eighteenth century—when a sack of rice purchased two gallons of rum. For European homesteaders, rice became "a cheap article of diet . . . everybody likes," selling for about four dollars a bushel in the 1850s.[74] Organized cooperatively, two to five extended families of kinsmen camped near the rice lakes, and a "rice chief" supervised harvesting to ensure that "what serves the rice is law; what harms the rice is illegal." European farmers saw the celebration, singing, and dancing that accompanied cooperative harvesting as "unproductive." For decades European-Americans sought legal access to rice lakes reserved by law or treaty for the Chippewa. Ethnic cooperation worked: Chippewa harvesters first marketed to a trader in Minneapolis or Bemidji; one, Harvey Ayer, worked intensively with the Mille Lacs Indians to this end in the 1930s, and in 1936 Schoch's Grocery Store in St. Paul advertised wild rice as a harvest-time special.[75]

Cooperating California farmers also disturbed American businessmen with their "un-American" practices. Japanese who settled near Stockton's Wholesale Produce market at first rented individual stalls and received individually numbered plates to put on their produce wagons or trucks. This market was chaotic—a place where a Japanese child remembered that buyers "came out running, shouting orders to farmers," producing "bedlam everywhere as the men yelled, honked, and gestured." All that changed when Chiyo Shimamoto's father joined together with other farmers in a Japanese Vegetable Growers' Association. In the reorganized market, the Japanese growers had two rows of stalls, the Greek and Italian gardeners their own rows.[76] As late as 1943, John Brucato, the head of a West Coast Victory Garden Council and the operator of a Sebastopol ranch and winery, found himself accused of being "a lousy Sicilian Communist" when he created a market for farmers selling directly to consumers.[77]

Ethnic niches in agriculture particularly struck—and puzzled—observers. By 1920 Japanese farmers raised 90 percent of snap beans; 50–90 percent of artichokes, canning beans, cauliflower, celery, cucumber, fall peas, spinach, and tomatoes; and 25–50 percent of asparagus, cabbage, cantaloupes, carrots, lettuce, onions, and watermelons. At that time they made up 3 percent of the farmers in California.[78] In Walla Walla, by contrast, onions were monopolized by Italians; in California's Central Valley Italian specialties included grapes, cabbages, and ultimately broccoli, garlic, and cauliflower.

Niches like these developed because bonds of ethnicity shaped labor recruitment, not just marketing. Chinese, Japanese, and Italians typically hired themselves out in gangs, working for a boss or subcontractor of their own ethnicity, who might also provide them with their food on the worksite. Italian family truck farmers operated boarding houses for their employees, and they preferred Italians. Employers leasing large tracts and needing hired harvesters to supplement family labor almost always turned to contractors, and thus immigrant harvesters, of their own background. One student of Japanese agriculturalists claimed that Japanese employers could hire laborers cheaper than other groups since ethnic ties eliminated competition among labor contractors.[79] Ethnic ties spread agricultural expertise and linked wage-earner, small-producer, and retailing cooperatives into a vertically integrated ethnic chain of production that ultimately delivered to a multi-ethnic and American marketplace.

Labor recruitment through ethnic channels produced ethnic niches with a few visible "kings" and large numbers of humbler producers. Chinese farmers in the California Delta cultivated tracts of up to 500 acres, employing Chinese labor. Typical was Chin Lung, who came to California in 1882 at the age of about 18 and worked for a rice importer while learning English. Because he spoke English, he could negotiate leases for his ambitious laborers as well as provide housing and food for hundreds of Chinese laborers at harvest time. Eventually known as "the potato king," Chin Lung had his equivalent in the Japanese farming community—in "potato king" George Shima.[80]

Labor recruitment worked a similar effect in the urban restaurant trade. The three immigrant groups establishing niches in restaurants—Chinese, Italians, and Greeks—included large numbers of male sojourners, who created a high demand for boarding houses and restaurants in enclave economies and who also sought jobs there. In the restaurant trade, as Sermolino noted, Italian-style service (in contrast to American cafeterias and automats) generated as many as twenty dishes per eater, thus providing ample employment for low-wage waiters, busboys, and dishwashers. All were immigrants recently arrived from Italy; many lived behind the restaurants, where they also ate. Many wage earners in these humble positions saw their employment as an opportunity to learn the restaurant trade, and some went on to start restaurants of their own.

Explaining why Greeks dominated the diner business in New York, Peter Drakoulias (whose grandfather founded the Empire Atlantic Supplies Company to furnish paper goods and chinaware to diners) also emphasized the influence of labor recruitment: "Someone came over from Greece, worked as a counterman, and then brought over his brother." In a pattern familiar in the South's candy stores and cafes, George Fallis arrived in New York in 1930 at age 18 to work as a dishwasher in a restaurant owned by his father's brother; two months later he became the chef's assistant, then the short-order cook, then apprentice to the baker. In 1940 he opened his own diner.[81]

Enclave foods, enclave businessmen, and American consumers of a wide variety of backgrounds all crossed over culinary boundaries in large numbers in the early years of the twentieth century. Crossing over produced new, regional creole foods; it also created ethnic niches in multi-ethnic, regional food markets. Wage labor recruited from within the ethnic community created considerable competition in these niches, but it also gave businessmen the capital and know-how they needed to spring out of their enclave economies and into a wider multi-ethnic market.

Cross-over businessmen usually "carried ethnicity with them," so their business niches gave regional marketplaces an ethnic flavor, even in the culturally homogeneous South. Ethnicity was no longer confined to enclave economies where consumers bought from producers and retailers of the same background. Ethnicity had instead become a dimension of multi-ethnic cross-over exchanges.

Ethnic foods also left their enclaves, to be purchased by a wide range of American consumers. They, too, often remained marked by an ethnic label, even as they gradually found mixture with other ingredients in multi-ethnic creoles. The ethnic origins of foods like pasties, deli, and chili remained identifiable, even when people of a variety of backgrounds ate them, alone or in combination with other ethnic foods.

Both the ethnic cultural conservatives we first viewed in their nine-teenth-century enclaves and Americans with deep historical roots reach-ing back to the colonial era participated in the cross-over exchanges of the early twentieth century. Immigrants and minorities seemed eager to bal-ance their search for familiar foods (in enclave groceries or in the form of processed flour and meat) with the pursuit of pleasure, recreation, and novelty through cross-over eating. Native-born American eaters with lit-tle sense of their own ethnic roots were as intrigued by novelty as were the enclave conservatives. Different consumers sought different identities by eating new foods: robber barons and middle-class New York Jews wanted their own versions of cosmopolitanism; Bowery boys and Italian mothers wanted camaraderie and sensory pleasures heightened by lager beer; bohe-mians wanted hedonism and "wine, women and song"—the pleasures they believed Victorian middle-class culture forbade them.

With businessmen and consumers of so many backgrounds regularly shuttling back and forth across ethnic boundaries, and with new creoles and ethnic markets emerging not just in cosmopolitan New York but in Cincinnati and Charleston, the meanings of ethnic, regional, and national identities entered a period of intense scrutiny and confusion in the early twentieth century. Eventually, the nation itself had to come to terms with its many cultural and economic cross-over residents, and try to determine what—if anything—defined Americans of the twentieth century.

But not before nativism and xenophobia—both prominent features of U.S. politics in the early twentieth century—had expressed themselves in opinions about the foods Americans should consume. Between 1880 and 1940, a veritable "food fight" erupted over what it meant not only to be, but to eat, American. Here again, however, the preference for variety and novelty would win over those intellectuals and home economists who would define patriotic eating by the regional eating habits of the New England past.

CHAPTER FIVE

Food Fights and American Values

In 1939, an unemployed writer charged by the Federal Writers' Project to describe New England's foodways lamented the decline of traditional foods—"forced out," he claimed "by the products of the fast freight and the canning factory and to some extent by the influence of immigrants." As proof, he described a trip to his local supermarket. There, "near the cans of Boston baked beans and codfish cakes" stood "cans of spaghetti and chop suey." "Or is it chow mein?" he concluded wearily, clearly not caring about the difference, and wishing he could instead return to a culinary past when superior, and unquestionably American, foods reigned.[1]

With immigrants, Americans, and ethnic foods regularly crossing over ethnic boundaries by the turn of the twentieth century, the confrontation of values represented by America's many cultures of eating seemed inevitable. Vast food corporations increasingly dominated the food marketplace, though they did not attempt to define a single national cuisine. That was to become the task of well-educated American women, who sought to convince enclave eaters that the simple, abstemious fare of Puritan New England provided a scientific, modern, and patriotic diet. Other reformers took more direct political action to stop the spread of enclave foods. But after a fifty-year food fight, the reformers' foray into culinary nationalism collapsed.

Between World Wars I and II, America's intellectuals and other self-appointed guardians of national culture gradually developed an alternative philosophy of American eating which was respectful of difference and pleasure, and thus reconcilable with both America's cultural diversity and its corporate food processors. At least in the culinary domain, intellectuals abandoned their notions of Americanizing immigrants and working-class outsiders and decided instead to celebrate culinary cultural pluralism.

W hile middle-class observers had long noted, and decried, the eating habits of poor Americans—and had begun to study them as early as the 1870s, in their efforts to define an American standard of living—fear and loathing of immigrant foodways crescendoed around the turn of the century. Just before World War I, nationalist demands for "100 Percent Americanism" intensified reformers' interest in immigrant kitchens. Sauerkraut became "Victory cabbage," and a visitor reported an Italian family as "still eating spaghetti, not yet assimilated."[2]

Just what was wrong with the way urban immigrants ate? First, Americans saw foreign diets as being dictated more by hidebound custom than by dietary or financial rationality. Mabel Kittredge, the founder of a model flat in New York City, believed that ignorance, more than poverty, rendered the meals of the foreign-born inadequate. Another reformer, Lillian Betts, noted that "ignorance prevents [an immigrant mother] from buying or preparing the kind of food that would give nourishment and satisfy the cravings of hunger."[3] A New Yorker insisted that immigrants did not understand the impact of migration and life in a new country on their dietary needs. A diet adequate to sustain life in Italy, wrote one, "is not suitable in the colder winters of this country. Animal foods form but a small part of their diet, [resulting in] a gradual but sure deterioration in stamina."[4] Immigrant cooks did not appreciate American foods like corn, or know about vitamins or "preservative" foods. They ate too little meat and too little milk; they drank too much coffee and alcohol; they ate too many sweets and rich, fatty foods. And the women responsible for cooking meals knew nothing of order and routine. "Poor little tenement girl, she does not know that in the well-managed home, breakfast is bought the day before," Kittredge lamented.[5] In this view, the education of women could end the power of culinary conservatism in ethnic communities around the country.

The consequences of female ignorance in the kitchen were supposedly grave. Jacob Riis believed that "half the drunkenness that makes so many homes miserable is at least encouraged, if not directly caused, by mismanagement and bad cooking."[6] John Spargo, who found only 7 percent of school children eating breakfast, compared children's craving for "stimulants" (mainly pickles) to the craving for alcohol in adults who did not eat properly.[7] The Depression of the 1930s raised further concerns that inadequate diet weakened the nation's youngest citizens. In New York, estimates of rickets rates among school children exceeded 50 percent, of decayed teeth more than 90 percent. Health officials in the public schools judged 20 percent of New York City school children to be underweight. Defining malnutrition as the "constant use of improperly chosen food," health workers at the Mulberry Health Center in New York judged malnourished fully 30 percent of "apparently well" and healthy Italian children. Home visits revealed that 227 of 275 families "needed instruction in preparing food, including assistance with marketing and greater economy."[8] Armed with height/weight data, Dr. Josephine Baker of the Department of Health concurred: Malnutrition "was the most serious and widespread physical defect found among school children."[9] Thus the reformation of foreign foodways seemed necessary for national strength and health.

Most shocking to American sensibilities was the lack of interest in milk among Asian and southern European immigrants. Welfare workers urged milk-avoiding Italians that in America "latte per tutti" was possible, and that canned, evaporated milk should be substituted for coffee.[10] Noting that Japanese families consumed only half the milk of native-born Americans, Carey Miller, a dietician, concluded that "milk, either fresh or evaporated, markedly improves the quality of the average Japanese diet. Not less than a pint a day for every child should be the goal . . . Children should be taught to drink milk without added sugar or flavoring such as chocolate."[11]

Those who criticized immigrant diets argued that immigrants did not eat like Americans. But how did Americans eat? What was the model to which immigrants should aspire, and toward which education should lead?

In culinary matters, regionalism reigned. Thus, reformers faced a glaring problem—the absence of a widely accepted national cuisine.

The United States had become an independent nation without creating a national cuisine that matched its sense of uniqueness. Its eating habits were firmly regional. Perhaps the yeoman farmers idealized by Thomas Jefferson found anything national—even a cuisine—a violation of their enthusiasm for the local; perhaps cuisine simply seemed too exalted a term for simple, republican eating habits. Americans did on occasion link patriotism and eating: In New England, for example, old residents eager to celebrate the special American origins of their new republic ritualized summertime clam roasts into clambakes, claimed they had originated with Native Americans, and then carried on their invented tradition to celebrate a town's founding or the Fourth of July. A few patriots even renounced foreign wines and spirits, or pledged "to drink no other strong liquor than [corn] whiskey," produced in the United States.[12]

Only in reaction to the arrival of immigrants in the late nineteenth century did the cultural elites of the Northeast attempt to define what American eating should be. The alternative seemed to be national suicide: "Will Uncle Sam be swallowed by foreigners?" one concerned cartoonist challenged, choosing an appropriate metaphor.[13] Educated American women instead proposed to Americanize the foreigners, by teaching them what, and how, to eat, and by developing a "domestic science" or "home economics" appropriate for American citizens. Domestic science emerged almost simultaneously from many sources: middle-class cooking schools in Boston and New York, the cookbooks of their organizers, the new middle-class women's magazines, and the social settlements that worked closely with poor and foreign-born communities. Collectively, these efforts defined the years between 1870 and 1900 as the era "that made American cooking American."[14] By proposing a national cuisine, domestic scientists helped arm a variety of reform movements aimed at limiting, or even turning back, the tide of cross-over foreign foods and eating customs.

As scientists, these culinary reformers did share some core values with the developers of modern, corporate food industries. In particular, they shared a concern with efficiency, careful planning and measurement, and scientific solutions to practical problems, all of which found a place in their domestic science textbooks and training programs. "Chemical analysis should be the guide for the cookery book," wrote a lesser known expert in the field, while Ellen Richards, the founder of modern domestic science, wanted rational cooking to form one branch of "the business of housekeeping."[15]

Still, culinary reformers saw but little place in the national cuisine for either corporate foods or consumer pleasures. For culinary inspiration, domestic science turned instead to the austere traditional cooking of rural New England. Ellen Richards, in her 1900 book *The Cost of Living as Modified by Sanitary Science*, argued that the rich shared with the poor a "temptation to spend for things pleasant but not needful" and that "nutrition should be aimed at but not overstepped." Richards wanted all American cooks, regardless of class, to teach at the table "the virtues of self-control, self-denial, regard for others, good temper, good manners, pleasant speech."[16] New England's simple dishes—cod fish, brown bread, baked beans—symbolized a restraint that domestic scientists hoped all Americans would learn and practice.

Indulgence and pleasure had no place in domestic scientists' recipes for workers, immigrants, and poor farmers of the South or Southwest. Just as home economists wanted the poor to purchase simple, wood furniture and bare linoleum, they recommended particularly spartan versions of the New England diet as the model for modern American cooking. Financial necessity meant that a woman providing food at 5–15 cents per person per day could purchase nothing canned, and little more than potatoes, rye meal, corn meal, wheat flour, barley, oats, peas, beans, salt codfish, halibut, meat at 5 cents per pound, oleomargarine, and skimmed milk. Still, Richards worried that those with incomes under $500 wasted the most food. In her *Fifteen Cent Dinners for Working-Men's Families*, published in 1877, Juliet Corson, superintendent of the New York Cooking School, described a day's menu as broth and bread for breakfast, mutton and turnips for dinner, and barley boiled in broth for supper.

In Richards's New England Kitchen, cooks prepared the traditional foods of New England with a scientific concern for standardization. By selling these foods cheaply, women reformers hoped to educate the poor. Richards described the kitchen as "a friendly but strictly educational establishment where neighborhood people could purchase at low cost a few different soups and stews, perhaps a rice pudding or a nourishing broth . . . the kitchen would provide not only impeccable New England cookery but absolutely invariable New England cookery . . . every portion of tomato soup and beef stew to be exactly the same from day to day."[17] The menus of the New England Kitchen, according to food historian Harvey Levenstein, were "resolutely New England, featuring fish, clam, and corn chowders, 'Pilgrim succotash,' creamed codfish, pressed meat, corn mush, boiled hominy, oatmeal mush, cracked wheat, baked beans and Indian pudding."[18]

At the same time that they sought to promote the regional foods of New England as a national cuisine for newcomers, some domestic scientists encouraged innovation, and even frivolity, in kitchens that were already firmly middle-class and American. While public school girls learned about baked beans and Indian pudding, middle-class ladies learned from Fannie Farmer and others not just the principles of scientific cooking but the pleasures of preparing and serving all-white or all-pink meals. According to one of her students, Fannie Farmer—known best for her insistence on careful measurement in the kitchen—also insisted that "if a cook can make a good cream cake, baking-powder biscuit, & creamed codfish, she can cook almost anything."[19] Cookbook writers for the middle classes of the late nineteenth century, including Farmer, supplemented such basics with white sauce and "composed salads." White sauces smothered everything from beets that had been "boiled all day, then reheated the next," to novelties like boiled "Frankfort sausages," to old New England standbys like roasted turkey.[20] Salads—once made mainly of meat or poultry—became works of art, with apples, nuts, cottage cheese, celery, slices of pepper, and asparagus tips arranged in "dainty" compositions on decorative plates. These salads formed a "fragile, leafy interlude that was something of a nutritional frill."[21] Composed salads made substantial use of canned produce, from sliced peaches and pineapple to olives and asparagus. While reformers urged new immigrants and poor Americans to learn the restraint and moderation of New England cooking as a kind of apprenticeship in American culinary life, they did not always want the middle classes to eat like new immigrants. Having already served their apprenticeship in culinary restraint, these Americans could be allowed the convenience of the modern marketplace, with its new processed foods, and the pleasures of innovation and creativity.

Domestic scientists did not stop with describing a national cuisine or demonstrating its dishes in model kitchens for the poor. They brought their program for culinary change into public school classrooms and health programs serving poor communities across the country. Educators attempted to tailor their advice to particular groups. Italians learned that "it is not right to cook meat, cheese, beans, and macaroni together" (since dieticians insisted that combinations hindered digestion).[22] Health workers urged Italian children to substitute bread and butter or milk and crackers or fruit for their highly prized "cheap cakes and candies" bought at the corner "poison stand." Health workers particularly disliked the European custom of eating sweets as an afternoon snack and warned that "sweet rich food should never be eaten except at the end of a meal."[23]

Dieticians especially emphasized the supposedly unhealthy qualities of traditional foods. For example, they attempted to persuade Mexicans to reduce their use of tomato and pepper, in order to make "a blander dish, easier to digest and not harmful to the kidneys." They discouraged Hungarian, Polish, and Jewish children from eating dill pickles (with their supposedly negative impact on the urinary tract). Bertha Wood deplored the sour and pickled flavors and the rich foods popular among Eastern European Jews; these caused "irritation," she argued, rendering "assimilation more difficult" in a people already so "emotional" that they went too often to their doctors.[24] Health care workers also found Jewish mothers too "indulgent" of children—by feeding them fine cuts of meats, and "Grade A eggs," they failed to teach self-denial.[25]

To create a scientific, healthful, and national cuisine, domestic scientists proposed somewhat similar programs of education for immigrants and minorities throughout the United States. School girls in St. Paul in 1920 learned in their textbook to analyze starch and to measure liquids properly while also learning that corn was an excellent, cheap source of fat and starch, that "vegetables are served with butter, salt and pepper, or with a medium white sauce," and that good breakfasts required oatmeal or corn-meal mush. When they prepared inexpensive classroom lunches (about 20 cents per meal), students could choose a menu of cream of pea soup, veal croquettes, creamed potatoes, cottage cheese balls, rolls, "snow pudding," chocolate cake, and coffee. The five suggested menus in the textbook included no green vegetables; canned produce appeared only as soups and fruit cocktail appetizers.[26] As late as 1940, the Home Economics Section of New York's Department of Welfare recommended that immigrants should eat the old colonial creoles: for breakfast, hominy grits with milk and sugar, bread with butter, and milk and coffee; for dinner, baked beans, coleslaw with carrots, bread with butter, and custard pudding with raisins; and for supper, cream of carrot soup with rice, cottage cheese and prune salad, bread with butter, and tea.[27]

Farm extension services and university-sponsored home-demonstration agents offered much the same advice to the country's sizeable populations of poor rural women. In the South, the Tuskegee Institute hired a farm agent in 1906, and classes at the residential Penn School in the coastal sea islands introduced principles of scientific cooking and farming to African-American farmers. In the Midwest, farm extension agents introduced better seed and livestock, the use of machinery and fertilizer, and principles of soil treatment, but also new techniques for canning fruits and vegetables, meat and fish, especially the water-bath canning method (which replaced the open-kettle methods of the late nineteenth century).[28]

Protestant missions to rural Catholic Hispanos, like most domestic science programs, focused on re-educating girls. They assumed that when they educated a boy, "you educate an individual; educate a woman and you educate a family." The Home Mission Board focused girls' education "on home economics and general training for homemaking" in order to produce "better housekeepers, more devoted mothers, and more intelligent and economical wives." Mission workers encouraged Hispanic sons and fathers to take over gardening and fieldwork from women. And they urged women to set American-style tables, with proper knives and forks, and to stop dipping with tortillas from a common pot. In the 1920s, Anglo home economics teachers in New Mexico quizzed students on "an inexpensive substitute for meat" and offered "baked potatoes, suet pudding, rice or baked beans" as choices. Their menus included a dinner of meatloaf, mashed potatoes and gravy, buttered carrots, bread with butter, baked apples, and a cafeteria lunch of salmon croquettes with white sauce, hot rolls and whole wheat bread with butter, Waldorf salad, milk and hot chocolate.[29]

Rural American eaters in the South and Midwest found the New-England-based cuisine as curious as did urban immigrants. At Atlanta University a northern teacher of southern blacks conceded, "To introduce soups and stews . . . roast beef, rare steak, Boston baked beans, Boston brown bread, codfish balls, creamed codfish, Johnny cake, Graham gems and hash was not by any means an easy task."[30] Midwest immigrant farm women preferred their own one-pot soups and stews based on homeland recipes to the home agent's peculiar "Project Dish" (a seven-layer casserole of potatoes, barley, rice, onions, ground meat, tomatoes, carrots). One Finnish boy, whose mother assisted a local agent, teased her, "Yes, mother, tell the ladies Anna Tikkanen is coming to tell them how to put vanilla into mashed potatoes."[31]

Even the peoples who had first cultivated corn in the Americas found themselves subject to campaigns for culinary Americanization. And they too viewed such programs with considerable skepticism. By the nineteenth century, groups like the Cherokees in North Carolina, Georgia, and Tennessee had already adopted intensive farming and animal husbandry based on European models. Forced removal from their eastern and midwestern homelands and relocation to "Indian Territory" (Oklahoma) and scattered western reservations destroyed newly developed strategies for subsistence. To prevent starvation, the federal Indian Bureau provided reservation food rations—and these typically did not include corn. Iron Teeth, an elderly Northern Cheyenne Woman, complained in 1916 that "I am given very little food. Each month our Indian policeman brings me one quart of green coffee, one quart of sugar, a few pounds of flour and a small quantity of baking powder."[32] While domestic scientists saw corn-eating as a way to Americanize new immigrants, they seemed eager to wean Native Americans off cornmeal, and onto white wheat flour and baking powder breads.

Between 1880 and 1920 the Bureau of Indian Affairs regularly taught cooking to girls in Indian boarding schools. Commissioner Thomas Jefferson Morgan, appointed in 1889, wanted the schools to Americanize Native Americans. Training in home economics also provided female vocational training. Students at the Cherokee Female Seminary in Oklahoma ate austere but well-balanced meals and remained healthy. Still, worried parents, if they lived nearby, often brought "buttermilk, desserts, produce from their gardens and fresh fish from the Illinois River."[33] In another school, Anna Moore Shaw, a Pima Indian, thoroughly enjoyed her introduction to cornflakes. In general, food at the Indian schools drew little complaint from students, who were otherwise not shy about expressing sharply negative reactions to American clothing and language. But girls' culinary Americanization often could not survive the trip home: a Hopi girl shocked neighbors with a school recipe that wasted three eggs on one cake. Overall, then, domestic science succeeded in creating a vast program for culinary change among the poorest Americans, but without convincing many enclave eaters anywhere to accept the national cuisine it promoted.

W hile women reformers battled in campaigns to Americanize women cooks and consumers, other culinary reformers fought instead to limit the spread of ethnic foods, businesses, and eating practices. Typically, they perceived these as dangerous to the health and well-being of American eaters and the nation. Progressive-era reformers, many of them male, often turned to government regulation of the production and retailing of food and its associated business practices, especially those originating in ethnic communities, as another pathway to modernization.

Already in the nineteenth century, sanitary reformers like Ezra R. Pulling in New York had found the German and Irish Fourth Ward's market stocked with foods of terrifyingly bad quality: "piles of pickled herrings . . . exposed to the air till the mass approaches a condition of putridity" and sausages with "fragments of bread and other farinaceous food."[34] Although concern about corporate processors of meat in the "jungles" of Chicago also sparked new interest in federal inspection, the 1906 pure food and drug law actually passed with the active support of corporate meatpackers, along with mass food producers like brewer Frederick Pabst and canner H. J. Heinz. Corporate producers saw increased regulation as a hardship to small producers, and thus a way to diminish competition.

The strategy worked. A sausage company founded in 1919 in San Francisco by Luigi Managhi and his son provides a case study of the impact of regulation on a small businessman. Run by Luigi's son Mario and a business partner, the Swiss Italian Sausage Factory prospered until World War II, but it marketed its products only in San Francisco because it lacked a federal certificate to ship across state lines. Even with a Chicago-based corporate manager, the family chose to sell its remaining equipment to a corporate sausage maker and cease business when federal requirements again changed in the 1960s.[35] Even local codes could be exacting. New York regulations required that "all meats, poultry, game, fish and similar products . . . shall be kept within closed refrigerated display cases"—a not inconsiderable expense for small businessmen. Seventy-seven inspectors for the Bureau of Food and Drugs enforced 36 such regulations.[36] Small businessmen experienced regulation as harassment.

Reformers explicitly attacked immigrant businessmen as unsanitary when they worked out of their homes. In New York, progressives drove small-scale bakeries and pasta-manufactories out of tenement basements; they legally and precisely specified dimensions for floors, ceilings, and windows of factories, and the quality and location of furnishings, troughs, utensils, and ventilation. In response, a Brooklyn Polish-run bakery of the 1930s defensively changed its name to the Greenpoint Sanitary Bakery and Lunch Room. The head of New York's Bureau of Food and Drugs even claimed that modest restaurant owners along the Bowery had become so fearful of city regulations that they were cleaner than "the classy establishments on upper Fifth Avenue [which] . . . may be whited sepulchres."[37]

Campaigns to ban pushcarts affected immigrant businessmen almost exclusively, and reformers justified these regulations, too, on sanitary grounds. In 1905 Mayor McLellan appointed an investigating commission and tightened the licensing of street vendors. East Side peddlers, responding to what they claimed was police harassment, held meetings to propose counter-legislation. *The American Hebrew* supported the vendors, claiming that the food they sold was "as good, if not better" than supplies sold in neighboring stores.[38] New York then tried to end the sale of hot or cold street foods but quickly relaxed the ban as unrealistic: too many workers depended on them for their lunch. In 1936 New York's first Jewish-Italian mayor, Fiorello La Guardia, again succeeded temporarily in ridding the city of the pushcart markets he viewed as "colorful, shaggy and artistic" but also odorous, chaotic, noisy and unsanitary.[39] With WPA funds, La Guardia's administration herded Jewish and Italian pushcart vendors into new buildings, like the Essex Street and First Avenue markets. The city designed the buildings "for comfort and convenience of customer and merchant alike": they were heated, cooled, and well lighted, and "offending odors are banished by a suction system and each vendor must dump all refuse into huge Department of Sanitation trucks, loaded one after another all day long in a glass enclosed section of each building."[40] La Guardia and other New Deal reformers challenged the pushcart merchants to look at the change as a step up in the world: "Remember," he said, "you are no longer peddlers. You are now merchants."[41]

But when the Department of Markets told 900 Jewish pushcart operators they were a traffic hazard and must remove to the new Essex Street market, only 475 rented stalls.[42] WPA writers found that "despite the shrill cries of enterprising vendors and the persistent buzz of bargain-hunters, there is pessimism in the faces of the aged Jewish tradesmen who resent the change to order, cleanliness, and regulation that the younger generation has readily accepted."[43]

In a similar move in San Antonio in 1936, the Health Department removed the city's chili queens from market squares, on grounds that flies and unsanitary food-preparation techniques threatened the town's health. Outraged, liberal mayor Maury Maverick then helped build—and ostentatiously patronized—screened booths with central washing facilities, in the hopes that the chili queens could continue to attract local and tourist consumers. Ultimately, however, Maverick lost the battle with his health department, and chili queens disappeared from San Antonio plazas.

In San Francisco in the same years, city reformers sought to remove shrimp-cleaning operations from Chinatown homes. As in New York, San Francisco opposition emphasized both the sanitary threats of home production and the frequent use of child labor in family enterprises. A powerful poster of the period showed a small child, with bleeding hands, peeling a shrimp.[44] The implication was clear: Patriotic Americans would not eat foods produced in such foreign circumstances.

By far the most effective campaign in the food fights of the late nineteenth and early twentieth centuries was aimed at the drinking of alcoholic beverages, and thus at the largest and most successful of nineteenth-century cross-over businessmen. Prohibitionists, overwhelmingly of native birth and Protestant faith, succeeded in passing the Eighteenth Amendment to the federal Constitution in 1919. Responding to the significant consumption of alcohol typical since colonial times, moral reformers had worried already in 1815 about the United States becoming a nation of drunkards. After decades of arguing for individual abstinence and sobriety, reformers in the 1840s turned to regulation, like the famous Maine Law which licensed vendors of drink. But just as Americans appeared willing to change their drinking habits in response to religious revival and reformers' pleas, a new wave of immigrant Irish reintroduced customs like drinking at funerals, and the German brewers convinced urban Americans to take up beer drinking.

The arrival of millions of new Irish, German, and Italian drinkers, the growing popularity of beer, and the spread of the saloon spawned a national countermovement seeking "national unity through national self-restraint."[45] Natives complained of "the beer-soiled notes of the 'Fader-land,'" the salty pretzels of the saloon's free lunch, and the Limburger cheese that smelled as "if all the vile odors from the public sewers were mingled with those of Chicago's fragrant river and glue factories."[46] Sabbatarians like Billy Sunday reminded Americans that most cities had more saloons than churches, schools, libraries, jails, or parks, and more saloon-keepers than ministers. By the 1890s scientific racism added new founts of prohibitionist fervor, as when a Chicago minister in 1903 promised that "deliverance will come, but it will be from the sober and august Anglo-Saxon south, unspoiled and unpoisoned by the wine-tinted, beer-sodden, whiskey-crazed, sabbath-desecrating, God-defying and anarchy-breeding and practicing minions from over the sea."[47]

Immigrant Swedes, Finns, and Norwegians sometimes formed their own temperance movements. In North Dakota, Democratic pietist Norwegians set themselves apart from other immigrants by not drinking and by supporting both the Populist and prohibitionist movements which their German neighbors in the Republican Party opposed. Irish immigrants founded a Catholic Total Abstinence Union in 1872; an Irish priest had already toured the United States in support of abstinence twenty years earlier.

More often, however, immigrants mounted stiff opposition to a prohibition movement dominated by Protestant natives. Not surprisingly, Germans led the defense. Brewers had organized to protect themselves once already, in 1864, when the federal government imposed a tax of one dollar a barrel on beer and a licensing fee on brewers. Around the turn of the century, the most important German voice defending drink was the National German-American Alliance (founded in Pennsylvania), and its president, Charles J. Hexamer. The formation of state branches of the Alliance usually occurred in the midst of state prohibition campaigns in the early years of the century. Hexamer developed a defense of drinking that was both culturally German and deeply American in its references to natural rights, the Constitution, and the Bill of Rights. In 1912 Hexamer told Congress that "as devoted citizens of this country, we Americans of German birth or descent hold ourselves second to none in our devotion to the cause of true temperance and to all that makes for the sanctity and purity of the home, and decency and order in the States . . . as free and sovereign members of a free and sovereign people, we believe that we have the right to regulate our lives and our homes as we see fit. The right to drink our wine and our beer, and to import it, we consider as absolute an attribute of human liberty as is the right to buy any other food."[48]

Alas for Hexamer, World War I called his blending of German and American values into question. Patriotic Americans especially hated beer dynasties like that of Adolphus Busch, who died just before the war in Europe began. The Busch family, with its frequent trips to Germany and its very public enjoyment of its vast wealth, symbolized the arrogance of the kaiser to many Americans, and Anheuser-Busch sales fell from $17 million to $14 million in 1914. Sizeable charitable contributions, pledges of loyalty, and the removal of busts of Bismarck notwithstanding, the Busch estate was sequestered by A. Mitchell Palmer of the Treasury Department and title to the property was placed under the control of the federal government. Undermined still further by the anti-German sentiments of the war years, the brewers lost their battle against the prohibitionists.

Hexamer's 1912 predictions about the consequences of prohibition were nevertheless prescient. He had warned that "attempts at prohibition will cause contempt for the law, will create law-breakers, will be an additional incentive to try 'the forbidden fruit,' and, in prohibition States will drive people to the vile stuff of the smuggler, the bootlegger, the speak-easy, the blind tiger, the gambling houses, the brothels and other dens of vice."[49] In fact, immigrant home brewers of bathtub gin and dago red in the 1920s not only legally evaded prohibition (since production for home use remained legal) but illegally attracted enough new native-born consumers to make

Prohibition an era of good profits for those businessmen willing to become criminals.

Prohibition, along with almost all the other efforts of the nationalizing food reformers of this era, failed miserably. It is easy enough to see why. While adopting a language of business rationality, science, and technology in order to create a national cuisine, food reformers discouraged Americans from viewing food in the ways consumers, corporate food processors, and cross-over businessmen alike saw it—as a source of pleasure, novelty, stimulation, and profit. Few Americans were disposed to forgo the pleasures of the food marketplace for Puritan simplicity, self-reliance, and self-denial. As Dr. Victor G. Heiser, a nutrition consultant to the National Association of Manufacturers, ruefully reminded reformers, "Most people think of food as a form of recreation. Only a few look upon it as the fuel which keeps our body functioning," so few were sufficiently concerned to think mainly about what they needed "to function efficiently."[50]

Between 1920 and 1940, the food fight gradually waned as America's reformers and intellectuals, far more than America's eaters, changed their views on ethnic eaters and their foods. Intellectuals speaking for the nation gradually came to terms with America's diversity—a diversity no longer contained in enclave economies but reaching out into urban and regional marketplaces—and with the industrialization of America's food industries.

Cultural reconciliation began within the movement for social welfare and in some of the same institutions that had pioneered cooking classes as a form of Americanization. As early as the 1920s in San Francisco's Chinatown, Donaldina Cameron occasionally wore Chinese clothing and often ate the Chinese food of the women prostitutes she sought to rescue. Elite acceptance of immigrant contributions flowered briefly as "cultural pluralism" during the otherwise tribalist 1920s. While food was nowhere the centerpiece of pluralist thought—neither in Jane Addams's industrial museum nor in Horace Kallen's writings—culinary expressions of toleration nevertheless proliferated in the interwar years.

As a relatively short war, World War I required but limited sacrifices of American consumers. Still, for the first time the federal government—fueled by Progressives' enthusiasms for rationality, planning, and national unity—sought to manage food shortages and issued wartime directives to housewives facing shortages of wheat and meat. Patriotic eating required the substitution of beans for meat. To prevent consumers from "suffering protein and wheat shortage," the government distributed foreign recipes that were both rich and meatless. Dieticians, aware of the newly discovered vitamins in so-called "preservative foods," also pushed for greater consumption of fresh vegetables. No longer completely strange, and loaded with healthy vegetables, Italian cookery became a wartime boon to readers of women's magazines. But wartime recipes in local newspapers did not always reflect this sudden federal interest in culinary diversity. Food columnists in Pittsburgh were concerned to substitute other grains for wheat flours, too, but their featured recipes seemed more influenced by the "national cuisine" of the home economists than by recent immigrants: recipes for "seed bread, brown potato soup, spinach croquets" predominated. The most exotic suggestions were northern European treats like butterscotch and roast goose with gooseberry sauce.[51]

More sustained interest in immigrant culinary gifts subsequently developed during the 1920s at the International Institutes of the YWCA. A participant would later call the 40 institutes (which roughly resembled settlements) "the eatingest places ever known." The International Institutes popularized ideas with long lives in twentieth-century thinking about ethnicity, namely that "food and fellowship go together, whether in the home or in community life" and that ethnic food's main contribution to American life was "VARIETY—the spice of good eating as well as of life."[52] The Institutes created food programs to help immigrant women "develop a better insight into the problem of adjusting their food habits to those of America" but also saw immigrant foods adding "to our American dietary, giving it greater variety," as Lelia McGuire noted in her *Old World Foods for New World Families*, originally published in 1932. During the Depression they emphasized, "It is not the Institute's aim to change the diet habits of a family when their diet is excellent."[53] The Institutes even published cookbooks for American cooks, like St. Louis's *Menus and Recipes from Abroad* (1927), or Lowell's *As the World Cooks: Recipes from Many Lands* (1938). Notably missing were recipes from Jewish immigrants (who avoided the programs of the clearly Protestant "Y"). Milwaukee's Jewish-oriented settlements had, however, produced their own very popular *Settlement Cookbook* (1903), which provided a best-selling blend of American and immigrant recipes.

A number of the Institutes' programs moved beyond woman-to-woman contact to encourage cross-over business. The Boston Institute produced a tourist's guide to foreign food restaurants; by the 1930s its list of "nationality" shops and restaurants urged consumers, too, to remember that "understanding and friendship are often built around meals."[54] In St. Paul/Minneapolis and some other Institutes, workers sponsored Old World Markets, Festivals of Nations, and International Bazaars that sold foods and goods, offered by both ethnic women's organizations and by restaurant owners, grocers, and importers from immigrant communities.[55] These festivals grew into regular events and became even more popular in the 1950s.

With the onset of the Depression, the Institutes urged Americans to remember that immigrant communities held important culinary resources. "Under-privileged communities," they pointed out, had, by the mere fact of their poverty, "learned to know a lot about food substitutes and economies in buying."[56] The poor had useful skills—like the urban African-American woman who, drawing on her southern childhood experiences, reported that, for her, "during the Depression, fishing was survival."[57] Reformers urged native-born Americans to see themselves critically as immigrants sometimes perceived them to be—spoiled and indulgent—and to learn from their poorer neighbors. One observer noted that "Croatian immigrants, foreign-born people used to make disparaging remarks about the native American women sitting in the shade in the summer heat fanning themselves while the foreign-born women sweated in their kitchens putting up hundreds of jars of beans, tomatoes, preserves, jellies, pickles, beets, fruits of all kinds. Instead of putting up vegetables, meat, etc., for the winter native Americans bought canned goods from the store. None of the foreign-born women would be caught dead with store bread on the table."[58] These women knew how to "make do"—a skill much in demand among all Americans during the 1930s.

In New York, Depression-era social workers became enthusiastic advocates of multi-ethnic eating for low income families. Spaghetti entered the "advised" lists for inexpensive menus, distributed in Spanish to newly arrived Puerto Ricans.[59] The welfare department not only offered recipes in Yiddish for cooking oatmeal but praised the thriftiness of a kosher dairy meal like cheese blintzes, combination salad, bread with butter, and milk and coffee. Welfare brochures even included English-language instructions for making tzimes.[60] From Americanization, social welfare workers had rather quickly moved on to a celebration of the economic practicality, social rewards, and gustatory pleasures of culinary cultural pluralism.

Still, the food fight was not completely over in the 1930s, and nowhere was cultural confusion over the definition of American foodways more apparent than in the America Eats portion of the Federal Writers' Project. Begun in 1938, this project organized intellectuals (including writers like Nelson Algren) in 42 states to write a guide (never published) to American eating.[61]

Correspondence between administrators in Washington and their many employees in the states reveal differences of definition that marred the project from its beginnings. One editor in Washington complained that some states "could not get away from the idea that 'America Eats' was to be a cookbook . . . a few undertook to write dissertations on food in the worst women's magazine manner. One or two became fascinated with the commercial festivals supposed to give publicity to some local food-stuff. Yet others devoted too much attention to the food-habits of groups of recent foreign origins."[62] America Eats editors consistently requested descriptions of traditional American celebrations of community through food. What its writers found, however, was universal interethnic mingling and the popularity of corporate and "invented" foods. Were not these, too, "American"? Editors in Washington were reluctant to call them that.

Administrators of America Eats easily accepted that American foodways were regional. They requested state units to describe foods typical of their particular natural environment or agriculture. On the list submitted by Florida writers was terrapin, coquina broth, conch, grunts, rattlesnakes, key limes, oranges, wampus, and comtie. The files of Delaware and Massachusetts overflowed with stories of shore dinners and clambakes. For the vast midsections of the country, arguments arose. Iowa writers insisted there was no product or dish unique to their state; Washington suggested corn. Editors queried Montana about the possibility that miners there had invented ham and eggs with potatoes, "a unique American contribution to good cookery."[63] Trying to choose among recipes submitted from Kansas, Walter Kiplinger wondered if "buckwheat cakes and buffalo meat barbecue [were] representative." State writers informed him that the state grew very little buckwheat. They had found several buffalo barbecues near Milford, but these had been introduced three years earlier by Chamber of Commerce boosters. Nor could they explain "why Milford boosters hit upon the buffalo idea," since at most "the herds . . . in the old days paused there to satisfy their thirst at the old shogo-spring." Impressed that the 1941 Milford barbecue had served 10,000 barbecue sandwiches, Kansas writers reported also that "the buffalo idea" had spread to Czechs and their Sokol—which now sponsored its own buffalo festival.[64]

Federal administrators welcomed accounts of the historical evolution of foodways in colonial Massachusetts and Maine; without comment they accepted as genuinely American the reports on the eating habits of Native Americans and of frontier miners and ranchers. Even Spanish-origin foodways qualified if their roots were deep enough. The state file on Florida described the "creole" influence of Spanish and Majorcan settlement, and included descriptions of popular "pilau" dinners of rice and chicken (or what writer Stetson Kennedy termed "A ton of Rice and Three Red Roosters") "cooked in large iron pots over open fires." Southwest writers recognized a regional cuisine that blended Mexican, Indian, and Spanish into barbecue sauce, a "dark crimson blend of tomatoes and chili peppers," and that included tortillas, chili con carne, tacos, enchiladas, tamales, and a variety of wheaten baked sweets and corn dishes.[65]

Reports from the American South proved both rich and thoroughly uncontroversial as descriptions of regional, but completely American, eating. Portraits of skillful white housewives unloading baskets of hams, potatoes, and fried chicken onto "snowy white" tablecloths for a rural church picnic or "all day preaching" alternated with rhapsodic, condescending descriptions of Negro cooks and servers, male and female. White writers praised the bounty of the simple food of white housewives, but noted that "most everyone brings the same things, made much the same ways," so that "the ambrosia which Mrs. DeShazo is taking from her box is identical with that which Mrs. Ballew is setting on the tablecloth."[66] Whether barbecue, Alabama eggnog, fish fry, or "candy pullings," fine food in these accounts instead emerged almost exclusively from black hands. One WPA writer insisted that "the making of the masterpiece does not lie in the food, whether or not it be modern, but in the secrets of preparation, buried deep in the brain of many an ancient Negro retainer."[67] Sometimes this retainer was an Uncle Felix (who cooked for the white members of a Georgia "fish camp" clubhouse); more often it was a mammy or "mauma."

A few of the eating events described in America Eats—notably possum roasts and "chitlin struts"—were all-black. And in Delaware the white community's Big Thursday (celebrating the end of the yearly ban against oyster fishing) preceded the comparable Black Saturday by several days. Generally, however, patterned intermingling of the races prevailed, and few food items (with the possible exception of chitlins) found favor among only one race. In those parts of the South where immigrants had earlier settled, their adoption of the southern regional creoles was well advanced. In Savannah, the March Salzburger Gathering picnic no longer included "delectable sausages and puddings made with specially fattened smoked porks" or imported wines. Instead "year by year all the old German foods have been replaced by Southern American cooking. Even sour potato salad and Austrian jellies have disappeared"—replaced by "mulatto rice," chicken pilau, and "real home-made southern custard [ice] cream."[68]

In contrast to their positive reception of regional variations on American culinary themes, project administrators and writers were of two minds when faced with submissions that described hasenpfeffer, lutefisk, or other immigrant dishes as American food. Florida writers saw Tampa's Sicilian-Spanish-Cuban community of cigar workers, along with their arroz-con-pollo and Cuban bread festivals at the town's Asturiano Club, as recent expressions of a traditional regional creole. And New York writers proclaimed, without apology, the distinctive eating habits of their city, which was totally unlike the rest of the United States precisely because it had been so influenced by recent immigrants. Not so in New England. There, writer R. Cameron, in an awkward piece of fiction, described the travails of a Connecticut Valley working woman who sought to carry on a local, Protestant church May Breakfast in a town where foreigners and "their thick, dark sandwiches, their great hunks of soggy-looking cake," and "peppers and garlic fried in erl" overwhelmed and disgusted her. "'Foreigners'—she hated them all."[69] In Indiana, too, a local writer claimed that foreigners "have exerted little influence on the balance of the State, and almost none at all upon its eating habits," perhaps because "the true Hoosier doesn't like unusual foods; he sticks self-righteously to his meat and potatoes, corn, beans, and pie." But a second writer from Indiana in "a pitch-in Dinner after a Funeral Service," noted that the widow was "an excellent kraut maker," known also for her "cabbage relish with pepper"—both German specialties.[70]

The vast upper Midwest, with its predominantly immigrant-origin farmers, posed the toughest issues for the project's definitions of American eating. North Dakota's Thomas Moodie alerted project administrator Florence Kerr of the trouble his writers had in preparing a list of recipes "for popular traditional North Dakota dishes that do not represent recent foreign influence. The State's population has been so greatly influenced by foreign groups that few, if any, dishes have been developed that are traditional to North Dakota alone."[71] Editors in Washington actually sent Wisconsin writers in search of "a typical German New Year's Even feast," only to be disappointed that "they had never heard of such a feast." The same administrators turned down the Milwaukee proposal that herring salad and mulled wine, both commonly served in German homes for New Year's, be included. (These, sniffed Mrs. Florence Kerr, were "not peculiar to Germans.")[72]

The Wisconsin unit instead gained Washington's permission to explore lutefisk suppers when "several members of the staff . . . indicated their willingness to eat the fish in their eagerness for basic research." But Washington then turned down Iowa's request to include lutefisk (along with Amana bread) as "not representative enough for our purpose." Writing to Washington in 1941, Administrator S. L. Stolte passed along the editors' sense that "the Norwegian LUTEFISK supper and the German 'booya' are more interesting as examples of traditional community eating in the state than the Kolacky or sauerkraut events."[73] Only Mrs. Kerr knew why.

In fact, lutefisk—a Norwegian codfish Christmas dish made notorious most recently by Garrison Keillor—appeared as representative in submissions from all over the upper Midwest. A dish of codfish soaked first in lye, then in water, then cooked, then served with melted butter or cream sauce, lutefisk had wide appeal as a novel dish for multi-ethnic eaters. Church and community groups all over the Midwest held lutefisk dinners in the fall, not merely as a Christmas celebration. The Minnesotan who described these events noted, "Its traditional Scandinavian features are more or less incidental" as the third generation understood not a word of their native language. Neither were they the largest group of eaters at lutefisk suppers. Instead, he wrote further, "Torgrim Oftedal's German wife is there because she hasn't missed a parish function since she was married. Henry Bleecker, who came to Minnesota from up-state New York and married Anna Olson, is there because he always goes to church with his wife."[74] Wisconsin writers too believed that lutefisk church dinners had become so popular, beginning in the 1920s, that humorous Norwegians had formed "a Norwegian Lutefisk Protective Association to make sure that Germans and Irish don't get more than their fair share of the traditional Christmas delicacy." Immigrants and their children apparently delighted in introducing newcomers to the "gastronomies of lutefisk." "They will tell him, with an air of complacent knowledge, 'You won't like it. Nobody likes lutefisk at first. You have to learn to like it. Better take meatballs.' For Swedish meatballs are served the uninitiated who have yet to grow to a liking of the strong fish."[75] (In the South, "possum" feeds, chitterlins, "Kentucky oysters," and Brunswick stew with squirrel sometimes provided the same moments of occasional culinary frisson for middle-class, and usually urban and male, white cross-over eaters.)

While happy to welcome as American any foods that originated in colonial America, and while being somewhat confused and ambivalent about ethnic customs, America Eats editors vigorously rejected foods or events they regarded as commercial or corporate. Contributions from California sparked particular anger in Washington. Faced with descriptions of California novelties like the burrito, French dip sandwich (invented by an Italian), and Texas Tamale Tommy's Ptomaine Tabernacle, and with an article on health food "a la concentrate," a federal administrator lost his patience. "What these contributions exemplify is the mongrel character of Southern California today—its eagerness to have traditions, the commercial character of its attempts to make such traditions."[76]

But California was not alone in liking cross-over and commercial treats: hot dogs appeared everywhere, even in the rural South; Oklahoma City boasted of Ralph A. Stephen, owner of the Dolores Restaurant and Drive-In, who had invented Suzi-Q potatoes and a machine to cut the potatoes into the requisite spirals. In Atlanta, a Georgia writer noted a recent development: ladies meeting between 11 and 12 in the morning for Coca-Cola parties, which included "trays of tall iced glasses filled with Coca-Cola" followed by "platters of crackers and small iced cakes."[77] Colorado found its drive-in restaurants sufficiently novel that the writer explained, "You 'drive-in,' honk the horn, read the menu painted on the high board fence in front of you, or accept one thrust into your hands by a pretty girl . . . wearing a jaunty slack suit," and then order hamburgers, hot dogs, or ribs with Cokes.[78] All of these entries were marked for exclusion from the final publication.

That publication never came, however, as the Second World War ended federal programs for unemployed intellectuals. The notes and files of the America Eats project, frozen in time, stand as a lasting reminder of the legacy of earlier food fights. Disagreement and discord, not national unity, still characterized the efforts of American intellectuals to define American eating.

The confusion about what constituted regional American, as opposed to ethnic, corporate or invented foods in the America Eats project resolved itself in the face of a national wartime emergency. Any and all foods that helped solve a food crisis caused by shortages and rationing found acceptance as sufficiently American. World War II intensified exploration of the nation's many eating communities, in large part because the Army had 15 million soldiers to feed, many of them of foreign descent. As one northerner noted, "I never ate grits or black-eyed peas or broccoli until I came into the Army." Another confessed, "I had never eaten eggplant. Fried eggplant's real good too. Broccoli I don't care for at all. You say it's called the aristocrat of vegetables?"[79] At the request of the National Defense Advisory Commission, the National Research Council (NRC) together with the U.S. Department of Agriculture decided to research food habits of Americans, and formed a Committee on Food Habits. Wartime researchers sometimes assumed that foreigners might still need special education, if only to handle the rules of rationing; the International Institutes in particular worried that "submissive" foreign housewives might not resist or report store owners who overcharged or operated black markets.

But the judgmental condemnation typical of many earlier studies by food reformers was entirely absent in the work of the NRC.[80]

On the home front, ethnic foods became central to campaigns to remind American cooks that "every time you cook you can help or hinder Hitler."[81] Under the auspices of groups like the Common Council for American Unity, public programs again stressed learning from one's multiethnic neighbors. Reported one Council worker, "In general, foreign-born housewives are more careful both in their food-buying habits and in the economical preparation of food." They also "know a lot about food substitutes and economies in buying, and might make a real contribution." She suggested neighborhood meetings where individuals exchanged experiences, methods, and food recipes.[82] At the close of one such meeting, foreign-born housewives offered newspaper reporters an attractive array of dishes they had prepared. A press release from Constance Gurd Rykert of the Common Council for American Unity emphasized that "European housewives had had to use meat substitutes or meat stretchers . . . Age-long shortages have conditioned them to rationing long before it became a war-time rule here in America, and they have evolved succulent dishes, rich in nutrition and low in point values." She appended to her release a recipe for eggplant "parmiciana," contributed by Miss Angela M. Carlozzi.[83]

The Council also sponsored a series of radio broadcasts as part of its Food Fights For Freedoms programming. Radio segments, and a special cookbook, encouraged the organization of "What's Cooking in Your American Neighbor's Pot" parties. One broadcast focused on "What Americans Can Learn from the Greek American Housewife"; it emphasized her thrifty ways and the value of putting several ingredients into one dish to eliminate waste. Other lessons from the Greek community included the use of cereals in meals other than breakfast, the use of low-point rationed meats, especially lamb, and the use of fermented milk (presumably yogurt) as a substitute for cream. A Council brochure called "War-Time Recipes Used by Our Foreign Origin Americans" included Czech lentil chowder, Italian pasta e fagioli, Norwegian smorre brod, and Polish "golarki" and "pierozki." The Council's cookbook listed the ingredients used by Greeks, Scandinavians, Western Mediterraneans, "Orientals," and Slavs to fulfill daily requirements for the seven food groups; it also suggested that local organizations sponsor an American regional party, with foods from New England (brown bread), the South (black-eyed peas), and the Southwest (hot tamales).[84]

With a diverse multi-ethnic food marketplace beneath their noses, New York's food columnists became especially enthusiastic about ethnic solutions to wartime problems. In 1942 New York's *PM* ran a week-long series focusing on Mrs. Daly (an active clubwoman in the Bronx Auxiliary of the American Legion who prepared "medium-price" wartime menus) and Mrs. Lederman (who lived in a federal housing project with her husband, an organizer for the Amalgamated Clothing Workers union and prepared "low-price" meals). Charlotte Adams, the author, noted that "we shall learn more from Mrs. Lederman than she can possibly learn from us" because "she's fond of what might seem to some of us strange foods," a trait attributed to her Hungarian mother. Including a recipe for "tzibla kirchluch" (onion cookies), Mrs. Lederman easily convinced Adams that these were "perfectly delicious and most easy to make."[85] The same series suggested that readers try dandelion greens fried with bacon, or broccoli, or pumpernickel bread. Meanwhile, at *The Times,* Jane Holt praised the greens readily available at any springtime Italian market—dandelions, mustard greens, sorrel grass, field salad, artichokes, broccoli rabe, spinach.[86] (Dandelions could even be purchased "in the grocery department of a dignified city store, neatly packaged in tins that bear the label of a distinguished Back Bay Boston firm of gentlemen grocers.")[87] Holt also touted a sugar substitute—the molasses of "the Deep South of long ago."[88]

With all their enthusiasm for culturally diverse patriotic eating, the reformers and food columnists of the 1940s nevertheless described ethnic foods as a new means to fulfilling old values. The cuisine they recommended was more inclusive, but the values remained those of New England's Puritans. Thus recipes for Spanish rice, Brazilian cabbage salad, and Norwegian Prune pudding ("a sugar saver") appeared as part of a "war on waste."[89] Simple, homemade, and thrifty meals using native American ingredients still drew the highest praise. When the West Side Children's Aid Center sponsored a competition won by Anna Abbattista, her meal (a fairly mundane but Italianate luncheon of vegetables, bread and butter, milk, and sliced bananas costing mere cents) earned praise while the more commercial American meal of her sister, who had prepared a home-economics text menu of creamed chipped beef and crushed pineapple with whole-wheat toast and milk, fell by the wayside as too expensive—at 18.5 cents.[90] Across town at the Madison Square Boys Club, Albert Hines declared the empanadas that his Colombian students prepared by blending meat, eggs, and corn far superior to his own expensive steaks. Foreign recipes thus "glamorized money-saving."[91] With a war on, one food writer insisted, "Every consumer must learn to exercise a kind of patriotic self-restraint in every act of buying and using."[92] Offal meats provided a particularly telling exercise in restraint and self-denial, carrying readers far from Puritan tastes, but not from Puritan values. In one article, Mrs. David Dubinsky, wife of the president of the ILGWU, shared her recipe for a Russian dish of mushrooms and chopped calf's lung, liver, and heart on a dough made with chicken fat.[93]

Food experts of the 1940s also kept consumers well informed about the use of new processed foods, relaxing their earlier objections to corporate products. By the 1940s nutritionists had agreed that citrus fruits, transported from far-off Florida or California, should be part of a healthy eater's daily diet. Even canned novelties could find acceptance if they perked up war-stressed appetites. Meat shortages created a temporary enthusiasm for soy bean products, both those familiar in Asian import stores and new corporate products like a spaghetti manufactured from soy flour in Chicago. Overall, food writers suggested that housewives, who might be returning home from wartime jobs, should feel patriotic—and efficient—when they opened cans of the baked beans, spaghetti, and chop suey (or was it chow mein?) that they found side by side on grocery shelves.

Thus, after fifty years of intermittent battling, American intellectuals decided that Uncle Sam could swallow immigrant and regional specialties and processed foods and actually grow stronger in the act. While still loathe to reject moderation and self-denial as key American values, or to embrace the hedonism of uncritical consumerism, even in the food marketplace, they now saw ethnic and corporate foods as alternative routes to old cultural ends. Efficiency, restraint, and moderation meant tolerating diversity and multi-ethnic marketplace exchanges. It meant welcoming, as well, the convenience of standardized processed foods. As the United States rejected isolation and rose to global power, it also accepted a peculiarly American, and fundamentally commercial, culinary cosmopolitanism. Corporate production and curiosity about "what's cooking in your neighbor's pot" now defined what was American about how Americans ate.

In the postwar years the two found even more common ground. Sometimes remembered as the decades of Jell-O and Twinkies, the postwar years instead saw ethnicity "go corporate" and become American in a newly tolerant culture, where eating had finally and truly become big business.

CHAPTER SIX

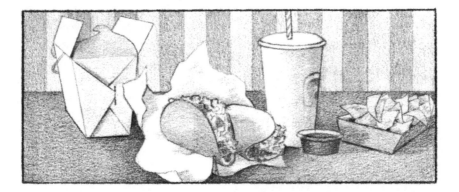

The Big Business of Eating

What better symbolized corporate food and American eating in the postwar period than the TV dinner? Standardized, quick-cooking, convenient, and marketed initially in a novel cardboard box that looked like a TV, the same TV dinner sold coast to coast. It was mass produced for mass markets, and it is one of several 1950s corporate novelties that continues to sell well, although in somewhat new evolutions, down to the present.

Swanson's, the inventor of TV dinners, was founded by a Swedish immigrant, Carl Swanson, who had arrived in the United States in 1896. He moved from an early job as a grocery clerk to success first as a wholesale grocer and then as the largest processor of turkeys in the United States. With the development of freezing technologies and the spread of community freezer lockers and then home freezers after World War II, Swanson's sons began manufacturing frozen potpies, hoping to extend sales of turkey beyond the holidays. In 1954 they marketed their first frozen TV dinner of turkey with dressing, green peas, and mashed potatoes.[1]

It is unlikely that anyone anywhere in the United States thought of Swanson's TV dinners as Swedish. Swanson's was not an enclave business, marketing to persons of Scandinavian descent. Nor was it interested in cross-over marketing of Swedish-inspired dishes to the multi-ethnic consumers of the Midwest. Swanson's sons made no effort to market their dinners as ethnic fare; they did not care about the ethnic ties of their customers. They took on the role of all-American businessmen, in an all-American corporation, completely devoid of ethnic labels or regional distinctiveness. Their TV dinners were quintessentially all-American food, acceptable to a wide variety of tastes: turkey or fried chicken with mashed potatoes and a tiny compartment for soft vegetables or applesauce on the side. They offered it in the mass-produced, standardized forms of the modern American food industry. And they offered it everywhere in the United States.

In the same period, Chef Boyardee spaghetti in cans became a popular item with baby boom children and with their suburban moms, who sought to add variety to kids' meals without spending long hours in the kitchen. Chef Boyardee products had originated with Hector Boiardi, a chef from Piacenza, Italy, whose brother worked in the hotel business and helped him get started in the United States. Hector Boiardi first had his own Italian restaurant in Cleveland. He decided to can and distribute his sauce, initially packaging it with dry spaghetti and a packet of grated cheese, through his own business Chef Boiardi Food Products Company. Boiardi changed the name of his company (and its product) to Boyardee in the 1930s, mainly to ease pronunciation by non-Italians, as he sought a regional, cross-over market of multi-ethnic consumers. By the late 1930s, Boiardi was successfully selling canned spaghetti to A&P stores and reaching a national market. Boiardi even became a supplier to the U.S. army during World War II, further building a taste for Chef Boyardee among returning GIs. Its consumers assumed they were buying Italian food when they purchased this spaghetti in a can. But the boomers and their mothers who ate canned Boyardee spaghetti in the 1950s no longer bought the product from immigrant businessman Boiardi. In 1946 he had sold his company to American Home Foods, a large conglomerate. Boiardi served as an occasional consultant and adviser to American Home Foods, but he was neither a shareholder nor a manager in the corporation. American consumers recognized spaghetti's Italian origins, but its production, packaging, and marketing now rested in non-Italian hands. Its profits, furthermore, went to an all-American mix of shareholders.[2]

In somewhat different ways, Swanson's TV dinners and Chef Boyardee spaghetti mark the final phase of the march of enclave businessmen and ethnic foods into the national marketplace and the cultural mainstream of

American life. While both represent a clear departure from the past, when immigrants and racial minorities worked only in the lowest levels of food corporations, both also reveal a paradoxical relationship between the corporate and the ethnic or regional in the national food marketplace. While Swanson's sons remained in active control of the family business in the 1950s, they and their product had completely lost any ethnic or regional labels and seemed quintessentially all-American. Chef Boyardee's canned spaghetti retained its Italian label and associations, but its Italian inventor no longer controlled its mass production within a modern corporation. In both cases, though in different ways, the local or ethnic seemed somewhat out of place in mass production for mass markets. When the sons of immigrant businessmen remained in control of production, their foods no longer bore ethnic labels; when ethnic labels remained attached to mass-produced food, their producers were no longer the ethnic businessmen who developed them.

The integration of enclave businessmen into the nation's large corporations and the mass production of enclave foods for the national market were the last phases in a rather lengthy process of market consolidation, mobility, and cultural change. Before World War II, ethnic businessmen who succeeded in national markets most often did so by selling either products with no ethnic labels attached or products marked by origins in an ethnic group other than their own. By contrast, it was typically businessmen with no obvious ethnic affiliations who popularized ethnic foods for consumers nationwide. Going corporate in order to become American thus required not so much the eradication of ethnicity as the uncoupling of enclave foods from enclave businessmen.

In the nineteenth century, immigrants and other outsiders, whether African-American or Mexican-American, were central actors in the history of modern food corporations. But the role they played was that of poorly paid wage-earners, either working for vast agribusinesses as field laborers, or in the canning or baking industry, or on the meat-processing floor. Most of them produced foods that had no ties to their own enclave foodways, and very few succeeded as founders of modern food corporations. The occasional immigrants who made their fortunes in mass production or mass retailing were often outstanding innovators, but they too rarely achieved their successes by specializing in foods unique to their own culinary traditions. On the contrary, success in the national market in the nineteenth century seemed to require the production and marketing of foods with no ethnic associations or labels.

In corporate life, as in American life generally, immigrants started near the bottom of the food chain. Agribusiness on both the West and East Coasts could not have developed without foreign laborers, and even today this economic sector depends on new immigrants from the Caribbean, Central America, Mexico, and the Philippines to raise, plant, and harvest crops from large factory farms. In nineteenth-century California, a succession of immigrant groups labored in the earliest of these agricultural corporations. The Japanese replaced the Chinese, sometimes in competition with Italian, Greek, Portuguese, (East) Indian, and Korean harvesters around the turn of the century. After 1920 Mexican and Filipino harvesters arrived in ever larger numbers. On Hawaiian sugar and pineapple plantations, too, Chinese and native workers eventually gave way to Japanese, Korean, and Portuguese laborers at the turn of the century. On the East Coast, migratory Italian labor in the early years of the century was replaced by African-American and then Caribbean labor in New Jersey and Florida beginning in the 1920s.

As one employer of immigrant labor explained, large farms located far from urban centers where most immigrant populations lived found it difficult to recruit enough laborers. Most turned to immigrant labor contractors, who provided large gangs of workers of a particular background. Owners maintained this segregation of harvesters by "race" when they set up camps. On one large California farm, an owner recalled building "an American camp for white people. We had a camp for Japanese. We had a camp for Mexicans. We had a camp for Filipinos." When asked why workers were segregated by ethnicity, he explained that it "had to do with the eating habits of the people . . . They each require different types of food and prefer them. And so we had to have cooks of the proper nationality in each of those camps."[3]

The jobs of migrant farmworkers included some of the worst in the American economy. Demand for agricultural labor was heavily seasonal, so migration remained a way of life for workers in agribusiness, even after they arrived in the United States. One migrant remembered, "After the grape pruning season . . . we would go to the asparagus camps in Stockton's Cannery Ranch . . . [Then] pear picking started in Walnut Grove . . . After pears came peach packing in Marysville . . . Apple packing came next in Watsonville . . . From Watsonville we moved on to Pismo . . . We worked for Maxuoka-san picking peas."[4] Today many of these seasonal migrants are undocumented immigrants, or they are recruited under immigration exemptions that allow employers to import seasonal labor as needed. Owners and workers alike expect their stay in the United States to be temporary. Nevertheless, conditions of work and life in the fields and in migrant camps continue to appall journalists and social welfare workers alike.

Only slightly more stable were jobs in food processing, like canneries and meat-packing plants, which numbered among the most highly capitalized of American industries in the nineteenth century. Food industries actually employed more workers than the steel industry as late as the 1920s, and their employees—like those in steel—were also disproportionately immigrants or the children of immigrants, working in unskilled and semiskilled positions as machine operators. As late as 1929, 875,000 laborers (or about 10 percent of all American workers in manufacturing) worked in 58,148 food processing establishments, which constituted about one-quarter of all manufacturing establishments.[5]

In Chicago, packinghouse workers in the huge meat-packing plants, with their mass-production disassembly lines, were overwhelmingly immigrants from Central and Eastern Europe—first Germans and Irish, later Slavs, and then Mexicans and eventually African-Americans in the years just after World War I. In Pittsburgh canneries, Irish and German women gave way to Polish, Slavic, Italian, and African-American laborers. In California, the women who processed the bountiful harvests of agribusiness included Jewish, Italian, Portuguese, Japanese, and Mexican workers. Pecan-shellers in Texas were also Mexican women—and on San Antonio's west side in the 1930s they worked so cheaply that owners actually replaced mechanical shellers with women.

Not all immigrants remained at the bottom, even in the nineteenth century, however. Immigrant entrepreneurs were especially important as investors and innovators in the production and marketing of novelty foods, and many of the snack foods that we think of as characteristically

American emerged from immigrant pushcarts in the late nineteenth and early twentieth centuries. For example, the German immigrant F. W. Rueckheim invented Cracker Jacks after opening a popcorn and candy stand in Chicago in 1871. In the 1890s he combined all the treats he sold (popcorn, molasses candy, and peanuts) into one, and his new product found favor at the city's Columbian Exposition. It became even more popular when Rueckheim began marketing Cracker Jacks as a ballpark treat.

In a somewhat similar evolution from pushcart to national marketplace, the Italian immigrant Amedeo Obici, having learned the nut trade from an uncle in Wilkes-Barre, in 1896 decided to install a peanut roaster in his California fruit stand. After adding salt and chocolate to some batches, he soon found he sold more peanuts than fruit. By 1906 he and a partner, Mario Peruzzi, had formed the Planters Nut & Chocolate Company, which exists to this day.[6] Like immigrant workers in agriculture, canning, and meat-packing, Rueckheim, Obici, and Peruzzi worked with foods that had no obvious ties to the eating habits of their homelands. Even as innovators and investors, these immigrants did not "bring ethnicity" with them into the corporation or the national marketplace. Their foods carried no ethnic labels at all.

Some other exceptional foreigners succeeded in mastering agribusiness and industrial food processing and could claim to have helped build a national market for mass-produced foods in the nineteenth and early twentieth centuries. In California, native-born Americans dominated the extensive planting of oranges and wheat, but Irish and German immigrants also occasionally did well as agribusinessmen. The Swiss rancher John Sutter transformed his cooperative New Helvetia ranch into a "principality" where he grew hundreds of acres of wheat just to feed his Indian and Kanakan (mainly Hawaiian) laborers. Somewhat later, the German Henry Miller and the Alsatian Charles Lux became the largest landowners in the state; they were butchers who had expanded into extensive ranching.[7]

Probably the most successful immigrant agribusinessman before World War II was Joseph Di Giorgio, who revolutionized the distribution of fresh produce throughout the nation. Joseph Di Giorgio's father, Salvatore, had been a landowner in Cefalú, where he raised lemons commercially for export to the United States. Dissatisfied with both his lemon broker (in

Baltimore) and his son (who did not want to study for the priesthood), he sent the 14-year-old Joseph to New York with a cargo of lemons in 1888 or 1889. (Di Giorgio himself later claimed he ran away.) When Di Giorgio arrived in the United States, few urban Americans ate much native-grown citrus or other fruit. Until about 1870, urban Americans were as likely to see lemons and oranges from Sicily and dried fruits from the Mediterranean—as well as pineapples, coconuts, and bananas from the West Indies, Cuba, and Central America—as native varieties. With the help of co-ethnic *paesani* in Baltimore, the young Di Giorgio rented a store to sell his lemons. Since he could market these only in the summertime, he sought a winter occupation, and became interested in importing bananas from the West Indies.

Duplicating a marketing practice common in Europe, Di Giorgio set up auctions for his imported fruits in New York, Baltimore, Pittsburgh, Chicago, Cleveland, Cincinnati, and St. Louis. Eventually, fruits came also from California and Florida to these eastern cities; they traveled, furthermore, on the same refrigerated cars that delivered meat from these cities to the agricultural hinterlands. According to Di Giorgio's nephews, auction houses near railroad terminals in large cities received shipments of fruit, catalogs, and bills of lading during the night, and set up samples in different rooms in the early morning. Sales followed between 8 A.M. and 12 P.M., with deliveries to local businesses beginning at noon. Within 24 hours after fruit arrived in New York, it was in the hands of thousands of retailers, from municipal markets to street vendors. The auction collected a commission on all sales. Some auctions like these survive today, but many more went out of business as chain stores and supermarkets began to purchase fruit independently in the 1930s.

As the oral historian Ruth Teiser noted of Di Giorgio, "His success was due to the fact that he knew first what the market was, and then worked back to supply what the market wanted."[8] In 1910 Di Giorgio began to expand vertically, acquiring lands and canneries in California; by 1920 he had purchased the Sierra Vista Ranch, a large farm that was still desert, along with orchards in the Pacific Northwest, totaling about 24,000 acres. Later he purchased citrus groves in Florida. Linking auctions, shipping, and growing, he formed the Di Giorgio Fruit Company in 1920. Like his American counterparts, Di Giorgio depended heavily on immigrant labor to grow, transport, and can his produce. But most were not Italians. In fact, in the 1960s his company would become embroiled with Mexican laborers organized by Cesar Chavez.

According to Teiser, Di Giorgio "marched along with or a bit ahead of, much of our agricultural history."[9] His expertise and familiarity with fruit came from his Sicilian past, and his system of auctioning fruits seemed to be borrowed from European precedents. But the products he sold carried no ethnic labels, and he sold them to Americans across the nation, regardless of their cultural food preferences.

In the history of American canning, Henry J. Heinz (born in 1844 outside of Pittsburgh to German parents) presents a comparable case of early success in the modern food industry and the national marketplace. Heinz got his start as a bottler of horseradish, celery sauce, and pickles—foods broadly popular with both English- and German-origin peoples in Pittsburgh. After some initial business reverses, he opened a Pittsburgh plant in 1876 to can tomato ketchup, and he quickly added red and green pepper sauce, which was popular in the oyster bars of the period. By the 1880s Heinz was exporting to England and had expanded his products to include vinegars, apple butters, fruit jellies, and mince meat. An early master of modern advertising gimmicks, Heinz attracted flocks of visitors to his Columbian Exposition booth by giving away miniature pickle pins; in 1896, he began to advertise his famous "57 varieties" (a meaningless number he had pulled from his hat) of canned sauces, pickles, and preserves and to develop a Heinz pleasure pier at Atlantic City to keep his brand and its "57 varieties" in the public eye.[10]

Just as Joseph Di Giorgio did not produce or market foods deemed Italian, Henry Heinz did not produce or market German ones. These were not businessmen using their ethnic origins or enclave ties to sell products labeled as ethnically distinct. Nor did their customers share their ethnic backgrounds. Still, Heinz, in particular, was quite aware of his cultural roots, and proud of them. He took German lessons to perfect his knowledge of the language before his first return trip to Europe; he then traveled yearly to Germany to enjoy its many health spas. The Heinz family maintained ties to Germany into the twentieth century; Heinz's sister even married a paternal cousin from their father's hometown.[11]

The businesses of Heinz and Di Giorgio resembled smaller-scale ethnic enterprises—and differed from most modern food industries—in remaining family firms and employing many family members for two generations, sixty or eighty years or more. Their business operations grew to national and even international stature under direct family ownership, well before they incorporated. H. J.'s cousin Frederick Heinz, trained as a florist and gardener in Germany, long had charge of Heinz gardening operations; his brother oversaw manufacturing and canning for the firm. The Heinz family business became a corporation only in 1905, and the existing family partners remained the main stockholders in the new company: these included H. J., his cousin Frederick, his son Howard, his brother-in-law Sebastian Mueller, and two old associates, W. H. Robinson and R. G. Evans.[12] In 1919, upon H. J.'s death, son Howard, who had trained in chemistry at Yale, where he learned the new techniques of modern food production, managed the new food laboratory he established at the old plant.[13] Only the passing of the second generation marked the waning of active family control of the corporation.

Joseph Di Giorgio also involved many members of his family in his expanding business even after he went public and incorporated in 1920. Di Giorgio had no children of his own, but his brothers and nephews operated auction houses, managed orchards and farms, or handled banana imports. As founding "father" of a family enterprise in which he personally maintained 51 percent ownership, Di Giorgio liked to believe that "he built the business and his brothers and sisters built the family." "We always spoke with one voice about the company and the family," one nephew insisted; until Di Giorgio's death in 1951, "no important decision was made that it wasn't first submitted to him either in writing or on the phone or in person." Even before Joseph's death, his eldest nephew, J. S. Di Giorgio, became the main decision maker for the company, and he oversaw diversification of the company into processing, wine making, and canning. Like other growers in the 1950s and 1960s, faced with challenges from organizing farm workers, the Di Giorgios concluded that "farming of this type of specialty crop [grapes] is not suitable for a corporation, to a corporate setup—it is better suited for families and partnerships with individuals."[14]

Only in the 1960s, and again with the passing of the second generation, did the Di Giorgio family recruit outsiders from corporate America to prepare a managerial succession. "At some point," his nephews sadly concluded, when telling an interviewer that an outsider, Peter Scott, was now chief executive of the corporation, "every family has to change and go."[15]

The companies founded by Di Giorgio and Heinz represent a pattern that can be seen in many twentieth-century American corporations. Though both men seem to have identified with their immigrant family roots, they found success in national markets by mass producing and marketing products with no identifiable ethnic markers. Unlike cross-over businessmen, neither man hired his laborers through ethnic networks. In the second generation, family members remained employed in managerial positions, but within businesses organized as corporations. By the third generation, family members might own stock, but outsiders managed and represented the business to the corporate world. Whatever ethnicity or ethnic associations Heinz and Di Giorgio had brought with them as individuals into their corporations disappeared with their children.

Di Giorgio and Heinz themselves created large and modern—if initially family-controlled—corporations that helped create a national market for their products. But most entrepreneurs who got their start in regional cross-over markets followed a different path to the corporate world and the national market. This path, too, uncoupled ethnicity both from the businessman and the product. Successful entrance into the national marketplace most often occurred through sale of a family firm to a corporate food conglomerate, managed and run by native-born Americans with no cultural ties to the products they produced and marketed.

Indeed, this is how modern food conglomerates began to form in the late nineteenth and early twentieth centuries. Typical of the nineteenth century is the history of Charles Louis Fleischmann, a Jewish immigrant whose family had specialized in distilling and in yeast production in Hungary. In the United States, Fleischmann became a major provider of compressed yeast for the many German, Jewish, and Central European bakers who popularized Vienna and other European-style breads in the aftermath of the Philadelphia Centennial Exposition of 1876. Fleischmann's fourteen yeast factories supplied an extensive distribution network for its own perishable products, along with other brands it had acquired—including Royal Baking Powder and Chase and Sanborn's coffee. By the 1920s the family-owned company had 900 distribution centers with 1,700 delivery routes to bakeries and hotels and to 20,000 retail units in over 33,000 towns. In 1929, Standard Brands, part of J. P. Morgan's expanding corporate empire, purchased controlling interest in the family-owned company.[16]

The same pattern is seen in the early mass-production of spaghetti. The first commercial canner of soups and Italian foods, twenty years before Hector Boiardi, was a company called Franco-American. Founded by French émigré Alphonse Biardot in 1887, along with his sons Ernest and Octave, the business began as a commercial kitchen in Jersey City, near the tomato fields of the Garden State. Having worked as a major domo in the Greek royal household, Biardot set as his goal to "market foods that would introduce Americans to French traditions of masterful cooking." His Franco-American company canned higher priced specialty goods aimed at a cultivated palate—if not robber barons, then those who at least knew of the sophisticated associations of French foods. Among Franco-American's most successful products, however, was a food widely perceived as "Italian": spaghetti á la milanaise—a tomato, cheese, and macaroni combination that became popular nationwide only after Arthur Dorrance purchased controlling interest in Franco-American. Arthur was the younger brother of the founder of Campbell's canning and processing company, nearby. In 1915 Arthur sold his Franco-American stock to brother John, and in 1921 Franco-American was merged with the Campbell Soup Company, its competitor, giving an Italian food, first canned by a French immigrant, access to Campbell's national distribution system.[17]

National marketing of Tex-Mex food followed a similarly multi-ethnic path to corporate success and a national market. William Gebhardt, a German from Essen who arrived in Texas around 1885, began serving chili to Germans at a cafe in back of a popular saloon in the German town of New Braunfels in 1892. Chili, at the time, was still a seasonal specialty in San Antonio, made with fresh produce. Gebhardt began importing ancho chiles from Mexico, and—using a meat grinder—pulverizing the chiles so they could be dried successfully and used year round. For several years, Gebhardt marketed his Tampico Dust—which a 1925 critic claimed had been "tamed for the timid tongue"—around San Antonio in his own wagon. A tinker and mechanic, Gebhardt subsequently developed 27 machines for the manufacture of Tampico Dust, and after opening a factory in San Antonio he began, in 1908, to can a chili concoction for wider distribution and sale. (Gebhardt was not the first: in the 1870s a Texas Anglo had marketed a canned chili with goat meat as "Montezuma Sauce.")[18]

In 1911 Gebhardt sold his company and his Eagle Brand chili to his brothers-in-law, who expanded their product line to include beans, tamales, and other local specialties. In the 1920s they introduced to the tourist trade Gebhardt's Original Mexican Dinner Package. Priced at $1.00 and packed in a colorful box, the souvenir contained a can of chili con carne, a can of Mexican-style beans, a can of shuck-wrapped tamales, 2 cans of deviled chili meat, and a bottle of Eagle chili powder. This marketing strategy, along with a widely distributed cookbook, helped spread the taste for chili into the upper Midwest. In 1962, after being purchased by Beatrice Foods, Gebhardt's Eagle Brand products became available nationwide.[19]

So strongly were Eagle Brand foods associated with Mexican-Americans that a journalist in 1976 described shock and surprise when he visited Gebhardt's. "I arrive hungry, ready to be filled with enchiladas and filled with nostalgia: stories of little Mama Esperanza Ramirez Lopez Gonzalez who ground corn for the first 10 million tamales by hand. The three loyal sons who took over the business from ailing (perhaps arthritic) Mama, and who still taste a bit of every refried bean to make certain it meets Mama's standards." Instead, the journalist met Gebhardt manager Lyle Van Doozer, who admitted, "I really don't know too much about Mexican food. Before Beatrice transferred me, I worked for La Choy."[20]

The uncoupling of ethnic producers from ethnic products often began very early in the history of their mass production. We do not know the name of the Mexican-American who taught Gebhardt, the German, to cook or enjoy chili; the innovators and inventors of ethnic foods more often than not are lost to history. It was, for example, a nameless African-American chef on the Southern Pacific Railroad who in 1930 first gave a General Mills salesman the idea for blending lard, flour, baking powder, and salt as a quick mix for southern biscuits. The salesman had sought an off-hour meal on a train and was surprised to receive his order of fresh biscuits so quickly. When he asked how this was possible, the chef showed him the biscuit mixture he kept in the train's ice box. Once the General Mills chemists had worked over the recipe, substituting sesame oil for lard, the product became known as Bisquick.[21]

Even in companies firmly in family hands, under the supervision of the children and grandchildren of immigrant founders, ethnicity came uncoupled from product as it found success nationwide. The German butcher Oscar Mayer and his brothers had made a successful business selling sausages to Chicago groceries, beginning in 1883. By 1904 eight company salesmen sold to northern Illinois and Wisconsin groceries. But it was Mayer's Harvard-educated son, Oscar G. Mayer, who began moving the company toward mass production by purchasing a meat-packing plant in Madison in 1909, and then by pioneering in prepackaging technology to facilitate marketing through chain stores and supermarkets. Initially, Oscar Mayer promoted its products with oompah bands, appealing to German-origin consumers. By the 1930s, however, the company dropped its German-tinged advertising strategies and introduced their slogan, "I wish I were an Oscar Mayer Wiener." Their advertising jingle appealed to children familiar enough with hot dogs that they would eat them even when called wieners.[22] A German wiener had become just another "American" hot dog.

As these examples suggest, ethnic foods had already found a limited place in national food markets by 1940. The creators most often succeeded in mass production and mass marketing when they either left their ethnic affiliations at home, handled products with no ethnic labels, or sold out to corporations with no enclave ties. These patterns did not change significantly as culinary cultural pluralism broadened markets for ethnic foods and as toleration of ethnic diversity increased after World War II. This new openness was inspired in part by the multi-ethnic experiences of many GIs, who had been in combat units with fellow Americans of diverse ethnic backgrounds and had been stationed in posts outside the United States for the first time in their lives. It also owed much to GI's actual eating experiences during the war, when many of them had no choice but to eat outside their own enclaves. While stationed in the Pacific, for example, young men from the mountains of Georgia and the Carolinas found themselves eating rice and other foods to which they were unaccustomed. The "discovery" of cultural diversity during World War II, and the big business of foods associated with that diversity did, however, encourage corporate leaders to rethink their philosophies of both mass production and mass marketing and to rediscover the power of ethnicity to influence consumer decisions.

New initiatives in food service and retailing fueled the postwar growth of food corporations. Profits now came more from new processing techniques (especially freezing) than from the production of raw food products themselves. By the 1970s and 1980s, production of many more foods had left small enclave firms linked together by market ties and had become an integral part of corporate systems characterized by exclusive contracts, vertical ownership, and joint ventures. Large food corporations grew even larger as they created a unified flow from production and processing through final marketing. Direct sales to supermarkets increasingly replaced wholesalers; retailers now more often bought or contracted with their own producers.[23]

After World War II, American corporations also began to worry that the mass production and mass marketing of highly standardized products—symbolized by Coca-Cola and by Henry Ford's Model T—had reached their limits in generating profits. Theorists argued that higher profits in the future would come from forms of corporate decentralization (such as franchising) or through marketing a wide variety of branded products to specific demographic groups with rather precise consumer tastes. This change in corporate thinking about the marketplace paralleled the nation's wartime tolerance of ethnic diversity as the distinguishing characteristic of American culture.

However belatedly, corporations suddenly recognized the persistence of enclave markets and attempted to sell to them as effectively as enclave entrepreneurs had in the past. In the 1960s, growing corporate concern with consumers' diverse tastes meant that conglomerates became even more eager than in the past to purchase successful enclave businesses. It meant that corporate leaders began to read new journals like *American Demographics* for a glimpse of the diversity of American consumers, notably "Negroes" and "Hispanics." By the 1980s, corporations even generated "boutique" labels to appeal to very specific groups of consumers. In 1987 one analyst told corporate leaders there were no consumer niches defined by ethnicity among very high and high socioeconomic groups, but the suburban middle classes included an "ethnic industrial" subgroup, while the urban middle classes included both black middle-class and "high-rise" (unmarried, young, or "Buppy") blacks. The analyst pointed to large but lower-income ethnic markets, too: he differentiated "young Hispanics" from "Metro Hispanic Mix," and "Urban melting pot" and "black urban fringe" from the "teeming tenements."[24]

Corporate interest in ethnic groups as niche markets had actually developed slowly before World War II. Perhaps because Jewish communities had long contained significant numbers of middle-class consumers, large department stores in the early twentieth century began to construct special Passover departments, packaging dried fruits into one-pound boxes (certified kosher by a San Francisco rabbi) and offering fruit preserves, matzos, nuts, meal, noodles, soup nuts, cakes, coffee and tea, cooking oils, fats, dessert pudding powders, and gift baskets.[25] As early as 1916, a Chicago study called *Winning a Great Market on Facts* gave potential advertisers advice on how to reach foreign-born consumers. In New York, Joseph Jacobs's advertising firm specialized in connecting corporations to Jewish consumers; Jacobs convinced Joel Cheek of Maxwell House Coffee to advertise in the Yiddish press, telling him that "the big chains and the big food companies did not know how to promote to a Yiddish-speaking population since they employed no Jews."[26] Jacobs also convinced Procter & Gamble to advertise Crisco to Jews as the perfect solution to their long-standing search for a kosher alternative to lard. The company's slogan— "Jews have been waiting 4,000 years for Crisco"—proved wildly successful.[27] Another advertising man, Joshua C. Epstein, convinced Heinz to make kosher vegetarian baked beans; together with Rabbi Herbert Goldstein and Heinz, Epstein then popularized the Orthodox Union's U symbol for kosher certification.[28]

While corporations attempted to reach into ethnic niche markets, ambitious enclave businessmen attempted to expand sufficiently to compete with them. Even in the 1990s, small firms with ties to the Jewish community often could compete successfully with large conglomerates. The company founded in 1921 by Yugoslav immigrants Bella and Elias Gabay (Gabila and Son's Knishes) remains a family operation: Bella first cooked up knishes (crispy square potato pies) for Coney Island pushcarts. Elias then patented a method for producing square knishes en masse, marketing them through delis and stadium concession stands. In the 1990s the firm produced frozen knishes, in four packs, for national distribution. "While the home of the knish will always be New York," a family spokesman explained, "we're looking forward to entering new markets" like Kalamazoo, Michigan.[29] To succeed, however, the company had to accept rabbinical supervision and certification for the first time: word of mouth could no longer assure their customers of the purity of their products.

Expansion into national markets could also generate considerable controversy within cultural enclaves, imposing pressures on small businesses that large corporations could not feel. Hebrew National hot dogs seemed to resemble Oscar Mayer wieners in many ways: its hot dogs had become firmly part of the American snacking mainstream—no longer marketed exclusively to Jewish or kosher consumers. But when Hebrew National planned to move its production from Queens to Indianapolis and to manufacture their beef hot dogs in a plant formerly used to process pork, its Maspeth, Long Island, unionized workers as well as the three rabbis it employed to ensure kosher criteria went on strike. One of the striking rabbis insisted, "Making kosher food in Indianapolis—such a thing is impossible to think." The company—and its many consumers—respectfully disagreed.[30]

The kosher niche itself was significantly transformed by commerce at a national level. Kosher foods now include a U on their labels—rather than a Hebrew letter—to certify that they have been prepared under rabbinical supervision. The reason for the change? Neither Heinz nor his Jewish counterparts wanted to discourage Gentile purchasers of kosher foods by appearing "too Jewish." As author Joan Nathan discovered when writing about kosher food production, "Of the 6,500,000 people who purposely buy kosher foods, only 1,500,000 are kashrut-observing Jews. The great majority are Black Muslims, vegetarians, and Seventh-Day Adventists."[31] Such consumers were little concerned whether kosher products emerge from corporations with ties to the Jewish community, from New York, or from non-Jewish corporations with plants in Indiana. They care only about the U.

Compared with small-scale enclave producers, however, corporations that uncoupled ethnic foods from their communities of origin often found themselves without much insight into the desires of ethnic consumers in the postwar period. The case of Frito-Lay, long-time manufacturer of potato and corn chips, is illuminating. Fritos originated in San Antonio, where they were a popular Mexican-American variation on tostadas (fried tortillas) but made from fried masa meal. In 1932 the Anglo Elmer Doolin (a floundering salesman of ice cream) paid 5 cents for a bag of them in a Mexican-owned San Antonio cafe. Locating the Mexican maker of the chips, Doolin claimed to buy the recipe with one hundred dollars borrowed from his mother (who had pawned her wedding ring). Doolin called his chips fritos; local Mexican-Americans had called them friotes or tamalinas. Doolin quickly acquired nineteen store accounts for his products, and he sold the rest out of the back of his Model T, expanding sales as far east as St. Louis.

In 1945 Doolin met Herman W. Lay, the potato chip manufacturer, who agreed to distribute Fritos for him. (Typically, Frito-Lay claimed not to know the name of the Mexican from whom Doolin bought the fritos recipe; some believe he was a man who returned to Mexico to manage a national soccer team.[32] Others claim the Mexican-American owners of a San Antonio masa grinding mill invented them.) From 1953 until 1967 Frito-Lay assumed that children were their target consumers, and Frito-Lay advertised the corn chips with the cowboy-clad but ethnicity-less Frito Kid. In 1963, with growing awareness of niche markets and how ethnicity might shape consumer tastes, the Frito-Lay Company switched to the Frito Bandito. This corporate strategy, a display of appalling ignorance about the targeted community that had invented the snack, backfired: the Mexican-American Anti-Defamation Committee accused Frito-Lay of insensitivity, stereotyping, and racism. The Frito Bandito soon disappeared. But Frito-Lay, undaunted, in 1965 introduced Doritos, a chip they believed looked and tasted more like "authentic" tostadas, and they have become tremendously popular nationwide.[33]

Since enclave entrepreneurs still best knew ethnic tastes, some did succeed in building major postwar corporations to cater to ethnic groups scattered across the country, much as kosher industries had done somewhat earlier. An enclave economy, in other words, could still function nationwide. Typical was La Preferida; the president in 1995 was David

Steinbarth, a fourth-generation member of the founding Chicago family of Mexicans.[34] La Preferida had begun humbly, packaging foods for Mexican-Americans in glass jars; they had stocked canned refried beans, pinto beans, and the like. By the 1970s La Preferida was producing and marketing frozen foods to supermarkets. In the 1980s they introduced fat-free products to enhance their appeal to a mass market that included increasing numbers of non-Mexicans.

Even more successful was Goya Foods, the Secaucus, New Jersey, firm founded in 1933 (some sources say 1936) by the Unanue family. Selling initially to New York's Spanish, Puerto Rican, and Cuban residents, Goya expanded into an import and processing (canning, freezing) company with 600 employees and an annual business of $465 million. Family members still serve in key positions (including general manager) at Goya, and the corporation still distributes through small stores, employing a largely Spanish-speaking sales force. It dominates most of the market for the products it produces. But Goya also successfully negotiates contracts with supermarket chains, hoping to reach Hispanics who live or shop outside of their ethnic community. Thus, for example, it licensed its label to Frozen Desserts Resources, which then marketed a child's ice cream treat (with a sombrero) and the English advertising slogan "Oh Boy-A Goya."

Like Frito-Lay, however, Goya faced some real challenges in building ties to Hispanic consumers of increasing diversity, including those of Mexican and South American origin. Goya introduced frozen guacamole and new fruit juices to appeal to them.[35] At the same time, Goya hoped to attract non-Spanish-speaking customers interested in good prices for such basic items as olives, olive oil, beans, and rice. Not surprisingly, Goya's success makes it the focus of considerable corporate attention. The Campbell Soup Company developed its own food line (Casera) to compete with Goya in New York and Miami, while other corporations sought to purchase the company to pursue their own niche marketing strategies.[36]

Reflecting postwar trends in the marketing of all American foods, the mass production of ethnic foods by large corporations increasingly involved freezing. The most widely sold ethnic foods of the 1960s and 1970s have been ones that froze well and were thus convenient—egg rolls, burritos, quiche, bagels, and lasagna. In the world of fast food, freezing mattered to the franchise owner, who had to keep large quantities of food on hand.

The customer, on the other hand, cared more that frozen foods retain the visual appearance of their fresh counterparts. The most successful ethnic fast foods—such as tacos—were sandwich-like or burger-like and thus easily accommodated into broad, national habits of snacking and fast lunch-time eating.[37]

The development of freezing also gave small numbers of immigrant and ethnic entrepreneurs a chance to reach national markets, albeit with predictable consequences. The American Jew Charles Lubin had operated a chain of retail bakeries since 1926. In 1949 he formed a new company, named after his daughter, Sara Lee, to distribute premium baked goods through supermarkets, at first largely in Chicago. Then, through a personal connection to a Houston businessman, who wanted them shipped over long distances, Lubin began to apply freezing techniques (already used with vegetables and juices) to baked goods. His success opened possibilities for shipping Sara Lee products, including its popular cheesecake, all over the country. Supermarkets, in turn, had a new way of offering baked goods to consumers. Thoroughly corporate and geared toward mass production— one of its plants, in Rock Island, Illinois, is devoted entirely to cracking eggs—cheesecake lost its ethnic label in the process of going national. Like the bagel, this cakelike specialty, once known mainly to German and Jewish Americans, in the 1960s became popular throughout the country as "New York cheesecake" (even though it was manufactured in the Midwest).[38] Marian Burros, food columnist for *The New York Times*, confirmed that "I don't think anyone thinks cheesecake or bagels are Jewish foods anymore."[39]

In the postwar period, enclave businessmen continued to hesitate at the doors of corporate boardrooms, even those boardrooms that had every reason to want enclave entrepreneurs who could help them capture ethnic niches. When enclave businessmen made fortunes, it was still by selling foods associated with culinary traditions other than their own. Jeno Paulucci, for example, founded Chun-King, which raised the question—as one good-humored journalist put it—"Can an Italian American find success making Chinese food in a Scandinavian section of Duluth, Minnesota?" The founder of Chun-King was a fruit barker at age fourteen, known for his piercing hawker's voice. Later he became a salesman in a wholesale grocery firm and attempted without success to sell dehydrated garlic. In 1947 Paulucci borrowed $2,500 and began growing and canning bean sprouts; he eventually expanded to chop suey and chow mein. In 1967 he sold out to R. J. Reynolds for $63 million. (In an interesting twist, R. J. Reynolds sold the floundering Chun-King in 1989 to Yeo Hiap Seng, the largest food and beverage manufacturer in Singapore.)[40] Paulucci went on to develop Jeno's frozen pizza, which he then sold to Pillsbury in 1985 for $150 million. Experiments with ethnic restaurants, real estate, frozen dinners, and a Chinese-food home delivery business called China Kwik followed—and failed.[41]

Nothing better symbolizes the resistance of ethnic entrepreneurs to corporate employment and the persistence of uncoupling the businessman from his ethnicity than the contrasting stories of Tom Carvel and Reuben Mattus, two ice-cream innovators. Tom Carvel was born Thomas Andreas Carvelas in Athanassos, Greece; he came to the United States as a child in 1906. After living on a chicken farm in Connecticut with his family, he followed a pattern typical among Greek Americans. In 1934 he loaded an old ice cream truck with ice cream to begin peddling; his garage tinkering in the 1920s had resulted in a machine that could manufacture a soft, frozen custard, which soon found a good market. Carvel then built a small factory in Yonkers to manufacture and sell his frozen custard machines, but few understood how to use them, so in 1955 Carvel began training and licensing franchisees. Customers did not see Carvel's frozen custard as Greek; and in the business community Tom Carvel was viewed as a businessman eccentric, not as an immigrant—even though he worked in a field, ice cream, which had been a Greek niche for generations. Carvel had refused to use an advertising agency, and served as radio spokesman for his own product, earning Carvel considerable professional ridicule—to which he characteristically appended, "but who cares?"[42]

Reuben Mattus, the American-born son of a Jewish immigrant, was the inventor of Häagen-Dazs Ice Cream. Born in 1912, Mattus had been selling family-made ice-cream in the Bronx for thirty years. Like Carvel, he had started with a horse and wagon, peddling his ice cream to multi-ethnic New Yorkers. According to analysts of Mattus's later success with Häagen

Dazs, other entrepreneurs had realized that upper-income Americans in the prosperous 1960s were increasingly willing to pay more for a product they perceived as superior. According to a *New York Times* reporter, Mattus "was the first to understand that they would do so if they thought it was foreign. So he made up a ridiculous, impossible to pronounce name, printed a map of Scandinavia on the carton and the rest is history." (Although Danes had a long tradition in the United States of working in dairy, Mattus supposedly chose a Danish-sounding name because Danes had rescued so many of their Jewish population during World War II.) In 1993 Mattus sold out to Pillsbury, but (like Paulucci and others before him) he ventured off into a new business—Mattus' Lowfat Ice Cream.[43] Unfortunately, he died shortly thereafter.

By the late 1960s, large corporations were scrambling to buy up successful ethnic food enterprises like Stella d'Oro, Lender's, and Boston's Star Markets. They acquired regional brands and marketed their products nationally for quick profits. Kraft alone purchased Lender's, Celestial Seasonings, Tombstone Pizza, and Frusen Gladje, all in 1984–1987.[44] Progresso sold to Ogden Food Products, which was acquired later by Pet and then in 1995 by Pillsbury. When Pillsbury acquired Progresso, it assessed its ethnic appeal and decided to play up its Italian-American heritage—"The brand has an underlying Italian personality but it's not strictly Italian food"— presumably because Americans of a wide variety of ethnic backgrounds now eat Progresso spaghetti sauces and soups.[45]

While some foods occasionally, or at least temporarily, retained ethnic labels even in the corporate mainstream of mass production and marketing, the businessmen who had originally developed these ethnic products or labels remained the exception in corporate bureaucracies. The Lenders did not follow their bagels into corporate positions with Kraft, nor did Jeno Paulucci or Reuben Mattus apparently relish life as a Pillsbury executive. Quite exceptional is Rose Totino of Pillsbury. In Minneapolis, Rose and Jim Totino had opened their first pizza house in 1952 when no one in the upper Midwest knew what pizza was. Totino's Italian Kitchen restaurant used a thin-crust pizza recipe from Rose's mother and was a mom-and-pop operation. Rose Totino remembered her simple ways of handling money: "We'd just put it in a paper bag and write the date on it. The next morning we'd pay the milkman, the bread man, the meat man and all the bills. We'd always have some money left. I'd say, 'Look, Jim, I guess we're profitable.'"

In 1962 the Totinos used $50,000 in savings to start a frozen Italian entree business, making frozen pizza; they ended their first year $150,000 in debt. Borrowing money from the Small Business Administration, they then began producing a prebaked pizza crust, and found success. In 1970 Jim Totino became ill; Rose decided to sell to Minneapolis-based Pillsbury for $20 million. She became Pillsbury's first female vice president—in charge of advertising and public relations for her namesake brand. But the Totinos also retained their family restaurant: Totino's Italian Kitchen now sells nonfrozen versions of their crisp-crust pizza.[46]

Perhaps no sector better represents the popularity of ethnic foods in contemporary American eating than the fast foods industry. By the 1980s a typical American ate fast food nine times a month, and left most of his money in the hands of a few corporate purveyors of a few standard fast food items. Who could doubt that ethnic and regional foods had become fully American when the bright corporate logos, colors, and advertisements of Kentucky Fried Chicken, Taco Bell, Pizza Hut, and McDonald's grabbed consumer attention everywhere? Yet few of these corporate hits began as businesses with close ties to the eating communities from whence ham-burgers, fried chicken, or pizza came.

Pizza Hut, for example, started in Wichita, Kansas, where in 1960 two Italian-owned pizzerias served a town with a population of 250,000. The chain subsequently expanded through the Midwest, with its multi-ethnic, but non-Italian, eaters. Taco Bell originated in California in 1962 but long remained a regional chain with no clear identity; in 1983 John Martin, a man born in Atlanta and raised in Detroit who had already worked for a Wienerschnitzel drive-through in San Jose, for PepsiCo's La Boulangeree, and for Hardee's, Burger Chef, and Burger King, made Taco Bell's Mexi-can-origin dishes popular nationally through value meals and heavy dis-counting.

Alone among the most popular of mass-market fast foods, Kentucky Fried Chicken did achieve nationwide success in the hands of a southerner with long roots in the regional home of this specialty. Still, it was a white mechanical tinkerer, "Colonel" Sanders—who was fascinated with building a pressure cooker that could fry chicken quickly while still producing a crispy crust—who popularized the dish as fast food. Despite attaching the local status symbol of "colonel" to his name, Sanders's origins were humble rather than patrician. And few Kentucky "colonels" had probably ever fried chicken or made biscuits for themselves. Once again, the fried chicken and biscuit specialists of the South—black and white women alike—were not the people who introduced the American mainstream to their regional dishes.

By the late 1970s, the mega-conglomerate PepsiCo owned three of these four big purveyors of fast foods. PepsiCo, and its corporate equivalents, at first made no effort to attract consumers of particular ethnic tastes. Market analysts agreed: "You're not going to find Hispanics at Taco Bell; you'll find Hispanics and other second-generation ethnics eating cheeseburgers at McDonald's."[47]

Surprisingly, Ray Kroc, the salesman whiz who transformed McDonald's from a family-run, high-turnover local restaurant in San Bernardino, California, in the 1950s into a corporate giant was in fact very aware of his ethnic roots. In his autobiography, Kroc insists that "I have always believed that each man makes his own happiness and is responsible for his own problems"—a "simple philosophy" he attributed to the "peasant bones of my Bohemian [Czech] ancestors." Kroc got his start as a Chicago salesman for Lily paper products; there, skeptical immigrant restaurant owners responded to Kroc's early sales pitches for paper cups with "Naw, I hev glasses, dey costs me chipper."[48] Before moving into the sale of multimixers to ice cream and hamburger chains—which led him to San Bernardino and the McDonald brothers' hamburger stand—Kroc sold paper cups to Italian vendors of spumoni and to Polish chefs, who filled them with prune butter. But did his background or years of business experience in an ethnic marketplace make Kroc an ethnic businessman or McDonald's hamburgers a Bohemian food? Obviously not.

Corporate America continued, also, to generate a business culture that many businessmen with urges to tinker or innovate, or with close ties to family businesses or enclave communities, found distasteful. Kroc's comments on the fast food industry contain suggestive hints about the continued differences between business cultures of corporate America and local enclaves. Proud of his own success, Kroc also insisted to an interviewer, "It is ridiculous to call this an industry. This is not. This is rat eat rat, dog eat dog. I'll kill 'em before they kill me. You're talking about the American way of survival of the fittest."[49]

That was not the way of business in America's many ethnic and regional enclaves. Cuban immigrant and Pizza Hut franchisee Arturo Torres agreed with Kroc, albeit from a differing position within corporate America. Torres believed he had a firm agreement with Frank Carney (then president of Pizza Hut) that granted him somewhat unique powers within the southwestern chain of Pizza Hut franchises. Torres claimed to have made the agreement personally with Carney just prior to the sale of Pizza Hut to PepsiCo. He was astonished that PepsiCo, apparently concerned with maintaining consistency across its enormous network of franchises, showed no interest in implementing the arrangement. Torres, who obviously felt disappointed that his personal dealings with Carney had failed to protect his privileges under the new management, concluded that PepsiCo merely said "screw this." Standard procedures and bureaucratic consistency, not personal agreements, defined life in a mega-corporation, as Torres discovered.[50]

Jeno Paulucci saw things somewhat differently from Torres, but reached the same conclusions about corporate employment. Paulucci was uninterested in managing corporations, he insisted. He saw himself as an individual and as an entrepreneur hooked on the thrill of building businesses from scratch, risking failure (which he also experienced personally) each time. He wanted to achieve success individually, not as a "cookie-cutter" manager in a standardized chain of corporate authority.[51] Mass production by a corporate conglomerate might succeed in making pizza as American as apple pie in cellophane; but businessmen like Paulucci seemed determined that the same thing would not happen to them.

The changing linkages of enclave, regional, and national markets created a curious, and in some ways paradoxical, cultural relationship between the ethnic and the corporate in food exchanges. The historian Daniel Boorstin has lionized mass production by modern food corporations, and has seen in canning, meat-packing, and evaporated milk a praiseworthy "democratization of American food." Without doubt, food was relatively cheaper and more bountiful in the United States than in most other countries of the world in the nineteenth century; processing made beef, sugar, and white bread more widely available, more regularly, than had been the case in the past.

But in our own world, the logical evolution of Boorstin's culinary democracy is McDonald's french fries and Lender's frozen bagels. These are not the foods that contemporary food critics lionize. The foods of modern industry still rarely outrank those of local enclaves among culinary critics. Fast food today is called junk food, just as the snacks of immigrant pushcart vendors were called "poison" in the past. Critics like John and Karen Hess, Raymond Sokolov, and numberless other intellectuals writing on food describe mass production and standardization as threats to American taste, and encourage Americans instead to explore the superior diversity of its regional and ethnic cuisines. Ethnic foods often lose their ethnic labels, their "authenticity," and—critics argue—their taste once they are mass produced by large corporations. It happened to hot dogs, beer, eggrolls, and bagels; it is happening right now to pizza, salsa, hummus, and sushi.

In the nineteenth century, corporations sought to mass produce foods that all Americans might want to eat, and their advertising sought to encourage homogeneity of taste and choice. While ethnic businessmen reached outward from their enclave markets into multi-ethnic regional markets, corporations sought inroads into them. In doing so they had to come to terms with the distinctive culinary tastes of multicultural consumers.

And they did. By midcentury the most successful corporations had begun to diversify production and to acquire a mix of products, brands, and smaller businesses to market more successfully to distinctive geographic and demographic segments of the population. Business historians have viewed this change in corporate strategy as a logical evolution in market relations: once all Americans had accepted and begun to purchase their standard products, corporate producers could not expect increasing profits from them. Thereafter, many corporations encouraged diversity among consumers, in order to sell ever-new and more diverse mixes of products specifically developed for specific types of consumer. To Richard Tedlow this has meant that "there was no such thing as the Pepsi Generation until Pepsi created it."[52]

Had corporate strategies of "niche" marketing actually created the ethnic niches to which they marketed, in the way that PepsiCo supposedly created the Pepsi generation? Evidence from the histories of ethnic foods, brands, and businessmen suggests otherwise. Enclave businessmen had recognized and operated successfully in niche markets long before corporations knew how to get their products to the shelves of Mary Antin's grocer father. In fact, cross-over businessmen had pioneered both in introducing enclave foods to corporations and in marketing mass-produced foods to immigrant, minority, and regional consumers. Ethnicity in the marketplace was not the invention of corporate demographic marketing strategies.

Nor were corporations necessarily always the winners in their efforts to sell successfully to demographic niches of consumers with distinctive tastes. In many respects, ethnicity did not coexist easily with corporate life. Many enclave foods lost their ethnic labels once they were mass produced for a national market. And only rarely did enclave businessmen "carry ethnicity with them" into the corporate world. Many preferred to return to the high-risk, entrepreneurial small businesses from which they had emerged.

Both small businessmen and their clients, furthermore, seemed aware that the corporate and the "ethnic" ways of doing business were different, and perhaps even antithetical. Small businessmen, with ties to enclave communities, would continue to compete successfully with corporations in niche marketplaces, and to enjoy considerable success with a new group of postwar consumers—the "new ethnics"—who wanted "authentic" cheesecake, not the frozen, corporate version marketed by Sara Lee.

CHAPTER SEVEN

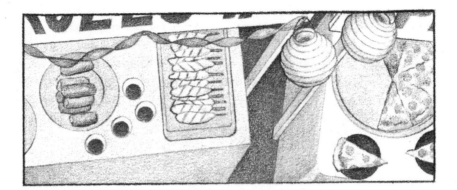

Of Cookbooks and
Culinary Roots

The advertising jingle that "Nobody doesn't like Sara Lee" proved over-optimistic. What mass-produced article could ever replicate Mary Antin's memory of her mother's baked goods? Antin noted that she could "dream away a half-hour on the immortal flavor of those thick cheese cakes we used to have on Saturday night," but she warned her readers that the cake could probably not be reproduced, even in their kitchens, and even though its recipe could easily be borrowed from her mother. Antin explained, "You have nothing in your kitchen cupboard to give the pastry its notable flavor. It takes history to make such a cake. First, you must eat it as a ravenous child, in memorable twilights . . . Then you must have yourself removed from the house of your simple feast, across the oceans, to a land where your cherished pastry is unknown even by name."[1]

Maybe corporate Sara Lee could stir up the proper ingredients and produce a delectable cheesecake at a price attractive to consumers all over the United States, but it could not sell the Jewish history associated with Antin's cake to African-Americans in Charleston. It certainly would not choose to devise an advertising jingle out of the history of intimacy and loss that suffused Antin's memories. Yet intangibles like these were exactly what the descendants of Mary Antin and other immigrants often sought with their food. They sought to recouple what had come uncoupled over fifty years: food, identity, and community. They did this even though many had also cheerfully participated in abandoning the foods, communities, and identities of their forebears. And like all Americans seeking to eat "what they are" in the late twentieth century, new ethnics turned to the marketplace to find their answers.

The ethnic revival that began in the 1960s was a cultural and political reaction of long-time Americans against the Cold War and its intensely nationalist celebrations of cultural consensus. It began with African-American critiques of a national history that had excluded them—some of the oldest of Americans—from participation and membership. Native-Americans, Asian-Americans, and Latinos also emphasized their exclusion from the celebrated benefits of American prosperity and democracy. Racial minorities initiated this ethnic revival or "new ethnicity" by demanding recognition for their unique histories and ways of life. The descendants of white southerners and immigrants from southern and eastern Europe soon joined the revival, and many also considered themselves new ethnics. They mourned a different history from that of the mainstream, notably the losses—of culture, community, and identity—they had experienced by voluntarily (or in some cases involuntarily) becoming part of the national group. For these new ethnics, the task at hand was to undo the cultural effects of three generations of assimilation. Not surprisingly, food became an integral part of that effort.

Foreign visitors of our own times still sometimes see in American ethnicity the power of culinary conservatism, which was powerful indeed in the nineteenth century. Wrote one, "Long after giving up all attachment to the land of his birth, the naturalized American citizen holds fast to the food of his parents."[2] Academics have sometimes concurred that "the only habit and custom which can be preserved in its entirety is diet."[3] Yet if enclave eating habits had truly been as conservative as these commentators believed, culinary loss could scarcely have occurred among immigrant and regional eaters, and the new ethnicity would have had no need of rediscovering foods like Mary Antin's cheesecake.

Observations like these were simply wrong, and they were probably based on quick visits to enclaves where new immigrants still predominated. As active consumers, the descendants of nineteenth-century enclaves in the twentieth century instead joined the multi-ethnic throng seeking novelty and pleasure from food vendors and corporate mass-producers. They changed their foodways significantly and voluntarily. By the 1970s, Italians in Philadelphia ate American-style "platter meals" most days, while reserving Italian-style "gravy meals" (with sauce) for one special day a week. Holiday dishes and desserts like ricotta wheat pie survived relatively unchanged, but most dishes of ethnic origin complemented or accompanied American and multi-ethnic specialties, even on holidays.[4] The culinary repertoire of Japanese farm women in California included Chinese chicken salad, chow mein, tamale pie, Jell-O mochi, and coffee azuki Jell-O,[5] while Passover dinners in Charleston, South Carolina, featured ham, rice, and challah.[6]

Even the many Orthodox Jews of the Northeast had invented a wide range of kosher-style foodways, by significantly adapting their eating to American life and market offerings.[7] According to one observer, kosher-style eating developed across the generations, with "the first generation being merely lax about the dietary laws without committing any willful transgression, the second disregarding the laws about the preparation of permitted meat, and the mixture of meat and butter, the third indulging in forbidden dishes only in restaurants, and the fourth introducing them upon the table at home."[8] Beginning in the 1930s, the Orthodox Union offered a regular "Kashruth Column" to educate Orthodox Jews as modern consumers, noting that "vanilla extract if made with alcohol is kosher, but if made with glycerine is trefa." It advised that "Heinz's vegetable soup is not kosher," and "Beechnut gum is not endorsed by us. We approve Wrigley's."[9]

Some of this culinary change occurred over loud objections from immigrant parents who were quite committed to preserving old ways. Leonard Covello's Italian father examined oatmeal sent home by a public school interested in improving his son's breakfast, and "to him it was the kind of bran that was fed to pigs in Avigliano. 'What kind of school is this?' he shouted. 'They give us the food of animals to eat and send it home to us with our children! What are we coming to next?'"[10] Other sources of change were friendlier, however, and reached into the heart of family life. Intermarriage meant that a Polish-American woman learned to make Scandinavian meatballs and krum kakes to please her Swedish-American husband. Schoolyard curiosity meant that a Portuguese girl in Hawaii asked a friend, "Sumiko, if tomorrow you bring me two sushis [rice cones] for lunch, I bring you some sweet bread and chorise [sausages]."[11]

No other eating event so symbolized the changing eating habits in ethnic enclaves as an immigrant family's first American Thanksgiving celebration. Here was one of the partial success stories of culinary Americanization, since many immigrant mothers prepared the feast when children requested it after studying the Pilgrims in school. An Italian daughter remembered, "Turkey with dressing. It took years before I make that dressing. When we first got a turkey for my little brother, my mother almost went crazy."[12] But in other families, the adjustment was a pleasant one: "How we did enjoy that delicious American turkey, with chestnut stuffing, giblet gravy, and sweet potatoes—all completely new to us."[13] Thanksgiving menus were gradually adapted to other celebrations, with culinary flourishes of their own added, too. A St. John's Day celebration in Frenchtown offered a "French-Canadian style" menu which included "turkey stuffed with potatoes, sausage and giblets in French Canada style; fluffy white mashed potatoes, golden sweet potato; carrot salad with green beans molded into a yellow gelatine; ice cream and cake, sometimes a carrot pudding but rarely pie."[14]

Thanksgiving was one of the largest challenges to the creativity of immigrant cooks, and much culinary change originated in the imaginative responses of creative cooks to American life and markets. An Italian from Argentina remembered his mother tricking a child, eager for a Thanksgiving celebration: "She bought the chopped meat, and she got, I don't know from where, two tongue depressors, and she sculpted a turkey, which was beautiful. The two tongue depressors were the legs. She basted that, then she surrounded it with potatoes and parsley. And there we had this turkey with my mother, father, and I winking at each other." This same woman, having once used her pasta pot to dye a pair of white pants, found that it subsequently turned her spaghetti purple. Ever thrifty, she washed the spaghetti until it was lavender: "As she washed it more and more it congealed into a solid. Not to worry. She poured the Italian tomato sauce over it and cut it into slices."[15]

As good cooks, immigrant mothers could scarcely resist the temptation to innovate with new ingredients, responding to the marketplace, their neighbors, their children's requests, and household emergencies. Children of many backgrounds were impressed with this maternal culinary creativity and remembered it. A Jewish child recalled, "She was ingenious about food, which meant we didn't suffer pangs of hunger, because she could buy a bunch of carrots and two potatoes and an onion, and we would have a vegetable soup. Then, she would take those soft vegetables, mash them up with an egg and fry them, and we would have vegetable cutlets." A West Indian woman, Rosanna Westing, remembered, "My mother wasn't a great cook, but she knew how to manipulate with food."[16] Ultimately, manipulation with food surpassed in importance the culinary conservatism of enclave eaters, putting them and their children on the road to the new ethnicity of the 1970s.

Most culinary change was voluntary, creative, and in both senses positively experienced. Where, then, did the new ethnics' very real sense of loss and sorrow come from? It seems to have originated as much in social and familial change as at the table. Although innovative as eaters, the descendants of enclave eaters remained human in associating certain foods—as Antin did—with the comfort, security, and love of their childhood homes. People turn to such comfort foods when they must cope with stress, and there was plenty of that in the culturally liminal, and changing, lives of immigrants, their children, and grandchildren. Change itself is stressful, generating a demand for comfort foods. When asked, "What do you do when you are feeling marginal, lost and sad?" a southeast Asian immigrant replied, "I shout at my children to speak Cambodian, I tell my wife to cook much rice and snao. Sometimes I drink beer. Then same day I feel better."[17] His sentiments differed little from the nineteenth-century German, who noted he had "just enjoyed a glass of beer, which what with all this pouring rain gives me time and the STRENGTH to keep on scribbling."[18] Mexican immigrants today sometimes go to considerable lengths to guarantee that children of working mothers come under the care of what they call a "tortilla grandma."[19] All need comfort, because they are changing.

Comfort foods are usually heavily associated with women as food preparers and organizers of the family's emotional life. Alvis Sancez, a Puerto Rican, felt it was the emotion that flavored the food of his youth, for "when your mother make the food, she put devotion to make the food the best for the family."[20] An Italian noted, too, that "everybody thought his [own] mom's cooking was best." Jewish immigrants in New York concurred—"It was the love with which mom cooked that made it taste good"—as did Bohemian farmers on the Great Plains, where, "With Mary, to feed creatures was the natural expression of affection—her chickens, the calves, her big hungry boys." Immigrants and their children glorified their mothers as "feast-makers" and culinary artists, in words that emphasize the warm sensuality that linked food to maternal love.[21] As Ernita James, an African-American woman, told a surprised interviewer, "Of course we have dinner together . . . I was raised that way. That's what families do."[22]

By the 1970s, however, that was frequently not what American families did. Faced with rapidly changing roles for women, and rapidly changing habits of family life, new ethnics expressed their concerns about the present by remembering, or merely imagining, a more comfortable past in the ethnic enclaves. Old ethnic neighborhoods had disappeared as the children of immigrants had moved to the suburbs and as rural southerners had moved north or to the city. Landmarks of urban ethnicity had disappeared beneath the bull-dozers of urban renewal and the new waves of immigrants from other parts of the world. Clearly, new ethnics hoped to recapture through food and eating the closeness of a bygone era, when families always ate a home-cooked, mother-served, meal and spent holidays together in a close-knit familiar world. Being consumers to their American core, however, they tried to recreate the past by buying it. Their efforts to reconnect food and fellowship led them to purchase cookbooks, festival meals, and "authentic" foods and in the process to rediscover the small businessmen who could deliver not just the required goods but the associations to community and ethnic identity that corporate producers could not.

No longer a nation of fussy, self-denying eaters, Americans by the 1980s devoured cookbooks describing the foods and cooking techniques of cultures around the world. Of greatest relevance to many new ethnics were "community cookbooks"—collections of recipes by civic, ethnic, religious, and women's organizations, often cheaply bound with bright plastic rings. The model for these cookbooks was indisputably American, even if their subject matter often was not. During the Civil War, northern Ladies Aid Societies discontented with mere bandage-rolling had for the first time collected their favorite recipes to sell at Sanitary Fairs supporting the Union Army.[23] Community cookbooks (also called "charitables" or "compiled" cookbooks) became favorite fund-raising projects of Protestant churches, women's groups, and women's clubs later in the nineteenth century.

Jewish and Catholic women hesitated longer, and foreign-born women or their daughters produced very few community cookbooks before 1960. Several German-language community cookbooks, such as *Chicago's St Paul's Bazaar-Kochbuch und Geschaeftsfuehrer* (1892), appeared quite early. But English-language cookbooks written by local chapters of the Council of Jewish Women (in San Francisco, Portland, and Waco) and by synagogue sisterhoods (such as Detroit's Temple Beth El, which produced *The Temple Cook Book* in 1903; and Temple Emmanuel of Yonkers Sisterhood's *Recipes Tried and True*, compiled in 1913) outnumbered the cookbooks of a few German, Norwegian, black, Moravian, Scottish, Swedish, Dutch, and Catholic parishes before 1915.[24]

Nor did writers and businesswomen in the nation's ethnic enclaves offer many commercial cookbooks for women linked to the orally transmitted cooking traditions of the Old World. We have a few examples from Czechs, Germans, Finns, and—later—Poles, Ukrainians, Italians, and Eastern European Jews in the native tongues of immigrants. There was, for example, Charles Hellstern's *Deutsch-Amerikanisches Illustriertes Kochbuch*, published in New York in 1891, and Marie Rosicka's *Narodni Domaci kucharka cesko-americka*, published in Omaha in 1904.

Somewhat more common were cookbooks for English-speaking daughters, like *Jewish Cookery* (Esther Levy's collection of kosher recipes, published in Philadelphia in 1871) or the Jewish *Aunt Babette's Cookbook* (published in Chicago in 1889) or Rosicka's translated *Bohemian American Cook Book* (from Omaha, 1925). Occasionally, too, companies like Manischewitz (*Tempting Kosher Dishes*, 1944) and Rokeach (*Rokeah kokh bukh*, 1933) published collections of recipes for their clients, making lavish use of their own products. It seems obvious that women still closely tied to their enclave communities did not need written cookbooks to learn to cook as their mothers did, since they learned from their mothers. The paucity of cookbooks on immigrant eating traditions in the 1950s, for example, stands in sharp contrast to a boom in cookbooks marketed to Americans learning the haute cuisine of foreign countries.[25]

Before the new ethnicity, much of what remained of regional and immigrant cooking was in the unwritten form of female art. In the words of the popular radio star Molly Goldberg, "When someone, Mrs. Herman, for an instance, asks me 'How do you make this or how do you make that?' do I know? Of course I know, but can I tell her? Of course I can, but easier to show her. So I have to say to her 'Come into my kitchen and I'll make you up.' That takes time, not that I begrudge such a dear friend my time, certainly not, but I mean if I'm going to show Mrs. Herman and all my neighbors how I cook something, who's going to make supper? My Jake would complain. So My Rosie had an idea. 'Ma,' she said, 'I'll stand on your shoulder while you cook and I'll write you down.'"[26]

Community cookbooks of the 1970s multiplied as hundreds of second- and third-generation Rosies committed themselves to "writing you down." The cookbooks thus served two purposes: to recover and celebrate the past and to teach lost culinary skills to descendants of enclave cooks. Recent immigrants from Latin America and Asia did not produce community cookbooks in the 1970s; they did not yet need them. Their oral traditions still sufficed.

Jews, Poles, Ukrainians, Greeks, and Germans from Russia wrote and sold far more community cookbooks than Italians, African-Americans, or Mexican-Americans, among whom (perhaps) the oral traditions of the enclave also remained stronger. Community cookbooks generally sold for two or three dollars in the 1970s, or for as much as eight or nine dollars by the early 1990s. Although evidence is patchy, most appeared in limited editions of 1000–2000 from a small number of midwestern presses specializing in the genre. A few cookbooks went through many printings, appearing over a ten- or even twenty-year period, suggesting that they were, at least in their creators' terms, very successful fundraisers. All were in English, although some included glossaries of foreign ingredients or gave at least the names of particular dishes in the native languages. Their compilers sometimes gave them names they found clever: *Czech Your Cooking; Shalom Ya'll; Wurst You Were Here*. More often titles were completely straightforward: *From Zion's Kitchen* (Baltimore, 1977), *The Badenfest Cookbook* (St. Louis, 1973). Women generally compiled these cookbooks, although they accepted contributions from men.

Cookbook compilers shared roughly similar goals, which mixed innovation and preservation. As innovators, they hoped to apply "modern methods of cooking and baking . . . to favorite Slovenian dishes of our grandmothers"[27] so that modern cooks would feel encouraged to try old ways, adapted for "ingredients and equipment readily available in the United States."[28] As preservationists, they hoped also "to make them readily accessible to those who have lost their mother tongue" (in this case Ukrainian).[29]

Cookbooks assembled by Philoptochos Ladies Societies of Greek Orthodox churches from the South contained chapters on "lenten recipes" and "religious foods," along with careful guidelines for fasting or producing pastries in bulk for festivals. Similarly, *Akiba's Kosher Cookbook* (no date, but assembled by parents of North Texas's first Hebrew Day School) taught the rules of Jewish kosher food preparation to descendants who had strayed from them.

Only rarely did compilers celebrate the ethnic group itself. A few described their purpose as celebrating "our Italian and American heritages"[30] or noted that "Lithuania, like other nations, possesses many treasures which merit fostering and preservation."[31] The compilers of *In Good Taste* (Women's Guild of the Balzekas Museum of Lithuanian Culture, 1966) saw their cookbook as only one element of a far more general, extensive "study of one's own heritage." More often, though, cookbook prefaces emphasized the compilers' desire to celebrate their mothers and families. Cookbook compilers routinely dedicated their cookbooks to their mothers and grandmothers, characterized as "those stalwart women"[32] or "valiant women" whose "efforts to provide recipes with limited ingredients, yet nourishing, need to be recognized."[33] Cookbook writers attributed good cooking specifically to women, not to a general ethnic tradition. In doing so, however, they acted out of no feminist impulse.

Instead, glorifying the female cooks of the past sometimes implied a critique of modern women. Community cookbooks offered "family-tested recipes" and "our husbands' favorite recipes," claiming "the way to your man's heart is in this book." The Women of the [largely Bohemian] Holy Trinity Mother's Club even boasted that "we make no claim as to the originality of these recipes. Our only claim to these tried and tested recipes is our husbands' and children's satisfaction."[34] Others saw their recipes as a desirable alternative to hastily assembled modern meals. These lines of doggerel appeared in *Our Swiss Pantry* (1967):

> Are you tired of instant food?
> Are you in a cooking mood?
> Store-bought cookies are no match,
> For the ones you bake from "scratch."
> Put away that instant mix—
> Take some pride in what you fix.

By celebrating women cooks, the new ethnic cookbooks promised the survival of "Italian holiday meals . . . prepared in the homes of . . . children, grand-children, and hopefully . . . great-grandchildren."[35] For cookbook writers, at least, ethnic survival lay in the hands of female cooks.

Dallas's Temple Emanu-El Sisterhood captured this connection among women, cooking, and a family-oriented past nicely when it called its cookbook *From Generation to Generation* (1992). It listed the cookbook's purpose as "continuing in the tradition of 5000 Years in the kitchen."[36] Similarly, the National Council of Negro Women called their collection *The Black Family Reunion Cookbook* (New York, 1991). In a cover-page blurb, Dionne Warwick pointed out to readers that "strong families and good cooking often go hand-in-hand," and she noted that the book celebrated both.

Producing cookbooks sparked memories and revivals of ethnic identity among their compilers, often transforming curious participants in a limited project into enthusiastic new ethnics. Lithuanian women in Chicago noted that "in the process of collecting these recipes, a considerable amount of probing and reviving of youthful memories of Lithuanian cooks was required to recreate some of the recipes."[37] The Temple Sisterhood of Dallas also saw itself presenting "favorite foods and memories." In some cases, recipes literally alternated with memories, pictures, and documents. Personal and familiar touches included hand-written or signed recipes, family pictures of relatives, homes, and groups of happy women cooks beaming over large platters of holiday food.

Catharine Tripalin Murray's collections of recipes, pictures, and oral histories from Italian-American residents of Madison and Kenosha, Wisconsin, are perhaps the richest illustrations of the new ethnicity's linkage of food and memory. A *Taste of Memories* documents what sociologists studying Boston's urban renewal in the 1960s called longing for the lost home. Madison's Bush neighborhood (where Murray's father grew up) had in fact been destroyed by urban renewal. Murray told a Madison reporter, "I did this book because I wanted to learn about my grandmother."[38] She described her larger motive in initiating the project: "I could recapture an era and its people . . . while becoming a part of the Italian/Sicilian community I so dearly loved, but was never a part of." Murray's work obviously struck an important chord; the Italian-American Women's Mutual Aid Society (with whom Murray worked, and which held the initial copyright to A *Taste of Memories*) earned approximately $25,000 from the first volume of the cookbook.[39]

Profits like Murray's tempted commercial writers to write for new ethnic consumers. Helen Jakubowski Rog's *Na Zdrowie! "To Your Health"* promised "authentic Polish recipes and memories of a Lackawanna tavern keeper." Stories of her family members, the Friday fish fries, canning, and soups made hers a "cookbook as legacy."[40] In a particularly elegant compilation of recipes and memories of Italian and Italian-American life, Helen Barolini wrote of her own motives in writing *Festa*. American interest in Italian food, she said, can be dated to the years following World War II, and she described her mother during that earlier period of revival as "dredging from her memory foods from her own mother's Italian kitchen." Barolini's assessment of the new ethnicity is a telling one. "Starting in her kitchen, my mother found her way back to her heritage, and this I sus-pected for many Italian-American families who were rescued from lives of denial by the 'ethnic explosion' of the 1960s." Barolini wrote her own book in response to the gradual dispersal of her daughters, nieces, and nephews on two continents. "I thought with some sadness and sense of loss about the complications of living, of the distances . . . that now keep me from setting a family table . . . I thought, what a shame if those customs and cookery are not recorded for our daughters . . . and for all those Italian-descended families in America."[41]

Commercial cookbooks focusing on immigrant food followed the exam-ple of community cookbooks in emphasizing the root of good cooking in family ties and loving mothers. Nancy Verde Barr's publisher advertised her book *We Called It Macaroni* as "a feast of gloriously flavorful Italian-American recipes and memories," and noted that the author "was raised on, and loves, the wonderful dishes, redolent of sun-drenched tomatoes and peppers, virgin olive oil and aromatic herbs—and the equally delicious and nourishing lore—that her grandparents brought from southern Italy." As proof, a small picture of Barr's "Nonna" (grandmother) in the 1920s appears in the upper corner of the ad.[42] TV's Frugal Gourmet, Jeff Smith, captured the sentiments of new ethnics rather well when he subtitled his own collection *Recipes You Should Have Gotten from Your Grandmother*.

Commercial cookbooks treated ethnic foods as discrete cuisines, fro-zen in some past time, unaltered by life outside the enclave community. Community cookbooks, on the other hand (whether intentionally or not), provided ample clues to what new ethnics actually ate in the 1970s. Cook-books dedicated to a particular tradition were surprisingly full of multi-ethnic recipes and ingredients; their recipes differed significantly by re-gion; and they were decidedly American in their high use of processed convenience foods. The same *Our Swiss Pantry* that urged women to take pride in their Swiss heritage and home cooking included recipes for American-Norwegian pancakes and Swedish Plattar (oven pancakes), em-panadas, arroz con pollo, Mexican wedding cookies, and Terrijaki ("Ha-waiian"). Alongside Swiss-origin recipes were ones for a "hamburger-Chi-nese vegetable electric skillet dinner" and a "local ingredients chop suey." Recipes called for cooks to use canned soups, beans, and fruits, gravy (and other) mixes, instant rice, frozen vegetables, and marshmallow fluff. A

Portuguese cookbook from Hawaii included a wide range of Asian-inspired dishes, along with pork and sweet potatoes, while *Recipes from the Portuguese of Provincetown* made use of the local clams. Compilers of such cookbooks obviously felt no contradiction between their search for roots and their fondness for regional, multi-ethnic, and convenient dishes.

In their ethnic intermingling, community cookbooks also differed from cookbooks created specifically to raise funds for public institutions committed to multiculturalism. These books seemed as committed to describing distinctive and codified ethnic cuisines as were the commercial cookbooks aimed at new ethnic consumers. The *Minnesota Ethnic Food Book*, for example, included recipes for groups ranging from the Ojibway to the Hmong. It presented their foods in a roughly chronological succession of distinct ethnic chapters. Similarly, *The Melting Pot: Ethnic Cuisine in Texas*, a cookbook published by the Institute for Texan Cultures, emphasized the many separate ingredients tossed into the southwestern pot, not their intermingling. The collection started with the African-Americans of Texas and ended—27 groups later—with the Yugoslavs.[43]

Recipes for *The Melting Pot* came from the ethnic societies participating in the yearly Texas Folklife Festival. Even the vast national Festival of American Folklife, held in Washington each year, produced cookbooks in 1994 and 1995.[44] This linkage of food with festivity was no more accidental than the linkage of food, in community cookbooks, with mothers and homelife. Ethnic festivals created temporary communities of consumers in search of authentic ethnicity, including food. They became a second important site for the commercial exploration of culinary roots for new ethnics in the 1970s. They not only connected food with community in ways new ethnics appreciated, but at the same time they gave new ethnics a way to demonstrate their commitment to the ethnic identities of other Americans. The search for roots occurred at festivals with a much larger agenda—already familiar to the International Institutes of the 1920s—of promoting cross-cultural communication through food sharing.

Communal celebrations of ethnicity, including celebrations of ethnic food, were nothing new in America. Celebrations of communalism in the United States had a long history, much of it distinctly commercial. This simple fact had confounded the America Eats Project in the 1930s. In Washington, project editors announced "that we are less interested in the commercialized feasts than in social meals attended by friendly groups— such as church suppers, school picnics, family reunions, and the like."[45] They had in mind the kind of church meeting Elise Waerenskold described in her rural Texas community in the 1840s, where Norwegian farmers' wives brought with them food in abundance, "to share and to pass." These pot-luck events were the simple origins of what became large, and often commercialized, food festivals in the twentieth century.

In the 1930s, some family reunions, church-sponsored camp meetings, and graveyard cleanings carried on this tradition in the form of picnics and covered dish suppers. At an Arkansas picnic, for example, a WPA writer reported that "one woman brings the meat, sometimes a roast or a fried chicken, more often a casserole dish combining meat and vegetables. Another brings the side vegetables; a third the salad; a fourth the cake; a fifth the pies or other desserts." But, alas, for the editors of America Eats, most such events in the 1930s were no longer pot-luck expressions of community solidarity. They had become fundraisers for enclave communities with eager multi-ethnic customers.

Lutefisk, for example, became controversial with America Eats editors not just because they were skeptical of its Scandinavian origins but because it was dished up for cold cash by Norwegian churches. In both Wisconsin and Minnesota, outsiders paid well for the privilege of trying the dish at ubiquitous annual lutefisk suppers. For Norwegian churches, lutefisk suppers were community celebrations, but they were also fundraisers no different from a rummage sale or Christmas bazaar.

Fundraising by religious and ethnic groups, like communal eating itself, had deep American roots. In a sense, it reached back to the U.S. Constitution itself: the separation of church and state forced all churches to raise money directly, and continuously, in order to survive, pay a religious leader, build a place of worship, or pursue missionary, evangelical, or social service programs. For immigrants accustomed to state-sponsored churches, a first step toward religious Americanization was fundraising—a task often taken on in the Protestant and Jewish communities by new "American-style" "ladies' aid" societies or sisterhoods. They often copied the practices of older, better established American congregations.

In the nineteenth century, Shakers raised money by drying fruits and vegetables, especially corn, for market (a skill they learned from the local Indians who had done the same in previous centuries); the Mormons operated veritable businesses in their community sugar beet processing plants. More common were the church Christmas bazaar, the New England May breakfast, the fund-raising pilau supper or strawberry social. By the 1930s 5-cent, 25-cent, and 35-cent suppers funded Missouri Sokol and Sänger-vereine (German choruses), along with immigrant parishes, congregations, and synagogues. Charleston's Hibernian Society raised funds with a St. Patrick's Day dinner, just as Charleston's (white) Elk's Club sponsored a yearly oyster roast to fund its recreation programs. North Carolina blacks held "chitterling struts" to repair a church roof, while in the mountains of north Georgia single girls decorated boxes or baskets "with enough of everything for two" to auction off (along with their own company) to the highest bidding men. The money went to their church.

Before the 1970s, larger-scale festivals rarely focused specifically on ethnic foods. In a 1950s guide to annual celebrations, sprinkled among descriptions of American historical festivals, rodeos, burgoo dinners, celebrations of local products, music events, and "old pioneer days," one finds only Tulip Time in Holland, Michigan (with gingerbread, braided bread, and morning teas), Flagstaff's All-Indian Pow-Wow (roasted game and huge kettles of "Indian pudding"), Kutztown's Pennsylvania Dutch Folk Festival (apple butter, rivel soup, shoo-fly pie, and "bot-boi"), the Chippewa Wild Rice Festival of Deer River, Minnesota, the William Tell Play of New Glarus, Wisconsin (Swiss German Kälberwurst and cheeses), and International-Institute-inspired multi-ethnic fests such as Cleveland's Folk Festival or St. Paul's Festival of Nations.[46]

Although not on this somewhat selective list, the Lindsborg, Kansas, Svensk Hyllnings Fest (Swedish Pioneer Festival) was also already in existence: its history was a dress rehearsal for the new ethnicity and its festivals of the 1970s. Svensk Hyllnings Fest began in an earlier moment of ethnic revival, which also centered around celebrating ethnicity and food, in this case a smorgasbord. Swedes had established a cooperative farming community in Lindsborg in 1868, and the town long claimed to be more Swedish than Stockholm. Still, the celebration of Swedish food was a long time coming. The first Hyllnings Fest, held in 1941, occurred when

Swedish was no longer spoken on a daily basis. It copied the Christmas activities of the local (Lutheran, pietist, and Swedish) Bethany College's Christmas smorgasbord of the 1920s. Initiative for the festival, however, came from businessmen boosters who wanted a homecoming event to promote the local economy. Lindsborg's Dutch-origin doctor successfully urged his Swedish neighbors to try a Swedish theme, explicitly emulating the Holland, Michigan, tulip festival.

Lindsborg had moved so far away from Swedish cultural practices in 1941 that initially it proved difficult to mount a full-scale smorgasbord with no evidence of how many visitors could be expected. The first festival was marred by confusion surrounding the correct dishes and presentation for the Friday-night event. Ample servings of a homemade Swedish drink made from juniper berries (which packed considerable alcoholic wallop) also produced many drunken visitors, to the horror of some temperance-minded festival organizers.[47]

Still, after a wartime hiatus, a second festival followed in 1948. In 1951 the Lindsborg Chamber of Commerce (believing that "this festival can be worth thousands of dollars in the advertising of the city of Lindsborg") assumed official sponsorship of the event. Roughly 900 visitors in search of entertainment and novelty soon outnumbered locals returning home for the yearly event.[48]

The Hyllnings fest reflected but also deepened ethnic revival among town residents. Town housewives learned to prepare most of the forty-plus foods for the smorgasbord, recollecting and recreating family recipes, and supplementing Swedish dishes with American favorites like potato salad and Jell-O. In 1961, the women of the Bethany College Auxiliary produced a cookbook that collected 100 smorgasbord recipes, *Measure for Pleasure*. Local boosters believed the event "put the town on the map," and that their Swedish heritage made that possible. The fact that minestrone and "south of the border" potato salad shared space with smorgasbord recipes in *Measure for Pleasure* in no way undermined the residents' heightened sense of their Swedish ethnicity.

The Lindsborg festival suggests that a small "new ethnicity" movement was under way among Scandinavians already in the 1930s, 1940s, and 1950s. Smorgasbords and similar events proliferated on the Great Plains and in the upper Midwest. Woodville, Wisconsin, for example, held its first Syttende Mai in 1952 to commemorate the adoption of Norway's constitution in 1814. The town's Lion's Club and the American Legion sponsored the event until a Sons of Norway lodge organized itself in 1982. The festival featured American-origin events—a "queen" pageant and fashion show—along with folk singing and dancing and ethnic food. The cookbook produced by the festival's sponsors included not only recipes for Norwegian chicken and potato sausage and dumplings but entertained readers with descriptions of local Norwegian humor ("Old Lutefisk eaters never die, they just smell that way!").[49]

The new ethnicity of the 1970s dwarfed these early predecessors. A recent guide to festivals lists 19 African-American, 31 Hispanic, 18 German, 7 Cajun, and 6 Irish festivals, along with smaller numbers of events for most other ethnic groups. These range from individual events like New York's Korean Harvest Folk Festival, held at Flushing Meadow in Corona Park, a three-day Italian festival (that evolved from church to business sponsorship) in Hartford, Connecticut, and an Armenian church bazaar near Boston that earns $20,000 annually, to a summertime full of festivals, like those sponsored by Toledo's Chamber of Commerce. There, eating begins with the multi-ethnic St. Vincent de Paul festival (pies, tacos, kielbasa sandwiches), includes an African-American Festival (with specialties from the American South, both creole style and chicken barbecue, as well as the food of a number of African nations—bean pies and fried croquettes), and a Hungarian festival in East Toledo's Birmingham neighborhood; it concludes with St. Michael's Ukrainian festival, which features pierogis, stuffed cabbage, and a chicken dinner.

Civic, ethnic, and commercial groups now work together so that ethnic food festivals "boost" local economies. In Clinton, Indiana, a small mining town in economic decline, the first Little Italy festival (1966) explicitly sought tourists to revive a declining town core that still boasted several Italian restaurants.[50] New York's Ninth Avenue International Festival of Food originated in 1971 with local merchants committed to reviving a deteriorating market area. Although the first festival in 1974 lost money, by the mid 1980s the festival was attracting a quarter of a million visitors, and the Association was clearing over $100,000 by charging vendors' fees ranging from $450 to $600. New York City collects an additional 15 percent of vendors' sales and in return provides sanitation services and electrical hook-ups. Despite their high costs, vendors of everything from Filipino shish kebab, heroes, kokoretsi, cotton candy, roast suckling pigs, and yackisoba noodles manage to make profits. The profits made by the Association in turn support Covenant House and other charities located in nearby Hell's Kitchen.[51] The festival's many supporters insist, "This is not a commercial fair—it's a community fair. It brings money into the community, but the most important thing it does is crystallize our community and bring us together."[52] Social workers at the International Institutes could not have said it better in the 1920s.

"Festival Marketplaces"—like San Antonio's Riverwalk area—represent a somewhat similar mix of civic, ethnic, and business goals. But they make the celebration of ethnic food a permanent fixture of urban life, and an important attraction for a growing population of tourists interested in purchasing ethnic variety as part of the fun and adventure of travel. In San Antonio, a meandering river, surrounded by wild vegetation, had required control after it flooded the downtown area in 1921. The area was not a center of commerce or eating at the time, but local architect Robert H. H. Hugman argued for the creation of a riverside shopping center to be called the "Shops of Aragon and Romula" and a "Foods of All Nations" development on the west bank. The Depression initially dashed Hugman's plans, although the 1936 Fiesta San Jacinto celebrated with a river parade, which again focused attention on the area. Hoteliers then took initiative for river beautification with WPA and city funds between 1939 and 1941. Until 1960, the Riverwalk still had an unsavory reputation as a dangerous area, and photos show it almost deserted—and off limits to military personnel. Only one restaurant (where a German family offered Mexican food) operated successfully. With ethnic revival in the 1970s, however, San Antonio's Chamber of Commerce saw its Riverwalk become a major tourist attraction. Developers had not anticipated how many visitors would see the Riverwalk as part of the "atmosphere of old Mexico" and "Spanish culture" typical of the town. Newly opened outdoor cafes offering Mexican, Italian, Chinese, French, and Texas foods contributed to its romantic, peaceful atmosphere without destroying tourists' sense that the Riverwalk was part of San Antonio's Spanish heritage. The city in turn coordinated a series of monthly festivals to entertain the tourists crowding hotels along its length; only a few focused on the town's Latin roots.[53]

Commerce was not the purpose of the largest ethnic festivals of the 1970s, which were funded by state and federal governments to encourage multiculturalism, but these undertakings, too, became important money-making events. Like the International Institutes in the 1920s, professionals working for government cultural agencies saw food-sharing as an opportunity for cross-cultural education and communication. Thus, the purpose of the yearly Festival of American Folklife evolved as the new ethnicity grew in importance. At the first festival, in 1967, performer Alan Lomax seemed uninterested in promoting ethnicity, and instead noted that "this is the festival of the democratic art. This is the art that American people have made out of their experience." A 1973 Smithsonian pamphlet also emphasized the creative, artistic, and democratic dimensions of the festival, which had as its goal "to increase public appreciation of the richness and viability of American grass-roots creativity," but added as well its recognition that "American cultures are varied. The population is diverse." By 1976, and the huge bicentennial festival, the Festival of American Folklife more clearly celebrated multicultural ethnic diversity, and hoped "to stimulate cultural self-awareness and inter-cultural understanding."[54]

Throughout the 1970s, festival exhibitions in Washington on "old ways in the New World" aimed "to reflect accurately one of the principal facts that has made the U.S. so unique in world history, [namely,] that America is the first unified yet genuinely pluralistic civilization in the history of mankind."[55] Special exhibits focused on ethnic groups, regions of the United States, other parts of the world, occupational groups, and particular states. The exact balance of topics, and the mix of folk arts and folkways, changed over the years, as did the financing and planning of the festival (especially with increased participation from the National Parks Service). Food, however, remained a constant in festival exhibitions, and almost as popular with visitors as the music and dance exhibitions.

Each year, the festival staff at the Smithsonian Institution seeks to include food presentations to illustrate and accompany its art, dance, ethnic, and occupational programs. In 1993 one festival theme was life in the U.S.-Mexico borderlands. With borderlands defined rather broadly, people from the area came to Washington to demonstrate candy making, South-Mexican cooking, the cuisine of New Mexican natives, the making of asadero cheese, Gulf fisherman cooking, and black Seminole cooking.[56]

Food demonstrations did not feed the festival's million visitors, however. Demonstrators could not provide food for sale in sufficient quantities, at appropriate prices, or under the rigorous conditions specified by local health and sanitation regulations. Instead, food for hungry festival visitors came from profit-seeking vendors recruited by festival planners. Folklorists on staff at the Smithsonian work closely with vendors, seeking to guarantee ethnic authenticity while also satisfying the hunger of eager consumers. In some cases, the Park Service has provided food for sale through its own vendors, but the Smithsonian staff has preferred to negotiate with enclave businessmen or community groups rather than rent booths to commercial vendors. The Smithsonian staff fully recognize that their negotiations often blurred already unclear lines between communal and commercial enterprises, hastening the transformation, for example, of a church group into a private catering business.[57] In 1995, when festival themes included the Czech Republic, the Afro-American Diaspora, Cape Verdeans, and American Indian Women and Music, administrator Barbara Strickland explored contracts with a Cape Verdean local caterer, and with a well-established commercial purveyor of Memphis barbecue (who got his start by vending at folk festivals) as well as working with the Baltimore Indian Center, a voluntary ethnic organization eager to provide a Native American menu.[58]

The difficulties of feeding 50,000 visitors daily placed real restrictions on which foods could be successfully vended. Smithsonian staff connected community groups to suppliers, educated them about sanitary requirements, found insurers, and even helped plan menus. Summertime festivals meant real risk of spoilage; the festival also had fixed numbers of electrical hookups, limiting the preparation of fried foods. In the case of the Baltimore Indian Center, its menu quickly evolved into a rather simple one of fry bread with honey and berries and buffalo burgers (scarcely a traditional food for East Coast tribes). Smithsonian employee Barbara Strickland and her co-workers in Baltimore had concluded that other Native American foods might prove uninteresting, or even unappealing, to the multi-ethnic crowd the festival draws.

Balancing a desire for authenticity is the promise of good profits. Festival food vendors operate up to 10 cash registers during lunch hours, and total profits can reach half a million dollars. Sponsoring government agencies receive 20 percent of food sales, and—beginning in the early 1990s—food profits contributed about $100,000 to future festival budgets (which currently equal between 3 and 4 million dollars).

The Institute of Texan Cultures (ITC) in San Antonio feeds visitors to its popular festival somewhat differently: it encourages exhibitors to sell the food they demonstrate in their exhibits. An outgrowth of planning for Texas's Hemisfair in 1968, the ITC sent representatives to Washington to cooperate with Smithsonian staff producing a special Texas exhibit for the American festival that year. One of the Texans in this delegation, O. T. Baker, returned from Washington convinced that Texas should have its own festival, expanding ITC permanent exhibits into an annual fairlike event. The ethnic revival had scarcely started at that time, and Baker remembers that "some folks were reluctant to be represented at the Institute back in the beginning, because, well, they appeared not to take as much pride in their origins as they should."[59] With some hyperbole, Baker by 1993 nevertheless proclaimed, "It's the biggest folklife festival in the world."[60] He dreamed of its expansion to occupy Hemisfair Park, as a kind of permanent festival marketplace, not unlike San Antonio's Riverwalk.

Food quickly became a major attraction at the festival, and the festival itself became a financially significant undertaking for all the community groups involved. The ITC employs a three-person staff to solicit applications, choose participants, and organize the four-day event. The festival collects general admissions from visitors (who peaked at 120,000 but have declined in numbers in recent years). Forty ethnic groups are represented with 10,000 exhibitors of foods and crafts, and performers on eight stages. Food vendors get three-quarters of the food proceeds, the remaining quarter falling to ITC so it may provide water, electricity, and other services. Exhibitors typically earn more than $1,000; some have earned $70,000.

A 1988 Festival magazine title—"A Cultural Marketplace"—nicely summed up the festival's easy-going acceptance of ethnicity as a form of commerce. Festival guidelines require that applicants are "bona fide ethnic groups," or established interpreters of Texas customs, but the guidelines do not discriminate between profit-making and voluntary groups, as all participants must have federal ID numbers and declare as income the money they earn. Guidelines permit other festivals boosting a local crop or product (like the Yamboree in Gilmer, Texas) to exhibit. Pioneer and local crafts and oddities are all represented.

Festival organizers insist that fun must characterize all its educational activities, but Joanne Andera admits that folklorists, as a consequence, sometimes dismiss the Texas event as a "fakelore" festival.[61] Not all festival exhibitors, in other words, focus on the ethnic customs of the past, and many feel free to improvise in the interests of fun and excitement. One year the festival gave free admission to any person who brought a live chicken for a chicken-flying contest; the origins of this competition in Texas folk customs may not have been particularly well established, but many excited fair visitors did appear with live chickens for the event. Andera, like earlier festival directors, sees their approach to authenticity, and innovation, as democratic—not just fun—and thus a realistic representation of Texas folklife, including ethnicity, in a commercial society. O. T. Baker started a tradition of bragging that the festival has no folklorists on staff. "I AM folklife," the charismatic east Texan, and first festival director, declared. Second festival manager Claudia Ball concurred more modestly: "I have no formal training in folklore, but I grew up with it without knowing it. I grew up with Texas traditions."[62] Andera dates her own festival activism to the early 1970s when she first appeared as a Lebanese belly-dancer. As director, she insists that participants are "bona fide" ethnic groups, but allows those groups to define largely for themselves how to adapt their ethnicity to consumer demands.

ITC staff insist that exhibitors explain and demonstrate, not just sell their food. Andera says consultation between festival staff and participants helps prevent too many from offering nothing but hot dogs. Cotton candy, funnel cakes, and "Hawaiian shaved ice" do not appear on festival menus. In 1990, visitors could buy food coupons that purchased dishes of Alsatian, Belgian, British, Cajun, Chinese, Czech, Dutch, Filipino, German, Greek, Hungarian, Indian (Asia), Irish, Italian, Japanese, Jewish, Lebanese, Mexican, Polish, Scottish, Soul Food, Spanish, Swedish, and Wendish origin. They could eat Texas specialties—yams, chili, poultry, ice cream, chuck wagon, peanuts, and chicken fried steaks—served up by community groups like All Saints Episcopal Church and the San Antonio Pod of the Chili Appreciation Society.[63]

San Antonio's annual festival is as much a commercial success as is New York's Ninth Avenue Fair. These huge festivals, like the burgeoning sale of ethnic cookbooks, revealed the considerable consumer power of new ethnics. Regular businessmen too took notice of this new market niche. Selling ethnicity year round for profit reproduced in some respects the competition between corporate and enclave economies of the nineteenth century. But in these competitions, again, new ethnic consumers often preferred to buy from businessmen with ties to a specific ethnic community rather than from a corporation with no ethnic authenticity to its credit. The ethnic revival encourages, in turn, a revival of small businesses as a growing segment of the American economy.

Competition between food corporations and small-business purveyors of ethnic foods quickly heated up again in the 1970s under the impact of new market demands from new ethnic consumers. Typical is the story of pizza consumption during these years. Corporate Pizza Hut first encountered real problems in marketing its product when—lured by new ethnic dollars—it ventured out of the Midwest to try to sell pizza in the Northeast. There, unlike in its home city of Wichita, Italian-American businessmen had been selling pizza in large numbers to their multi-ethnic neighbors since the 1930s and 1940s. According to Jamie Coulter of Pizza Hut, "Pizza Hut originally went into the East with a thin crust, which is a cracker-thin crust, and a spicy sauce and once it operated there for a couple years it realized that the palate of the consumer was different in those markets. Eastern customers at Pizza Hut declared, 'This stuff isn't pizza, it's matzoh with cheese on it.'" Pizza Hut responded with a great deal of new market research, developing a "thick'n'chewy" pizza for eastern consumers who "did not like the midwestern style chain pizza."[64]

Eastern consumers who disliked Pizza Hut also found a new generation of immigrant entrepreneurs eager to sell them a pizza more to their taste, and to do so in a less corporate, more community-oriented ambience. In Connecticut and parts of eastern New York, recent arrivals from Greece became the new cross-over merchants of the pizza trade. Whereas Connecticut had only 152 pizzerias in the early 1950s (mainly operated by

Italians and Italian-Americans), by 1975 there were 482 of them, and 40 percent of these were operated by Greeks. By the 1980s, furthermore, 80 percent of Greek immigrant families in the state operated small businesses, and three quarters of these sold pizza. Greeks' pizza parlors successfully competed not only with Pizza Hut but with second- and third-generation Italians' pizzerias. While small Italian pizzerias prepared large quantities of dough, cutting it into standard pieces and then hand tossing and spreading each "pie to order," "Charlie" (the Greek from Albania who opened the first Connecticut Greek pizzeria in 1954) instead put dough ahead of time into 10 inch pans, preparing the entire day's supply of pizza crusts in the morning. (Pizza Hut used the same technique later in the Midwest.) Charlie developed a chain of pizzerias before moving on into a bakery equipment supply company that served Greeks' pizzerias.[65]

The recoupling of ethnic food with community-oriented business values—not just taste—made mom-and-pop pizzerias different from Pizza Hut. About his corporate competition, one Greek pizza operator noted, "I'm going to try the best for my customers, and that's it . . . If you make good pizza, or you take care of your customers, you never lose them. The Pizza Hut opened. Everybody go. Everybody they want to try it. And they told me, they went over there and they say, 'Don't ever change your pizza.' They still come back here."[66] Even in the Midwest, small mom-and-pop businessmen—some Italian, some Greek—succeeded in challenging Pizza Hut's near monopoly. Standardized costuming and interiors and bureaucratic fast-food encounters in Pizza Hut simply could not satisfy customers who associated ethnic food with ethnic businessmen—and with their personal approach to customer service.

Throughout the nation, new mom-and-pop restaurants, groceries, and hotels duplicated on a smaller and more geographically-dispersed scale the food businesses of older enclave economies. Many of their clients were new ethnic consumers seeking to purchase the foods, and associations, of the more personally satisfying ethnic communities of the past. In its promotional materials, the New York Hungarian-owned Paprika Weiss Importing Company acknowledged that their "family business has always operated to sell pleasant memories." By the 1970s, Paprika Weiss did much of its sales through mail order, its clientele "no longer a local one, but it is a faithful one."[67] Italian-American businesses, too, catered to the nostalgia of new ethnics; in Boston, a food store announced, "Welcome to the 19th century, we have no freezer."[68] Businesses like these lured new ethnics back to what remained of old ethnic neighborhoods. On Arthur and Allerton Avenues in the Bronx, pastry and sausage shops catered to Italian-American eaters dispersed throughout suburban Westchester County. As one customer unhappily noted in explaining his weekly pilgrimage south to the Bronx, "You can't get anything up there."[69]

Among American Jews, the new ethnicity was especially visible and pronounced, since returning to culinary roots in this group meant a growing interest in returning to orthodoxy and to kosher eating. When New Haven's popular kosher Crown Supermarket closed, its owner lamented, "People are crying, they're so sad to see us leave. It's like a family." But the market for kosher food had not disappeared with Crown, and the rabbi who supervised Crown's bakery remained optimistic: he already knew of several people who were working to start smaller versions of the Crown store. He concluded, "The Crown Supermarket has been an institution, a staple in the community, but Jews are very resilient people. They always come up with solutions to problems."[70] Indeed they did. While Catskill hotels like Grossinger's foundered, new Florida hotels opened, and according to one visitor, "The Catskills have nothing to compare."[71] A resident rabbi at the Hyatt Orlando guarantees that even such nouvelle dishes as poached salmon with tomato coulis and wild rice pancakes meet the conditions of kashruth. The rabbi at Crown Supermarkets was correct. In the cultural dynamics of the food marketplace, ethnicity seemed never to die. It continually assumed new forms, and generated new conflicts between corporate and more communal ways of doing business.

When new ethnics went in search of their roots, they published community cookbooks as a fundraising activity; in their search for authentic dishes and ingredients, they began to patronize new and old enclave businessmen; they revived festivals sponsored by small businesses and ethnic community institutions. They sought pizza from Greek pizza makers, not Pizza Hut, and tacos from a local, immigrant taqueria, not Taco Bell. New ethnic consumers spurned standardized foods mass-produced by major corporations as insufficiently tied to the communalism and personalism they sought along with their food. In short, they continued to guarantee that enclave and regional markets flourished in new forms—as new market niches or "segments"—within a national marketplace.

Here, again, however, ethnicity and American food industries appear linked, but in an uneasy cultural tension with each other. The early twentieth-century drive to "Americanize" enclave businessmen and consumers underwrote modern food industries' efforts to build a national market by standardizing consumer taste for their standardized products. They entered enclave markets, and competed with enclave businessmen, but did not destroy them. On the contrary, as corporations responded to enclave businessmen and consumers, they developed niche marketing strategies to sell to consumers with a diversity of tastes.

But corporate strategies did not themselves create the new ethnicity. It is true, as one critic of an ethnic food festival noted, that in a consumer society "to present ethnicity (or anything else) is to provide the public with an opportunity to purchase things."[72] Certainly new ethnics were enthusiastic consumers. But the history of their search for authentic foods "from the good old days" provides little evidence that corporate marketers themselves created the new ethnicity as a market segment. On the contrary, during the 1970s and 1980s, the ethnic and the corporate still remained somewhat at odds in the marketplace, and major corporations rarely monopolized new ethnic consumer dollars in new ethnic market segments.

The new ethnicity demonstrates that the association of food with culture and community repeatedly generates anticorporate initiatives, especially in the form of a strong market for small, immigrant businessmen who deliver food in an ambience flavored by enclave life. Immigrant minorities have long been over-represented as small businessmen in the U.S. economy; they are even more heavily represented in small-scale food production and retailing. In the nineteenth century, foreign tastes gave foreign-born entrepreneurs especially valuable cultural capital, and created quasi-monopoly market conditions for entrepreneurs in immigrant enclaves. The business cultures of enclaves—marked by personal clienteles and familist or communal forms of business organization—continue to contrast with the mores of corporate America down to the present, and to make small businesses attractive purveyors of ethnic authenticity to new ethnic consumers.

The rabbi at Crown Supermarket was right about the tenacity of ethnicity in yet another way. Just as new ethnics demanded foods from businessmen with ties to communities, new immigrants were again arriving in the United States in unprecedented numbers, creating new markets for entrepreneurs of their own kind. The 1980s would demonstrate, once again, that in the culinary world, the more things changed, the more they duplicated the patterns of the past. In the 1990s, American eaters' desire for the familiar remained in anxious balance with their search for the new. New immigrants guaranteed that both enclave markets and cross-over eating and business would remain characteristics of American life into the twenty-first century.

CHAPTER EIGHT

Nouvelle Creole

The passage of the Civil Rights Act of 1964 and the revision of U.S. immigration laws in 1965 opened a new era in ethnic relations in the United States—and a new round of ethnic exchanges in America's food markets. The newest groups of immigrants come from Asia, Latin America, and the Caribbean; they enter a United States now firmly dedicated to racial equality and cultural diversity, at least in the legal arena. In both these ways, the exchanges of the present differ from those of the past.

But in most other respects, the cultural and commercial dynamics of American eating remain surprisingly familiar. Like earlier immigrants, to-day's immigrants bring with them distinctive eating habits, unfamiliar to older Americans; these distinctive tastes continue to create enclave markets for immigrant entrepreneurs. Today, too, ethnic businessmen still create important economic niches for themselves as producers and retailers of food. The result? More diversity, new creoles, and American foodways again in rapid transformation.

As in the past, ambitious immigrant entrepreneurs often succeed by reaching out to multi-ethnic consumers with cross-over foods of appealing novelty. The taco is arguably the latest ethnic icon en route to status as an American food—sold and eaten everywhere by and to people of all ages and backgrounds. Yet only forty years ago, the owner of a Mexican restaurant in Minnesota had to teach public school classes on Mexican food in order to build a clientele for her tacos.[1] Will *satay* or jerked chicken be next? It seems possible. The cartoonist Jim Unger in 1988 was already poking fun at midwesterners who would not try Indian curries because they were foreign and "unpatriotic," even though they ate "spaghetti mostly."[2]

Today's ethnic businessmen nevertheless buy and sell in a world somewhat different from the past. Immigrants now cook and eat in a culture less interested in demonizing them than in enjoying their foods; it is hard to find, or even imagine, a modern-day counterpart of the home visitor who judged the degree of an immigrant's acculturation by the smells wafting from her kitchen. Even if consumers continue to choose selectively—snapping up tacos while disdaining menudo—ordinary Americans today are much more eager than in 1900 to entertain themselves with the culinary gifts of new immigrants. They also continue to explore and to modify the cuisines of older ethnic groups. And, for their part, today's immigrants are quickly discovering the microwave, take-out pizza, and Coca-Cola—if they did not already know them as American products in their homelands. Businessmen within ethnic enclaves and at the largest American corporations eagerly gauge the emergence of new ethnic market niches whose food dollars they pursue. Food fights and ethnic revivals—should they come—seem decades away. For now, Americans of many backgrounds seem content to continue looking into one another's pots—as they have for the past four hundred years.

As in the past, too, culinary exchanges vary considerably from region to region, thus shaping the evolution of regional American eating habits into the next century. Rural areas and the Midwest attract relatively few newcomers, while the sunbelt South faces for the first time the challenge of incorporating new immigrants. Culinary change is greatest in American cities, and especially those most affected by the new immigration. Miami, Los Angeles, and New York vie for the label of the city most transformed, but even Minneapolis has its new population of Hmong, and Charleston has its Central American construction workers and gardeners. As in the past, the mix of immigrants varies east, south, and west. West Coast cities house Mexicans, Central Americans, and new immigrants from across the Pacific—Chinese, Samoans, Filipinos. Miami has mixed Cubans, Central Americans, and Haitians. In New York, Dominicans and Puerto Ricans have crowded into old Jewish and Irish neighborhoods, while new arrivals from China have engulfed its Little Italy. Indians, Colombians, Russians, Haitians, and Jamaicans have completely revitalized older decaying neighborhoods, particularly in Queens and Brooklyn. In the New York suburbs, enclaves of Japanese and Korean businessmen have reminded New Yorkers that this was not just a migration of the "huddled masses." The inevitable food exchanges among these groups guarantee that American eating on the East Coast will continue to differ from that on the West Coast and in south Florida well into the future.

N ew York's new immigrant enclaves require many of the same services as immigrant enclaves in the nineteenth century, including imports from their homelands. West Indians, for example, demand freshness in the tropical fruits and vegetables they eat. As a result, the importation of tropical products by air from Jamaica has increased in recent years; 4 million pounds now go to New York and 14 million pounds to Miami. Still, small shops like Mara's West Indian Market in Brooklyn must struggle to deliver produce of the quality her customers seek. Another West Indian grocer explains, "Jamaicans like [breadfruit] when it is not fully ripe and brown. Even if picked green, it ripens rapidly and must be kept submerged in water or wrapped in plastic, or it will spoil immediately. Even so, it ripens so fast that much of it is unacceptable to Jamaicans in New York." Its price is also high. Will Florida-grown breadfruits follow?[3] Undoubtedly. In Maryland, a Vietnamese immigrant has begun manufacturing soy sauce to draw immigrants away from imported brands. As ambitious as earlier entrepreneurs, he told a reporter, "My dream is to become the Colonel Sanders of soy sauce."[4]

Immigration from Africa, the Caribbean, Latin America, and the Mideast has raised demand for goat meat, and rural entrepreneurs have responded in predictable ways. In Bladenboro, North Carolina—a rural area almost completely untouched by international migration—Ahsan Mohyuddin's Halal Meat and Food Corporation specializes in slaughtering goat according to Islamic law.[5] His market remains largely among the foreign born, and quite distant; so it seems unlikely that he and other goat processors will anytime soon challenge the hegemony of pork, particularly barbecued pork, in this part of the country.[6] As in the past, the eaters of the rural South (and to a lesser extent Southwest) remain more tied to the creoles of the Columbian exchanges than much of the rest of the nation.

Similarly, it seems unlikely that long-time Americans will be drawn to the new markets for live poultry that again dot New York's poorer neighborhoods. "We're used to live ones," a woman from Ghana explained as she bought from a Bronx storefront replete with squawking birds and men in butchers' smocks. Once popular among New York's Jewish and Italian consumers, fresh poultry markets in New York saw their numbers plummet from about 200 in the 1930s to fewer than 20 in the 1970s. But numbers climbed again with new immigration. According to a reporter accustomed to supermarket shopping, these markets "resemble a cross between pet shops and automobile garages, with hundreds of birds stacked in cages in cavernous, unadorned rooms."[7]

Small groceries catering to immigrant consumers in New York, like their earlier counterparts, quickly become important community centers. They also compete rather successfully with the city's chain supermarkets. Bodegas began appearing with Puerto Rican settlers in the 1930s; Cubans operated large numbers in the 1960s and 1970s, while the huge migration from the Dominican Republic make this group the most important among 8,000 New York bodega-keepers today. When they first opened their businesses, Dominican grocers became "like part of the extended family, when everybody knew each other and credit was honored," according to one customer. Or, in the words of Michale Concepcion, "A bodeguero has to treat people with love." They market the soft drinks, white cheese, plantains, pigeon peas, rice, beans, olive oil, goat, pigs' heads, and boliche that customers demand. Easy credit disappeared, however, as these small businessmen expanded, adding frozen food compartments and regular American produce. Like grocers of the past, Dominican grocers also cooperated, forming organizations like the Metro Spanish Food Wholesalers (founded in the Bronx in 1967) to purchase products in bulk. With such support, small businessmen remain optimistic that they will continue to compete with the larger chains: it has been estimated that New York's Hispanic families spend 55 percent of their food dollars in bodegas.[8] The fact that chain supermarkets hesitate to compete for low-income consumers, who generate very slim profit margins, contributes as well to the strength of the bodega in immigrant enclaves.

Even when firmly part of an enclave economy, New York's immigrant food entrepreneurs are nevertheless also busy adapting the foods of their homelands in response to local market availability and to the changing tastes and composition of their consumers. An Egyptian restaurateur confessed that while his mother "made melokhia from the fresh leaves of the actual melokhia plant that grew in her backyard in Cairo," he instead uses a prewashed, precut, frozen variety imported from Egypt. He buys the ingredient in Middle Eastern grocery stores. The same man confesses that he no longer forms falafel balls by hand, since consumers will accept mechanically produced ones.[9]

But he does eat hamburgers, and enjoys them. Immigrants' adaptation to American dishes often began before they left home, so ubiquitous have corporate purveyors of American fast food become around the world. Recently arrived foreign students, for example, reported little difficulty in eating the new foods they encountered in the United States in the 1970s, even though three-quarters of them also missed homeland foods. Most Asians in this group ate western-style breakfasts and snacks, but large numbers, regardless of background or previous cooking experience, chose to prepare an evening meal in order to produce approximations of what they might have eaten at home.[10] Many Cambodian families, too, adopt American food for breakfast and lunch, while eating Cambodian-style foods from a plastic tablecloth arranged on the floor in the evening; the children accompany their meal, however, with Sprite and precede their meal with a sweet cereal—Kix. West Indian families in New York today mix black-American traditions with those of the Caribbean for Thanksgiving, serving mashed turnips, turkey with bread dressing, cranberry sauce, and apple pie, alongside plantains, saltfish, and red snapper.[11] In modern-day San Antonio, "tamales meet the turkey"—in a turkey stuffed with tamale dressing. All these forms of adaptation occurred in immigrant homes in earlier generations, too.

Cross-over eating regularly occurs among recently arrived immigrants. In the Queens neighborhood of Elmhurst, residents openly talk of their community as a melting pot or mixing bowl. There Louie Antonio (a

Greek) operates Singa's Famous Pizza restaurant; most of his customers are immigrants recently arrived from India. A *New York Times* visitor to his multi-ethnic neighborhood repeats the slogans of the American Folklife Festival, insisting that food shopping is "a means to learn English, a way to feel at home, a chance to experiment, to bridge between vastly different cultures." The owner of the nearby El Molino Panaderia Argentina Confiteria (which sells Argentine breakfast pastries, characteristic flat sandwiches, and caramel-filled pastries) is a Korean, Sung Hong. But most daily customers at El Molino stop in to buy a croissant or bagel before work. "I don't know why," Paul Hong told a reporter, "but my father learned everything he knows at a Jewish bakery."[12] In familiar fashion, today's cross-overs resemble those of the past in including food, businessmen, and consumers of many backgrounds.

Somewhere in this Queens neighborhood, or ones like it, the twenty-first century equivalents of New York deli—the new foods that will symbolize the city or region—are probably now being bought and sold. In the South, observers have already identified Miami's Cuban sandwich as a ready symbol of south Florida's regional cuisine.[13] Calling their cuisine Nuevo Cubano or New World cooking, Cuban chefs take tropical ingredients and the ethnic foods of earlier immigrant generations—notably pizza and pasta—and use American cooking techniques, especially grilling and smoking, to create Florida dishes like blackened red snapper with orange sauce and key lime pasta. Says restaurateur Efrain Veiga, "All these ingredients were here just waiting to be used in different ways."[14] The participants of the Columbian exchanges could not have said it better four hundred years ago.

As innovative as their earlier counterparts, immigrant inventors of cross-over foods continue to compete quite successfully with fast food franchises in multi-ethnic cities. As business analysts have noted, "The gleaming McDonald's assembly line is not substantially more productive than the traditional diner," and, in any case, it is not in production efficiencies that McDonald's realizes its profits.[15] In New York, Chinese restaurants in particular continue to attract attention for their equally assembly-line production. One *New York Times* writer labeled an 8000-square-foot commercial kitchen that produced 100 varieties of dim sum an "infernal machine."[16]

Low prices remain the key to success in immigrant businesses. So does family labor. Family restaurants in Dominican or Chinese neighborhoods of New York are well known for their low wages, poor benefits, and limited job security, at least for workers who are not relatives.[17] But the same is true in fast-food franchises, which have the highest rates of labor turnover of any American employers. While the discrepancy between executive earnings and those of female, minority, and teenage workers are enormous in companies like McDonald's, this is scarcely a source of conflict in family-run businesses. And unlike the waiters and kitchen help in Chinese and Greek restaurants, few McDonald's workers expect to open their own restaurant someday with expertise learned on the job.

Nationwide, consumers of inexpensive meals spend $29 billion in small mom-and-pop restaurants and $23 billion in fast food chains. One study of new immigrants in New York concluded that New Yorkers patronize national fast food chains less often than other urban dwellers precisely because family-based, small-scale ethnic restaurants provide tastier, more varied fast food, at prices only slightly higher than big corporations. According to Elizabeth Bogen, "New Yorkers seem willing to pay for their tastes," and "it is hard for a national chain to meet the widely diverse food tastes of New York's ethnically mixed population. Those tastes are more easily served by small, locally owned specialty shops."[18]

Managers of the warehouses that service national grocery chains also admit they are hard pressed to stock the range of products on their shelves that New Yorkers demand. Their difficulties leave open a market niche for smaller, more specialized, often immigrant competitors. Nor is this phenomenon completely new. During the frenzy of chain-grocery-store expansion in the 1930s, 28 percent of grocery retailers still operated out of their living quarters and had no employees except family members. A study at that time concluded that these stores "lead all known retail organizations in economy of operation."[19] Members of enclaves still seem to understand and to target the tastes of multi-ethnic urban markets more effectively than corporate readers of *American Demographics*. The long hours worked by "Mom and Pop" keep their groceries as competitive as their restaurants.

American tastes also remain firmly regional, even after one hundred years of cross-country transportation and trade. Americans in the Northeast consume five times more pasta than those in the Southwest. Fried fish is a popular fast food in the Southeast and Northwest but not in the South Central or Rocky Mountain states. Fried chicken still enjoys its strongest regional market in the South, though its ethnic market is probably strongest among black Americans throughout the nation.[20]

Corporations geared to mass production for a national market must take these regional differences into account if they are to succeed. In the 1970s market research showed, for example, that, nationwide, 40 percent of Americans like a thin-crust pizza, 40 percent like a thick-crust pizza, and 20 percent recognize no difference. The Northeast was thin-crust pizza territory, but within 100 miles of Long Island, along the New York/Connecticut border, Pizza Hut had to develop three different varieties of pizza crust and sauce to compete successfully with smaller pizzerias. And in Cincinnati, McDonald's reluctantly concluded it had to introduce a fish sandwich or lose all its numerous Catholic consumers on Friday to Big Boy's.[21] Chesebrough-Pond discovered that southerners wanted a "thick and hearty variety" of their Ragu sauce (purchased for $43.8 million in 1969 from its developers Giovanni and Assunta Cantisano of Rochester), while Californians preferred the much lighter Ragu Fino Italian.[22]

Today as in the past, the street vendor still seems closer to cross-over consumers' complex and regional taste buds than corporate America, and this petty entrepreneur often continues to introduce novelties and low-cost culinary adventure. Most of New York's 7,754 licensed food vendors are recently arrived immigrants. They sell the snacks of Mexico and dozens of other countries alongside long-time "American" specialties: pretzels, crab rolls, Philippine lumpia, pickles, knishes, empanadas, calzones, gyros.[23] A fairly typical vendor is Tony Stanacich, who despite his South Slav name, is an Argentinean dishing up burritos, tacos, and "Acapulco salad"—all Mexican-inspired dishes—to those in search of a fast lunch near Wall Street. "Beethoven played the piano, but the piano maker was Italian," Stanacich concluded, trying to explain the multi-ethnic blend he represents. Competitors to Stanacich's Latin foods include West Indian roti, served up by the Badall family (who came to Brooklyn from Trinidad), and pizza from Hispanic vendors working for a small chain of street pizza carts owned by Michael Paparo, an Italian-American.[24]

"Fast food makes good business," said Afghani Mohammad K. Rouzyi about the food he serves from a pushcart, and later in the day from his own restaurant: flat bread, kebabs, and grilled chicken. But to sell in multi-ethnic New York, even Mr. Rouzyi has had to adapt his cooking. "If you want real Afghan cooking you come to my home," he recommended. For his restaurants, he chose simple dishes, reducing the seasoning and the size of his flatbread. He worries that Americans will think of Afghanistan as a land only of kofta and chicken, flat bread and kebabs. And he is aware that Americans will not eat this food as his fellow Afghanis might. Nearby, in an Israeli restaurant, for example, tourists from Israel amused themselves watching American students eat a common Israeli breakfast bread as an accompaniment to their evening meal. And visitors from Italy cannot understand the American penchant for drinking cappuccino (a morning coffee in Italy) at any time of the day or night.[25]

While market exchanges are slowly pushing urban eating in New York, San Antonio, and Los Angeles toward new creoles, national attention continues to focus instead on consumers' interest in foods and drinks still firmly labeled as ethnic. Cross-over eating became so popular among Americans in the 1970s and 1980s that food writers, cultural critics, and business analysts alike talked about a nationwide craze for ethnic foods. They identified the fad with young, well-educated consumers—baby-boomers all—who fall roughly into two groups: the hippies and political activists of the 1960s–1970s generation, and the young urban professionals (yuppies) of the 1980s, who included both recent law school graduates and ex-hippies and activists moving toward comfortable, middle-class, middle-aged lives. Probably the most surprising cross-over enthusiasm among hippies and yuppies was not a dish introduced by a new immigrant group but a drink: wine. Inexplicably and rather suddenly, hippies in the 1970s and yuppies in the 1980s made wine a totally acceptable and even stylish American beverage, as popular with middle-class Americans as lager beer had been one hundred years earlier.

The change was a long time coming from the days when robber barons and the urban elite preferred French imports and when only immigrants and bohemians drank domestic "dago red." Key players were the largely Italian, Italian-American, and German vintners of California, who survived Prohibition by producing grape juice, sacramental wines, table grapes, and "wine bricks" (for home wine manufacture) and held tenaciously to dreams of expanding markets. Their sons surveyed the wreckage of Prohibition, tested the marketplace, and in the late 1930s began to modernize. Seventeen of the 32 men listed as "wine pioneers" of the modern California wine industry had technical or scientific training, many at the University of California at Davis or Berkeley.[26] Others proved adept at reorganizing family businesses to produce a safe and standard product for national distribution.

Men like California's Mondavi, Gallo, Rossi, Petri, Mirassou, Martini, Lanza, Fromm, and Cella had fathers, or even longer family traditions, in winemaking. Family ties continued to be important in the post-Prohibition world, but they assumed new forms. Often brothers or brothers-in-law shared management of family businesses—as did Peter and Robert Mondavi, Ernesto and Julio Gallo, Otto Meyer and Alfred Fromm, and Norbert and Edmund Mirassou. In each family, one man, the technician, specialized in winemaking, while the other pursued new marketing strategies or oversaw the reorganization of the business as a shareholder-owned corporation. In most cases the winemaking brother stayed with his machines and in the fields because he strongly disliked corporate life. Elie C. Skofis summed up this feeling: "I was a winemaker; I wasn't going to become an officeman, even though I realized there was a lot of good things about it."[27]

Sometimes disagreements rooted in the differing concerns of technically educated winemakers and their market-oriented brothers threatened to destroy family businesses. For example, all the children of Cesare Mondavi worked at some point in their family business, begun in 1923. In 1943 the Mondavis bought the Krug winery, and two sons, Robert and Peter, transformed the business into one of California's leading producers of wines. When father Cesare died, mother Rosa, now president of the company, invited a widowed brother to come and live with her and manage the company. Rosa Mondavi remained a businesswoman on traditional models. She oversaw the business from her kitchen, and cooked meals for board members and business clients. Her sons developed diverging opinions typical in winemaking and marketing sibling teams. Quarrels between Peter and Robert over corporate strategy resulted in divisive law suits, which were ongoing when Rosa died in 1976. Similar family feuds shook other producers of bulk wines, notably the Gallo brothers. Frequently, the company stabilized only when its ownership went public and outsiders assumed management.

During World War II, when wine imports were disrupted, California's winemakers insisted that they could produce wines equal to Europe's. But as long as their main product was bulk wine sold in large jugs in supermarkets, mostly to immigrants, bohemians, and winos, they had a hard time convincing knowledgeable consumers (who could afford to drink expensive imports) that this was so. Beginning in the mid-1960s, California's vineyards changed their marketing strategy. They expanded production and started targeting college-age Americans, who traditionally had preferred beer—mostly because it could be drunk in large quantities for comparatively little expense. Jug wines, which had similar attributes, began to make inroads among college-educated baby boomers in the late 1960s and early 1970s. Young, and still living on limited incomes at the time, hippies and college students associated wine with the peasant cuisines they also admired. As they aged and their incomes rose, they provided a market for California producers of finer wines.

By the early 1970s, new and younger winemakers—few of them with family ties or ethnic traditions linking them to winemaking—began to raise standards and prices for California wines. These new "boutique vintners," following the example of European vintners, focused on developing fine wines for Americans with cultivated palates, familiarity with imported wines, and money to spare. They also began to dream of exporting their wares to Europe. In the 1980s, restaurateurs did their part to expand wine drinking by selling wine by the glass to consumers identified as yuppies; this made wine a standard option for sophisticated diners who did not want beer, Coke, or water with their meal but who rarely thought to order a whole bottle of wine either. Growth in wine sales fueled corporate competition and consolidation, and it also led to innovation and change in the late 1980s, as wine consumption reached a plateau and wine-coolers, spritzers, natural waters, and a bewildering variety of "New Age" drinks were introduced to compete with beer and wine as American recreational drinks.

Class distinctions in American drinking habits came sharply into focus with the decline of beer drinking and the rise in wine consumption in the 1970s. One study demonstrated that among women, "Wine drinkers are better educated and younger, with a higher income" than moderate users of beer, who are less secure financially and more involved with popular culture.[28] For hippies and yuppies—two comparatively affluent market segments—wine drinking went hand-in-hand with ethnic eating, and together they symbolized both a hedonist and nutritional critique of American eating habits. These same consumers also sought ethnic foods quite different from the humble, down-home foods that pleased new ethnics in the 1970s.

Hippies, as well as the yuppies and New Agers who followed and were influenced by them, viewed peasant cuisines from around the world as healthful and earth-friendly, unlike the preservative-laden, resource-gobbling, wastefully-packaged, homogeneous processed foods churned out by impersonal and perhaps immoral giant food corporations. Some hippies and their followers saw ethnic cooking as "a protest against American cultural imperialism around the globe,"[29] or a critique of capitalism. They objected to what they saw as the international corporations' exploitation of labor, their expropriation of other countries' resources, and their negative impact on the rainforest and other environments.

A boom in counter-cultural consumer cooperatives—sometimes built on their ethnic, left-wing predecessors, especially in the upper Midwest—occurred during the 1970s, and remnants of that movement can still be found in most large cities today. Hippies' concern with how food was produced opened new opportunities for communal forms of production. Thus, the Santa Ana Indians and the nearby villages that formed the Five Sandoval Indian Pueblos incorporated to grow blue corn, a discovery of New Age eaters in the 1980s. With revenues of $40,000 and profits of $7,000, they hoped to triple their business under the leadership of Denis Robinson. Robinson noted that the tribes "would like to become contract growers for a major processor or even make their own consumer products," although they still sold much of their corn through Indian fairs and advertisements in organic-gardening magazines. This change would require them to begin using contemporary farm machinery, Robinson admitted, and this would hasten their evolution toward corporate styles of business.[30]

Ethnic foods underwent yet another round of transformation to meet the health standards of the most nutritionally minded of young American consumers in first regional, then national, markets. In Michigan's Upper

Peninsula, health food stores and some pasty shops began to prepare vege-tarian pasties and pasties with whole wheat crusts.[31] As Warren Belasco has noted, anticorporate types of the 1970s successfully nudged American corporations to deliver the kinds of ethnic foods they wanted. Nearly half of Conagra's Healthy Choice frozen entrees now have ethnic flavor-ings; Campbell Soup's health-conscious "le Menu" brand includes His-panic and Asian flavors.[32] A 1994 controversy sparked articles with titles like "At Mexican Restaurants, Hold the Fat, Not the Taste" and "A Who's Who in Health Mex.[33] Corporations responded with "lite" ethnic foods that one southwestern wag labeled "fern mex." Even the Mexican-Ameri-can-owned El Chico restaurants stopped using lard for masa dough and tamales because of consumer resistance to animal fat.[34]

For some counter-cultural Americans, seeking a healthier way to eat returned them to their own ethnic traditions. Vegetarian and healthful versions of ethnic foods developed alongside the traditional ethnic fare offered at food festivals and featured in community cookbooks in the 1970s. For American Jews, a vegetarian tradition had been articulated a century before, in the 1880s and 1890s. The deeply rooted habits of kashruth, which separated meat and milk, in poorer communities gener-ally had required limited consumption of meat.

The Jewish Vegetarians of North America distributed a newsletter to hundreds of members in the 1980s, and the well-known Jewish vegetarian Jonathan Wolf, an Orthodox Jew, began teaching courses on "Judaism and Vegetarians" and celebrating the sabbath and other Jewish holidays with vegetarian meals. Vegetarian Jews on Passover could even turn to a "Hag-gadah for the Liberated Lamb" that reminded them that "vegetarianism is less a break with tradition than a return to an historical trend."[35] Maureen Goldsmith, who called herself a "twenty-five-year-old hippie-type young woman of Jewish ancestry (healthy Russian stock)," not only became a vegetarian but emphasized natural foods in her cookbook *The Organic Yenta*. She reported to those wishing to follow her recipes that "along with my change to natural foods has come a rebirth in my interest in Jewish cooking . . . I began to go back over my life to remember milchig meals we used to have when I was a little girl."[36]

Educated, well-traveled, and enjoying a higher income than most hip-pies had as young people in the early 1970s, yuppies in the 1980s searched more often for authentic and exotic, than healthy, ethnic food. Chef Boyardee spaghetti and Pizza Hut pizza were not what these savvy consumers had eaten in the quaint *trattorie* of Italy. Neither was the food offered at ethnic festivals and in many community cookbooks: Chow mein and spaghetti and meatballs failed the test of authenticity on yuppie palates. As critics noted, "They preferred to eat the latest from abroad rather than the culinary left-overs of *immigrant* cultures."[37] Their search for foreign, haute, or at least nouvelle cuisine created new opportunities for foreign-born and trained immigrant chefs. Typical were very young men, like Pascal Dirringer from Alsace, who at age 25 had already worked twelve years in great restaurants in France when he took a job at New York's Gauloise. "A chef has to know everything," he lectured, while one of his young, slightly more experienced colleagues at Palace concurred. "You have to get your base first before you can paint like Picasso."[38] One hundred years ago, young chefs like this would have worked at Delmonico's and served robber barons, who were the big spenders of their era.

When yuppies ordered dinner, however, their motives seemed as much like those of bohemians as of robber barons. For yuppies, like bohemians, a food columnist noted, "Eating is a form of travel, and no matter how high the price of cardamom, taste-bud tourism is a real bargain."[39] In Atlanta, the Imperial Fez Moroccan restaurant trumpeted its own exoticism: "Imperial Fez is a place for people of nostalgic and romantic dreams." Their advertising blurb cited a review that urged people to "take a mini-vacation to Morocco" and to "leave your shoes and inhibitions behind." Business analysts accustomed to thinking of the marketplace in demographic terms, at least since the 1960s, began to call the yuppie segment an example of "psychographics, not demographics." Market analyst Harry Balzer reported to his colleagues that "the only growth area in dining out is in the Asian and Mexican sector," because these cuisines meet baby boomers' "appetite for exotica" and perhaps allow them to relive—on a more lavish scale and at a higher price—their experience as $5-a-day backpackers, sampling the native cuisines of the world.[40]

Even well-educated professionals needed guidance in exploring new cuisines and other developments in the restaurant industry. Help came from many directions. In the 1990s the Naples Pizza Association and Milan's Associazione Pizzaioli Europei e Sostenitori visited the United States and agreed that American pizzas failed to meet their ten rules, which included a list of classic pizza ingredients. These rules gave thumbs-down to Sicilian- or Chicago-style deep-dish pizzas as well as to the focaccia and other flat breads of central and northern Italy. Still they noted, "Variations on the classics, which are inspired by tradition and fantasy, are accepted, provided they are not in conflict with the rules of good taste and culinary laws." Presumably pizza with shiitake mushrooms and Canadian bacon failed this test.[41]

Adventurous eaters in search of authenticity turned as well to academics and to native-born interpreters of foreign cuisines, like Diana Kennedy. After writing an authoritative study of Mexico's regional cuisines, Kennedy surveyed New York's Mexican restaurants, and found almost all lacking. They were, she warned readers, "more Mexican-inspired than authentically Mexican." After recommending three city restaurants to truly discriminating diners, Kennedy dismissed the rest for their "odd, eclectic and ineffective" food, and rejected Mexican pizza, fruit-flavored margaritas, and Montezuma croissants as examples of culinary experimentation gone awry. One Mexican restaurateur she interviewed, however, humbly reminded Kennedy of the market pressures he faced. Apologizing for tortilla chips on the table, he explained, "I have to do it that way. Our customers expect it."[42]

What Kennedy disdained, other up-scale New York consumers demanded. Much of it was "fusion food"—the nouvelle, and often pricey and faddish, creoles of the 1980s, often associated with California chefs. Yuppies could explore Alice Waters's or Wolfgang Puck's California fusions of Asian, Mediterranean, and regional American cuisines, all made with the finest organically grown California ingredients. They could sample the Asian/Italian blends of "Ciao Mein" at the Hyatt Regency at Waikiki. They could exalt in San Francisco chefs' explorations of Pacific Rim culture as a unique fusion cuisine, where sweet and salty marinades of Asia become attached to American grill and barbecue traditions, and where the hot and spicy foods of Asia meet the hot and spicy foods of Mexico and the American Southwest.

The yuppies' fascination with ethnicity in authentic or nouvelle forms eventually spread to more modest consumers in the mass marketplace. Ethnic and foreign foods invaded the middle-management coffee room of the comic-strip character Cathy, who "nuked" Thai food one day to cover up the smell of huevos rancheros prepared earlier by a colleague. Cathy complained that the day before, "Eveline had the burrito. I know because I had to disinfect the microwave before I made my pasta primavera." "Which, thank you very much, made my stuffed flounder taste like broccoli!" complained a third office mate. Cathy's boss, Mr. Pinkley, upset by the pretensions of his office staff, yelled, "What's wrong with you people?? Whatever happened to bringing a sandwich?" But Cathy soothed him with the voice of a midmarket yuppie wannabe: "There, there Mr. Pinkley, let me fix you a nice steamy bowl of chili."

Consumers like Cathy never traveled the world on $5 a day or shopped barefoot in '70s hippie food cooperatives; neither did they have the disposable income of yuppie consumers. For her, too, eating for adventure might require guidance, and one introduction to moderate-priced ethnic dinners promised "fearless dining in ethnic restaurants," which might otherwise be intimidating.[43] It is easy to imagine Cathy and her office co-workers enjoying an occasional lunch out at Benihana of Tokyo, with its knife-swinging tableside chefs. Here was a modern reminder of novelty's appeal in ethnic disguise. Benihana's was founded by Hiroaki (Rocky) Aoki, who came to the United States in 1959 as a college student and "discovered . . . that Americans enjoy eating in exotic surroundings but are deeply mistrustful of exotic foods." Modifying Japanese hibachi cooking (learned from his father, an owner of a chain of restaurants in Japan), Aoki promised "no icky, sticky, slimy stuff" and offered three "Middle American entrees— steak, chicken, shrimp." Japanese touches were architectural (his restaurants are built of old disassembled Japanese houses) and theatrical. His chefs were trained in Japan and learned to portray what Benihana advertising called "A man dressed like a chef but with the unmistakable air of a samurai warrior."[44]

Because it now appealed to almost all Americans, from the richest to the poor, ethnic food was a large segment of the food industry, which— with sales of $70 billion already in the 1970s—had become the third largest of American industries. Americans left $53 billion a year on the counters of inexpensive restaurants—$23 billion at the large fast-food chains but $29 billion at smaller ethnic and regional mom-and-pop restaurants. They spent another $10 billion in moderate-priced restaurants, including $4 billion in ethnic restaurants, and another $7 billion at expensive restaurants.

By the 1980s ethnic restaurants constituted 10 percent of all restaurants in the country, although they were most prominent in the Northeast and West. Chinese food made up 30 percent of the total, and the three cuisines of China, Italy, and Mexico represented 70 percent of all ethnic restaurants.[45] In every part of the country, chain restaurants also offered two or more cuisines, sometimes in combinations like "Mediterranean." French and Italian might appear together on a menu, or Spanish, Mexican, Greek, or kosher together with soul. Corporate restaurant chains tried to succeed with fusion dishes as diverse as Oriental- (or Mexican- or Italian-) filled potato skins or Gianni's Little Italy Blackened (that is, Cajun-style) Chicken Broccoli Alfredo. Or, for a still smaller tab, Americans in the immigrant-poor South could eat at Applebees, which experimented with Chinese stir-fry fajita-style, finished at the table; their advertising campaign called the food "stir crazy."[46]

Outside the restaurant industry, food writers have sought to educate customers interested in exploring ethnic food at home and on their own without the pressure of performing properly in a restaurant. In 1985 and 1986, in a number of articles, the food writer Nancy Jenkins instructed *New York Times* readers about "tracking down Oriental ingredients" and exploring New York's ethnic markets "in pursuit of the perfect ingredient." The suburbanite Vilma Chantiles combined similar guidance with recipes in her 1984 book, *The New York Ethnic Food Market*.

For yet more modest pocketbooks, far from the multi-ethnic groceries and restaurants of New York and Miami, other food writers have provided instructions for creating fusion cuisine in one's own kitchen, using corporate products. In the traditionally more conservative South, Jane Snow showed readers of the *Charlotte Observer* how to make "rapid ravioli" using frozen wonton wrappers. The food section of that day's newspaper also contained a recipe for "black-eyed peas and Chinese greens over rice," billed as the "ultimate fusion dish." It was indeed a three-way fusion of southern, Asian, and Mexican: its ingredients included jalapeno and serrano chiles.

Corporate processors quickly caught the fusion-food trend that had begun in upscale restaurants. One newspaper advertising flyer urged consumers to "have your meat loaf 3 ways—Italian, spicy, [or] cajun with salsa." Months before, the same page urged its southern readers to "try another mom's meat loaf for a change." Recipes included "tejano picadillo loaf," "Polish-style meat loaf," and "spicy sauerbraten meat loaf."[47] Food conglomerates saw fusion dishes as an ideal way to market several product lines at once: thus the invention and marketing of biscuit-topped Italian casserole (using Hungry Jack Buttermilk Biscuits, Sargento mozzarella, and frozen green beans). Doritos offered "Pizza Hut"-flavored tortilla chips for "pizza cravers." Fiesta marketed nacho-flavored bagel bites. Advertising flyers recommended Fettucine Alfredo Hamburger Helper, and Godfather's Taco Pizza or Beef Tortilla Pizza (which used a tortilla as pizza crust). American consumers were urged to transform frozen pierogies into a Mexican dish with salsa or picante sauce and to try Velveeta Italiana (with "the mild flavor of mozzarella and parmesan cheeses"). Coordinating marketing for their several ethnic labels, corporations couponed Azteca flour tortillas with County Line shredded taco cheddar and monterey jack for a special Cinco de Mayo advertising campaign.

Corporate production has made salsa the American success story of recent years, dethroning ketchup as the king of American condiments in total sales in 1991. The process took fifty years. Salsa's corporate story replicates that of many other ethnic foods. The first mass producer of salsa was Pace Foods of San Antonio, and its market was local. Founder Dave Pace was a native of San Antonio but not a Mexican-American. His company began bottling and selling salsa in 1948. Pace knew the market in San Antonio, where even Anglo eating habits reflected the long history of exchanges with Mexican consumers and marketers in the region. But mastering the technology of mass manufacturing for distant markets was more complex. He explained, "In '47, my sauce bottles exploded all over the grocery shelves because I couldn't get the darned formula right." Pace Picante Sauce remained popular mainly in parts of the Southwest until, according to one analyst, "the hippies came along" and business exploded.[48]

Searching for the ethnic origins of the rapidly spreading product in the mid-1970s, the Texas writer Randall Benham visited the Pace facilities.

He found a business managed (and soon to be owned) by Christopher (Kit) Goldsbury, the socially prominent Spanish-speaking son of a hacendado in Mexico—Dave Pace's son-in-law. The spice expert at Pace was a man named Lou Rasplicka, popularly known to his colleagues as "Dr. Pepper." Goldsbury explained the strategy behind the company's expansion into a mass market: "Our marketing philosophy is that people should put the sauce on anything that doesn't move. Sure, our name is Mexican; I guess I'll have to admit that. But we'd drop the word 'picante' in a minute if it wasn't already too late."[49]

In a familiar pattern, Campbell Soups acquired Pace Foods in 1994, when it was "the world's largest producer of Mexican sauces."[50] Pace had already turned down bids from Heinz and from Lea & Perrins. The deal cost Campbell's $1.1 billion. Other salsa producers (Old El Paso, Ortega) had already been bought by other corporate giants. Corporate observers did joke about the odd mix of corporate cultures brought together through the Pace buy-out, but they saw it as a Southwest/Northeast clash, not a Mexican/Anglo one: Would Pace executives wear their cowboy boots to the traditionally conservative Cambell's corporate center founded by the Dorrance family of Philadelphia's Main Line, or would they adopt the uniform pin-stripe suits associated with East Coast corporate life?[51]

In any case, Campbell Soups made no change in Goldsbury's marketing philosophy. "Pace belongs on everything except ice cream," it insisted. Apparently consumers agreed: "Thanks to their sharp taste and low fat count, the fast-growing Mexican sauces have been appearing on everything from pizzas to bagels."[52] Salsa producers began their own fusion experiments: One writer found Bubba Brand Y'Alsa (made with okra and black-eyed peas) and Grandma's Recipe Rugelach's El Rancho, a jalapeno jelly pastry billed as a Jewish-Mexican dessert.[53] In 1996 Pace even trumpeted its development of a "heatless" jalapeno pepper.

Some corporate analysts, aware of the growing Hispanic population of the United States, assumed that other Mexican-origin foods would follow in the wake of salsa. The milling industry's national newsletter predicted that tortillas would soon stand "bag to bag with bread in supermarkets and become a staple in American kitchens." That certainly seems possible in a country where people like Lisa Wong, the granddaughter of a Chinese immigrant and the operator of two popular Mexican restaurants in San

Antonio, can declare, "I was brought up with tortillas, and they are like sliced bread to me." Her grandmother even made them.[54]

But "becoming American" has traditionally required mass production. Some point out that tortilla factories were operating in San Antonio as early as the 1920s, while others trace factory manufacturing of tortillas only to the late 1960s when El Chico's Restaurant began making them for their chain. Will those with cultural expertise dominate production for the mass market, as they clearly do not for salsa? Some, at least, are trying to survive the stiff competition of a booming market. In Austin, two major tortilla factories are owned by in-laws Ernestine Galindo (of "El Galindo," with 80 percent of its grocery-store customers Anglos) and Joe Galindo (of El Lago, which markets mainly to Mexican restaurants).[55] If past patterns hold, however, it will be General Foods or Beatrice or Pet, not El Galindo or El Lago, that brings tortillas to the mass market, making them, finally, firmly American.

W ith more, and new, ethnic foods both popular and en route to becoming American through mass production or incorporation in new regional creoles, culinary Americanization in the late twentieth century does not duplicate the food fights of the century's early decades. Some things have, in fact, changed. When *The New York Times* reported on a culinary assimilation program for Westchester County immigrants, they featured a group of suburban Larchmont housewives who opened their homes regularly to Japanese neighbors to teach them how to make peanut butter and jelly sandwiches and pot roast. One participant said of the Japanese women, "They have to get hip because their children are plunged into the mainstream of American society . . . It's hard, and they're fed up." Many of the Japanese women believed that Americans put no time or effort into meal preparation and eat only fast foods. The housewives aimed to change that stereotype, by taking the Japanese women on trips to shop for food ingredients at local supermarkets. According to Lauren Groveman, the teacher of the class, some immigrant women "will travel miles to a Japanese grocery store just to buy a can of Campbell's soup that is written in Japanese letters." Quite unlike past Americanization courses, these upscale Japanese immigrant women paid $350 to attend five classes.[56]

Culinary Americanization work now more often emphasizes immigrant gifts and cross-cultural communication than the benefits of American food. Cornmeal and codfish have almost completely disappeared from nutritionists' lists of healthy foods. In a YMCA program for refugees at Eglin Air Force Base in Florida in spring and summer 1975, newcomers from Southeast Asia received instead a quick introduction to ethnic pride, American style. YMCA workers encouraged the refugees to produce a cookbook (*Happy in My Stomach: Toi vui trong Long*) as "one way of building a bridge of understanding" between the two cultures.[57] Social workers with low-income clients planned a cooking school for Vietnamese and attempted to show their clients how to prepare American and Vietnamese-style meals on a limited budget, but their guidebook urged them to "remember the importance of fellowship," for cooking "brings people together for both learning and fellowship."[58]

Dieticians and health workers continue to offer nutritional education, but they are careful to tailor it to the particular ethnic group. The Office of Navajo Economic Opportunity, through its Emergency Food-Navajo Homemaker Program, advised Native-American women on how to use commodity foods donated by the U.S. Department of Agriculture, and included pictorial recipes for modified native dishes and "guidelines for a good cook and homemaker" in its cookbook. Projects like Healthy Black People (of the West Tennessee Area Health Education Center in Somerville, Tennessee) suggest how to modify southern diets to diminish salt and fat intake, reminding African-American clients of their particularly high rates of hypertension and heart disease. During the 1990s the American Dietetic Association, together with the American Diabetic Association, published a series on "Ethnic and Regional Food Practices" which explained ethnic foodways to healthcare workers, so they could in turn help patients adapt traditional recipes to requirements of a low-fat, low-calorie, or diabetic diet.[59] Their cookbooks introduced new American-style recipes while also adapting traditional favorites like Navajo fry bread or Vietnamese spring rolls to a diabetic's special dietary constraints.

Contemporary Americanizers exhibit the respect for immigrant food gifts and traditions that one would expect of convinced cultural pluralists. There have been no real food fights recently. One skirmish, however, involved those controversial figures of the past—street vendors. In 1977 in

New York, new immigrant vendors—many of them operating illegally and selling shish kebab, felafel, quiche, and Asian foods—began giving hot dogs at licensed carts a run for their money. They precipitated what participants and observers jokingly called the Great Hot Dog War of 1977. At that time, John Zervas, an Athenian who had arrived in the United States in 1962, operated a fleet of Yum-Yum hot dog carts under a five-year $80,000 city contract. Like many Greeks, Zervas had begun his work in a diner kitchen, then operated seven coffee shops before turning to push-carts. In 1977 he and his 60 vendors enjoyed exclusive rights to sell push-cart hot dogs in Central Park. The city preferred dealing with one man, and believed they limited the number of vendors and the quantity of litter by doing so. Immigrants eager to break Zervas's special monopoly disagreed. When independent vendors invaded his turf, Zervas called in the police, the independents marched down Fifth Avenue, and Mayor Abe Beame eventually canceled Zervas's city contract. Consumers joined the newest immigrant entrepreneurs in calling the city's regulation of vendors "a repression of the free-enterprise system."[60]

Korean produce sellers have their own complaints about police harassment. They claim that the laws governing the sale of produce from sidewalk extensions of stores are impossibly complex, so that they find themselves unintentionally in violation even when they operate legal businesses. While agreeing they should obey the laws, Korean produce sellers find them "unfair, irregular and very cruel," and a real impediment to business. Policemen, they complain, "give tickets without warning . . . They should be patient with us, help us more." Like the vendors and their consumers, the Korean produce sellers draw effectively on deeply rooted American rhetoric to defend themselves. "There should not be so much red tape to the American dream."[61] These businessmen, too, strike a chord with consumer critics of American governmental bureaucracy. In this respect, they are a far cry from the Progressive Era, when native consumers created new governmental bureaucracies to produce the kinds of regulations about which Korean businessmen today complain.

Still, not every American consumer admires the new exchanges and blending now occurring from the lowest to the highest ends of the food marketplace. Multiculturalism has its outspoken critics, especially among those who fear the abandonment of a unified national culture and the concomitant "disuniting" of a great nation, to use Arthur Schlesinger's phrase. So too does multi-ethnic American eating have its critics—as it always has. In a diatribe worthy of Octavio Paz, Regina Schrambling of *Newsweek* rebelled at facing another meal of "Thai barbecue pizza, moo shu duck burritos, blueberry soup with lemongrass" or "Mexican tamales . . . stuffed with Norwegian farm-raised salmon." Defending her memories of her own mom's cooking and of authentic regional and ethnic cuisines, Schrambling blasted Americans' "nondiscriminating attitude toward ingredients" and "murkiness over restaurant types," and dismissed new creoles as insults to other countries' food and as the source of a new, dreary sameness in American eating. "In dog breeding," she concludes, "they would consider it mongrelization."[62] Other critics specifically associate this mongrelization with California, where, one chef complained, "they don't have any basics. They are always trying something new. Everything is mixed up."[63]

How can one not recall the WPA administrator of the 1930s, who had sniffed at the "mongrel character" of California cuisine sixty years ago? We are scarcely in the midst of a late twentieth-century version of that earlier food fight. Yet conflicts over food remain very real expressions of two perpetually conflicting visions of American life. The dream of a stable and unifying national cuisine is rarely at issue, and critics generally decry the mass-produced foods which in fact provide homogeneity and standardized eating across the nation. Instead, current conflicts about what we eat seem to revolve around two larger issues: whether the mixing and matching of cuisines and ingredients signify a spirit of toleration that is the greatest source of American unity and strength, or whether they represent just the opposite—a lack of respect for the ethnic and regional traditions that preserve the many differing histories of our people. These issues about what we eat, even when the voices that express them are quieter, more accommodating, and more civil than at the turn of the century, are important precisely because they embody larger questions about who we Americans really are.

Who Are We?

Anthropologists tell us that when human groups come together, fear and curiosity commingle. Fears generate hatred expressed as racial discrimination, immigration restriction, competition over resources, and violent personal confrontations; curiosity, on the other hand, encourages mutual exploration and accommodation. American foodways are the product of centuries of curiosity fueling exploration and accommodation in culinary forms. However much Americans have feared people different from themselves, we have ignored those fears when we believed we would find new pleasures by crossing cultural boundaries. Among other pleasures—from singing and dancing to making love—we have eagerly sought new foods and new tastes.

Jean Anthelme Brillat-Savarin—who in 1825 confidently announced, "Tell me what you eat, and I will tell you who you are"—would have no trouble describing American cultural identities. Our food reveals that we are cosmopolitans and iconoclasts; we are tolerant adventurers who do not feel constrained by tradition. We "play with our food" far more readily than we preserve the culinary rules of our varied ancestors. With the bagel changing from a distinctively Jewish icon to a national fast food, and the proliferation of Tex-Mex, New York deli, and "new Florida" creoles, Americans have no single national cuisine. But we do have a common culinary culture: What unites American eaters culturally is how we eat, not what we eat. As eaters, all Americans mingle the culinary traditions of many regions and cultures within ourselves. We are multi-ethnic eaters.

Two characteristics distinguish American eating habits from those of other countries: our tastes for standardized mass-produced processed dishes and for a diverse variety of multi-ethnic specialties. The former give a familiar and predictable homogeneity to supermarket shelves and roadside fast-food landscapes across the country. This is what first-time visitors from abroad, along with recently arrived immigrants, initially perceive as American food. But alongside the factory-baked spongy white bread, quick-frozen vegetables, and endless rows of identical tin cans, one discovers an extraordinary diversity. There is liver pudding in Carolina meat compartments and scrapple in Philadelphia; turnip greens in Charleston but lemongrass in San Francisco. A traveler who is willing to forgo a Taco Bell or Burger King can lunch instead at a small mom-and-pop diner in the Ozarks, or try the lunchtime buffet at a midwestern Mandarin Palace. And in the evening, a tourist or native almost anywhere in the United States can choose between chain-restaurant turf-and-surf and fusion cuisine prepared by a new immigrant chef from Vietnam, the Dominican Republic, or Central Europe. Eating homogeneous, processed, mass-produced foods is no more, or less, American than enjoying the multi-ethnic mixtures of particular regions.

These two varieties of quintessentially American foods correspond to our sometimes conflicting views of our own identities. While some Americans insist they are American because they have no ethnic or regional loyalties, others see their ethnic and regional ties as necessary components of their firmly national selves. The first view resembles the labeling of mass-produced American foods. Regardless of cultural origin, foods that are mass produced for a national market generally lose their ethnic identities in the United States. Hot dogs and Cracker Jacks, fried chicken and Fritos all emerged from specific cultural communities (German, southern, and Mexican) but lost their ethnic ties. Few people today think of hot dogs or Cracker Jacks as German, Fritos as Mexican-American, or Kentucky Fried Chicken as "soul food." Theorists of American identity, from Crève-coeur to Arthur Schlesinger, have suggested that immigrants and racial minorities should do the same, and that Americans are best united as a people when they lose their ties and loyalties to particularistic regional and cultural communities.

But other foods which seem just as quintessentially American retain their ethnic associations, even when they become widely popular with eaters across the nation. The chili of San Antonio is generally believed to be of Mexican origin; it provides much of the "Mex" in the region's Tex-Mex cuisine. Anglos and Spanish-speaking Tejanos, along with new immigrants to the region, have all enjoyed Tex-Mex foods equally. Now people across the United States eat them and consider Tex-Mex an American regional cuisine. There can be no "Tex-Mex" without its "Mex" ingredients, but Tex-Mex has a clear national identity that is American, not Mexican. In a similar vein, new ethnics of the 1970s argued that new immigrants had acquired ethnic identities in order to become American, and that their hyphenated, or creole, identities—like Tex-Mex, African-American, or Cajun—were a form of Americanization. In this view of American identity, loyalties to ethnic group, region, and nation complement one another.

The history of neither mass-produced foods nor regional cuisines shows Americans as people of conservative, unyielding ethnic tastes. It calls vividly into question Americans' most popular image of a multicultural United States as a mosaic of discrete racial and ethnic groups living in peace and harmony (or even in brotherly conflict) with one another. A food metaphor for this questionable view of multiculturalism might be the salad bowl, where each ingredient retains its own distinct appearance and taste. The most important and permanent ingredients in the American salad bowl have been its regional cuisines—New England, southern, Tex-Mex, midwestern, California, southwestern—not its ethnic culinary traditions. Cookbooks sometimes present American eaters as carrying on distinct ethnic traditions, with their separate chapters on "African-American" or "German-American" recipes. But in fact, both African-Americans and German-Americans eat a diet that mingles foods of their ancestors with those of their many neighbors. What makes the United States multicultural is not so much its many separate culinary traditions as it is Americans' desire to eat a multi-ethnic mix of foods, and to make this mix part of themselves.

In some ways, the old, and out-of-favor, metaphor of the melting pot provides the best description of American eating. The culinary melting pot can be a midwestern casserole, a southern gumbo, a New England stew, or a California "clay pot." In the regional cuisine of each pot, a tomato may give some of its flavor to a sauce or to its neighbor ingredient, be it rice, potatoes, or pasta; the flavor and character of the tomato changes when cooked with chiles, oregano, or soy sauce. Tomatoes blended with shrimp and rice give a low-country Carolina taste, while tomato sauce on rice-a-roni gives us a Mediterranean/Asian "San Francisco Treat." The culinary melting pot produces multi-ethnic diversity, not all-American uniformity. It produces Portuguese-Americans who favor pasta in New York and rice in Hawaii; it produces African-Americans who eat Chinese food on Tuesday, lasagna on Wednesday, and collard greens with pot liquor on Thursday. It produces identities that are blended creoles, not the culinary equivalent of five (or twenty-five) isolated ethnic groups, each with its own foodways. It makes a multi-ethnic American gumbo or stew, not a multicultural salad of discrete ethnic groups.

Blending in the culinary melting pot has produced little of the disunity and strife that opponents of multiculturalism warn of when they advocate uniform, un-hyphenated American identities for all. Culinary exchanges have been less violent than many other cross-cultural contacts. Food fights have occurred, especially during periods of rapid boundary crossing and creolization, notably in the aftermath of the mass migrations of the nineteenth century. But these food fights seem laughably mild, and limited in scope, compared with other cross-cultural battles. No one feared that fist fights might break out the first time satay appeared for sale on the Washington Mall. Such fights have been common enough when the first Irish Catholic entered a Boston public school in the 1840s, when the first Mexican or Italian moved into a formerly German or Irish neighborhood, and when a white daughter announced to her parents, "Guess who's coming to dinner." Americans have not been as tolerant of and curious about their neighbors as they have about their neighbors' foods. They have more often feared them, creating deeply entrenched, popular notions of firmly bounded racial and ethnic groups that demand exclusive loyalties from their members.

Such notions seem to deny that we are what we eat. They suggest that multi-ethnic eating is nothing more than a casual consumer choice, and quite unimportant when compared with the strength of primordial racial and tribal loyalties. But creole American eating is not an isolated example of multi-ethnic identity in American culture. It has important counterparts wherever Americans seek pleasure, most notably in the history of American music.

Music, like food, is an important marker of identity; as one Puerto Rican in New York told an ethnomusicologist, "My music is my flag." Blended musical forms like jazz, and cross-over performers from Vic Damone and Elvis to Vanilla Ice, are musical analogs to Cincinnati chili and Pizza Hut. Sharing and borrowing has been as common—and as peaceful—in the musical as in the culinary realm. And musical blends, like culinary ones, have varied regionally, largely because differing groups have blended songs and identities with one another in the Northeast, Southeast, and Southwest.

Key to identity and culture in both American music and eating is the tension between people's love of the familiar and the pleasure they find in desiring, creating, and experiencing something new. This tension preceded the commercialization of musical and food exchanges, but has become more obvious with the growth of musical and culinary marketplaces and big business at the national level. In the histories of blues and of ethnic foods, corporate producers and mass market consumers appropriated (or "co-opted") and adapted (or "adulterated") the cultural creations of ethnic or racial enclaves, from rumba to country ballad. In both cases, however, it was an enclave producer of music and food—whether black bluesman or Chinese chef—who first sought a wider market and initiated the transformation of their products.

In food, as in music, the marketplace followed and facilitated a long-standing human curiosity about new sensory pleasures. Market exchanges did not corrupt a natural or exclusive human preference for culinary conservatism, hometown music, or the comfort foods and melodies of childhood. Businessmen from within and outside enclave communities made profits off consumers' desire for novelty, but they did not invent that desire. Identities reflected in consumer choices should not be dismissed as superficial simply because they are expressed in the marketplace. Consumers' preferences for multi-ethnic food and multi-ethnic music remain an important expression of their identities as Americans.

Consumers of music and food did find that mass production by modern corporations could not deliver the complex associations that tied familiar music and dishes to their local communities or childhood experiences. African-Americans resented Elvis or Vanilla Ice for "stealing" black music for the same reasons that many Italian-Americans disdained Pizza Hut's crust and sauce. Both groups experienced a sense of loss as their cultural creations changed and found acceptance in wider circles. But both also responded to their losses as consumers; they went to market in search of a "mo' better blues," or a more authentic pizza crust. To the degree that American culture is a consumer culture, Americans will probably always hunger for the tastes and long for the sounds we believe we have lost to commercial producers. And our efforts to find "authentic foods" and "authentic sounds" will generate demand for small food stores and live jazz clubs, and for face-to-face relations between the shopkeeper and the consumer or the musician and the audience. Ethnic and local loyalties repeatedly generate critiques of mass consumer culture, even while the marketplace remains the arena for expressing ethnic and local identities. They guarantee that small businessmen and musicians with clear identities as immigrant, ethnic, and regional Americans will continue to compete successfully against big business.

Cross-cultural culinary contacts have been peaceful not only because they involve the search for pleasure but because they are commercial exchanges. Consumers come to American markets expecting bounty and diversity at a low cost. Most have found what they sought, along with a pleasant sensation of choice and of individual freedom. The impersonal rules of the marketplace help ease fears of cultural difference: buying and selling are limited, public, and highly ritualized forms of social interaction. In the marketplace, food becomes easily detached from its culture of origin, and from the people who first enjoyed it. Appealing sights, smells, and sounds suffice to win new customers. Consumers need not convert to Judaism or have Jewish friends to relish lox and bagels; they don't need to understand Islam or its faithful to enjoy babaganoush.

The pursuit of pleasure with minimal obligation encourages Americans to cross cultural boundaries and to incorporate parts of other cultures into our intimate lives. But it also exposes us regularly to the fears that cultural differences generate. Americans have been far more willing to celebrate multi-ethnic eating than the pleasures of cross-cultural sex and marriage. Still, throughout our national history, cross-over has occurred in this realm just as it has in food and music, and the numbers of Americans who are consciously multi-ethnic in a familial and genetic as well as a culinary sense are not trivial, and they are growing.

In the past, laws forbade cross-cultural marriage; more recently there have been battles over whether to include a "multiracial" census category or to maintain the convenient fiction that Americans are members of discrete ethnic groups. The battles are unlikely to end soon, as they are driven by forces that range from racism to legitimate worries or concerns about the loss of group solidarity, history, and cultural identity.

In a bountiful society where fears of cultural difference nevertheless persist, food remains the least controversial, the most typical and reliable, and the cheapest of all ways to find pleasure in life. Millions of ordinary Americans—not just robber barons, bohemians, or yuppies— have chosen its enjoyments, and with it culinary pluralism and gustatory cosmopolitanism. As eaters, Americans have long embraced identities that are rooted in interaction and affiliation with other Americans of widely diverse backgrounds.[1] The foods we eat commemorate a long history of peaceful cultural interaction; our multi-ethnic eating daily proclaims our satisfied sense of affiliation with one another. The marketplace, and its consumer culture, may be a slim thread on which to build cross-cultural understanding. But given the depth of American fears about cultural diversity, it is better to have that thread than not.

If our food tastes good, gives us pleasure, and connects us—if only commercially or sentimentally—to our neighbors, why not embrace those ties and the multi-ethnic identities they create? Americans have not proved to be strict culinary judges; we prefer the pleasures of novelty and blending. Such appetites keep corporate managers and small businessmen alike hopping to deliver the diversity that we Americans fear but also crave. As eaters, Americans reject uniformity or adherence to a single cultural experience. Why should we then insist that each American "belong" to only one cultural community, or that happiness can be found by narrowing, rather than broadening, the circles of American solidarity? Few would prefer a world where fear of the exotic or foreign again drew rigid racial boundaries in the form of Jim Crow laws or immigrant ghettoes. Nor would we necessarily live in a happier world if Americans chose to turn up their noses—or even spit out—the foods of newcomers. Rather than dismiss eating as a trivial consumer choice, Americans might do better to take our eating choices very seriously. Then we could recognize and celebrate that indeed we are what we eat—not a multi-ethnic nation, but a nation of multi-ethnics.

Sources
Notes
Acknowledgments
Index

Sources

Students of American culture have learned much from semioticians' and anthropologists' views of food as symbols, syntax, and grammar, yet these approaches represent only one small corner of the methodological possibilities for the study of food. By offering a culturally sensitive yet essentially materialist and economic view of American eating, *We Are What We Eat* seeks to remind readers at every turn, and in every chapter, of the mundane and everyday quality of much related to eating. To eat what we are, we must be able to produce the foods we want or we must create markets where we can buy them. To discuss American identity, at least as expressed through our eating habits, involves excursion into the histories of agriculture, business, and consumption.

American eating remains a huge yet relatively unexplored topic. For an excellent introduction to the range of approaches and questions in food studies, see Ellen Messer, "Anthropological Perspectives on Diet," *Annual Review of Anthropology* 13 (1984): 205–249. Readers will profitably begin their exploration of the topic with Charles Camp's helpful bibliography, "Food in American Culture: A Bibliographic Essay," *Journal of American Culture* 2, 3 (1979): 559–570. Useful as general studies are the early work of Richard Cummings, *The American and His Food* (Chicago: University of Chicago Press, 1940), and two more recent volumes by Harvey Levenstein, *Paradox of Plenty* (New York: Oxford University Press, 1993), and *Revolution at the Table*. In my own work, I have sought to steer between two interpretive poles in the history of American food—Daniel Boorstin's enthusiasm for mass production as the definer and democratizer of American foodways (*The Americans; The Democratic Experience*) and the preference of culinary critics like John L. Hess and Karen Hess, *The Taste of America* (Columbia: The University of South Carolina Press, 1989), for multi-ethnic regional cuisines as definers of genuinely American tastes.

Given my interest in the relationship of the ethnic, regional, and national in American eating, I pursued research in primary sources at all three levels. Yet I would never have completed this book had I attempted to explore every significant repository in the country, or to know intimately the eating habits of Americans from every cultural background or every distinctive region. A careful reader will certainly note that my analysis of national food industries, and national and multinational corporations, depends more heavily on secondary sources than my analysis of immigrants and southerners (white and black) and their economic enclaves.

Case Studies

Most of my primary research was undertaken as part of five regional case studies: in Minneapolis-St. Paul, San Francisco, Charleston, New York, and San Antonio. My goal was to choose cities and surrounding areas that represent the regional and ethnic diversity of American food markets. I wanted to encompass the culinary legacies of diverse physical environments (desert and swamp, mountain and plains, hot and cold), the complex legacies of three major early European empires (Spanish, English, and French), the African slave trade, and several major Native American cultures, and thus the regional cuisines of North, South, Midwest, East, and West.

Furthermore, I wanted my case studies to reflect the differing histories of regional integration into the national marketplace for foodstuffs in the nineteenth and twentieth centuries, encompassing areas of production, processing, and sale, of subsistence farming and of rapid urbanization, and of corporate and commercial evolution. Finally, I wanted my case studies to reflect a wide range of ethnic interactions: between indigenous peoples and colonizers, between native-born Americans and immigrant newcomers, between northerners and southerners, and between immigrants of differing backgrounds during the mass migrations of the nineteenth and early twentieth centuries and during the post-1965 migrations. By no means are all of my illustrations of general patterns drawn from New York, Charleston, San Antonio, San Francisco, and Minneapolis-St. Paul, but I have drawn heavily on my research in these five cities for stories of how family, community, and business intertwined in defining ethnic and national identities in particular times and places.

I chose Charleston because in its own peculiar way the city represents the regional eating of the Southeast. Settled early by English, Scottish, and French Huguenots, Charleston's European population quickly found itself outnumbered by the Africans they enslaved to raise the principal crop of the coastal Carolinas and Georgia—rice. The wealthiest plantation economy in the South in the eighteenth century, Charleston declined in the nineteenth century but never lost its reputation for good and extravagant eating among both white and black residents. Significantly for my study, Charleston never attracted large numbers of new settlers from abroad, but remained a largely biracial society—a declining port city with ties to its largely agricultural hinterland—well into the twentieth century.

In sharp contrast to Charleston was the burgeoning multi-ethnic city of New York, home of Ellis Island and the Statue of Liberty. North of New York lived some of the most highly organized Native Americans of the pre-Columbian era, but they were also representatives of a corn-based culture characteristic of much of the eastern woodlands. The New York area was colonized first by the Dutch and then by the English, and New York's unique colonial and commercial, and later industrial and corporate, development made it what it still is today—an astonishingly diverse "city of immigrants." Germans and Irish dominated the nineteenth-century city; Italians and Jews were prominent in the turn-of-the-century city. Native minorities from Puerto Rico and the American South joined the crowd of multi-ethnic eaters in the interwar years, while today Chinese, Korean, Puerto Ricans, and peoples from the Caribbean and South America—many of African descent—again make New York the urban East Coast melting pot par excellence.

The contrast between the relatively conservative eating habits of the Southeast and the rapidly evolving multi-ethnicity of New York City points clearly to the role of population movements in defining and altering regional markets and cuisines into the twentieth century. New York was a center for kosher food production and beer brewing, where rich and poor Americans alike first weighed the pleasures and dangers of eating new foods plied by exotic strangers, and where eager public officials tried, with only limited success, to convince foreign-born consumers that an American diet of cream sauces and simple New England staples was a necessary step along the road to full participation in American life.

Representing the Upper Midwest, westward expansion, and the vast wheat-based agriculture that changed American eating in the nineteenth century are the twin cities of Minneapolis and St. Paul. Colonized initially by the French, and subsequently by immigrant farmers from Germany, Norway, Sweden, and Finland, Minneapolis became my case study of the American heartland, of the interaction of foreign eating habits with a new American environment and of the relationship between large-scale commercial agriculture and food processing. Much of the grain that changed the United States from a nation of corn-eaters to wheat-eaters found its way to Minneapolis to be milled, and the city was home to some of the most important milling corporations of the country. At the same time, no region better demonstrates how immigrant communities experimented with noncorporate forms of food processing and food retailing, largely through producer and consumer cooperatives. Although this region has attracted some new immigrants recently, its local life and culture has been less affected—again, until quite recently—by the northward migration of African-Americans. It was rather the immigrations of northern Europeans during the nineteenth century that defined the region and the cultural mainstream of American (or more properly midwestern) eating. It also provided Garrison Keillor with much humorous material for his sketches about Lake Woebegon casseroles (with their mushroom-soup base) and the yuppie snobbery of the Cafe Boeuf. In a multicultural America, the eating habits of the

Upper Midwest and the South—regions relatively untouched by the significant migrations of the late nineteenth and twentieth centuries—seem oddly old-fashioned.

Selecting a city and region in the Southwest posed the most difficult choice in this study. I wanted a town shaped by significant, and long-term, immigrations of Mexicans. But having already settled on Charleston as an example of a city and region with a colonial-era local cuisine relatively unaffected by more recent migrations, I was careful not to duplicate that pattern for the Southwest, as I easily could have by studying Tucson or Santa Fe. Looking farther afield, I chose San Antonio. Although geographically outside the historical center of Meso-American corn cultures at their most elaborated (for example, in New Mexico), San Antonio shared with that region a common encounter of Native Americans with the Spanish empire and the establishment of missions on its frontier region, El Norte. In addition (and unlike Charleston), its food markets brought local Spanish speakers into contact not only with Anglo-Americans but with a variety of immigrant groups—both European and Mexican—in the nineteenth and twentieth centuries. Ultimately, then, I opted for a look at Tex-Mex regional eating, rather than at Southwest Sonoran or Hispanic cuisine (both of which did, however, find their way into my discussions of colonial era exchanges).

Having guaranteed attention to the Spanish empire and to Mexican immigrants in choosing San Antonio, I found it important to select for my West Coast case a city shaped by trans-Pacific exchanges. Los Angeles had its attractions, but San Francisco's multi-ethnicity made it a better counter-balance to New York in the East. The city has attracted large Asian and European immigrant populations, and it is located at the edge of one of the most important agricultural regions of the country. A further advantage is its nearby vineyards, whose quality quickly surpassed that of southern California and has made San Francisco the center of California's impressive wine industry today. While large-scale agribusiness was scarcely invented in California, it probably reached its zenith there, especially in the twentieth century. The state's truck farming, fruit orchards, and wine industry provide wonderful case studies of ethnic interaction, while San Francisco's urban elite bohemians and its tourist-oriented Chinatown also provide early West Coast examples of multi-ethnic eating.

My selections were not perfect. None of these cities falls firmly within the most intensive corn belt of the indigenous Native American world, nor within the later American corn belt of the pig-rearing, liquor-distilling region of the "Old Northwest" of Ohio, Iowa, and Illinois. To the degree that I may have neglected the place of salt pork in the settlement of the West, as well as the growth of the working classes in its large urban centers as well as the integration of the South and its slave population into the antebellum national economy, it is largely a result of this gap in my research. And finally, since I refer so often to America's creole eating habits, it may seem awkward that I chose not to study the city that actually calls its local cuisine a creole—New Orleans. This is a decision I now regret.

With all their limits, the eating habits of Americans in the five cities that appear and reappear throughout this book reveal surprisingly similar cultural dynamics at work. In each I found eaters looking to satisfy their tastes for the familiar and the novel; in each I found enclave businessmen balancing communal ties to their home communities with the search for wider markets; in each I found the identities of foods and producers, consumers and retailers, in considerable flux. Nowhere did cultural conservatism reign unambiguously, least of all in housewives' kitchens or "twixt cup and lip" at American dining tables. I believe I have not erred in taking these to be regional expressions of national, if not absolutely human and universal, patterns.

Libraries and Archives

For the local histories of food and business in my five case studies, I am deeply indebted to the staffs of many libraries and archives visited during the course of my research. So rich are the materials available in these repositories throughout the country, and so untapped are they for the history of American eating, that I will describe them in some detail here.

For the nation as a whole, I tried to identify sources that described both individual eating experiences and what folklorists call group "eating events." I systematically sampled autobiographies of food businessmen of many backgrounds, and I read extensively in the autobiographies of immigrant and minority women, since I had learned on an earlier project that men are less likely than women to write much about food, except in their childhoods. Perhaps this occurred because food preparation remained a more important focus for women throughout their lives. For twentieth-century business generally, I turned to the indices published by the Public Affairs Information Services, to the *Business Periodicals Index*, and to the rich CD-Rom resources of the New York Public Library's new Science, Industry and Business Division.

Although community cookbooks are not systematically collected or catalogued, hundreds of them appear in the Online Computer Library Center (OCLC) listings, and almost every local or state historical society has its own idiosyncratic collection. I examined about 150 community cookbooks from all over the country, representing about 30 ethnic, regional, and religious groups. The scholar wishing to locate and work more systematically with these cookbooks might want to consult private collectors, some of whom specialize in "charitables." Jan Langone of Ann Arbor, Michigan, for example, offers commercial help for those seeking particular types of cookbooks.

The papers of the "America Eats" project of the Works Projects Administration (WPA), housed in the Manuscripts Division of the Library of Congress, proved an invaluable source on community eating events and on the thinking of intellectual elites about the meaning of region, ethnicity, and nation in our eating habits. This collection deserves much wider use, and it should be complemented with other folkloric materials gathered by other Federal Writers' Projects in the 1930s, also housed at the Library of Congress. Its materials on community festivals, furthermore, sent me off in a direction I had not originally anticipated when I began the project, and led me to the American Folklore and Life Program in the Smithsonian Institution. Its staff and its small library of materials relating to the American Folklife festival sharpened my thinking on the place of food and scholarly professionals in the creation and re-creation of cross-cultural festivals celebrating American diversity.

Although I did not consult them, the records of Dun and Bradstreet, located at Harvard University, would also provide uniquely corporate perspectives on at least some immigrant, minority, and southern food businesses in the nineteenth century. Advertising and corporate materials at the Smithsonian and at Delaware's Hagley Library also need further exploration, as do aggregate census data on the niches of immigrant workers and businessmen in nineteenth-century food industries like baking, brewing, and butchering.

Another important repository from which I drew only lightly is Philadelphia's Balch Institute, which holds rich materials on immigrant and ethnic festivals, businesses, and foods in Philadelphia and Pennsylvania. Because I did not choose to focus on Philadelphia, the excellent materials—which include reports on German festivals and picnics, ledgers from an African-American family that catered to consumers as diverse as Catholic parish priests and the Philadelphia "main line," and the function of ethnic restaurants as community centers in the 1950s and 1960s—are not reflected in my footnotes. They deserve considerably more attention than I was able to give them.

In St. Paul, the Immigration History Research Center (IHRC), and Joel Wurl, IHRC Curator, proved a treasure trove, as did the library of the Minnesota Historical Society. Both contain a few—and exceedingly unusual, because so rare—collections from immigrant food businesses. Both offer rich oral histories, local cookbooks, and useful clippings on local restaurants and food businesses. The IHRC houses the most important collections on immigrant cooperation in the country, the papers of many of the YMCA's International Institutes (along with the papers of several leaders in this branch of social welfare work), and the papers of the American Council for Nationality services. The papers of Theodore Saloutos, who wrote several books on Greek immigrants and on American agriculture (including immigrant farmers), also contain important materials.

For the San Francisco area, I learned most from the oral history holdings of the Regional Oral History Office, Bancroft Library, University of California, Berkeley. These provide excellent descriptions of the lives of leaders in California's wine industry, along with scattered histories of bakers, restaurateurs, canners, and fishermen. The Bancroft also has a useful collection of unpublished theses on many aspects of California agriculture. The Special Collections of the San Francisco Public Library and the holdings of the San Francisco Historical Society offer guidebooks to the city's restaurants and tourist attractions, along with clippings, menus, and assorted memorabilia related to the city's celebrated bohemianism. Although I did not use them, the holdings of San Francisco's Wine Institute would be of interest to scholars studying the transition from family to corporate production of wine, especially after 1940. A visit to the University of California at Davis, which is home to an important enology department, would also prove worthwhile.

For the historian interested in pursuing a comparable history of beer's evolution in the nineteenth century, rich holdings on brewing are available in the Wisconsin Historical Society: I surveyed them but ultimately made relatively little use of them for this study. In St. Louis, materials on the Anheuser-Busch "dynasty" provide a necessary chapter in the history of this important nineteenth-century cross-over industry.

In Charleston, I found excellent collections of guidebooks and city directories for the nineteenth and twentieth centuries in the College of Charleston Special Collections. A scholar interested in the origins of the region's rice industry will also want to spend considerably more time than I did at the South Carolina Historical Society.

In New York, I drew—as I have for 25 years—on the inexhaustible resources of the New York Public Library. While its special collections are widely used, many scholars may not know that it houses a remarkably extensive set of cookbooks (as does the University of Iowa, the Schlesinger Library of Radcliffe College, Kansas State University, and Johnson & Wales College). For the recent past, and especially for my description of New York's latest immigrants and their impact on regional eating habits, I depended heavily on the *New York Times* and its food reporting. But since I also lived in the New York area during the first half of this project, I drew on my own experiences as consumer, diner, and cook in writing on this topic. I was surprised (and pleased), rather late in my research, to discover the enormously rich and useful—and microfilmed—notes and files of several of New York's Federal Writers' Projects at the New York Municipal Archives.

In San Antonio, most of my work was completed with the help of the staff at the Institute of Texan Cultures, both in its library and its Texas Folklife Festival Office. The ITC library has extensive, and excellent, clippings files on local food businesses, the chili craze of the 1970s, and the many street festivals for which the town is now widely known. The Texana and Genealogy Section of San Antonio's new (and architecturally stunning) Public Library was also helpful, and led me to explore the historical evolution of the city's river walk as an early example of a festival marketplace that highlighted both ethnicity and ethnic eating as tourist attractions.

Notes

In the interests of brevity, I have limited the notes to citations for direct quotations and to primary sources. Many of the latter are important archival collections, abbreviated as follows:

AE: Federal Writers' Project of WPA, "America Eats," Library of Congress, Manuscripts Division.

FtC: Federal Writers' Project of the City of New York, WPA "Feeding the City," Municipal Archives of the City of New York.

INY: Federal Writers' Project of the City of New York, WPA, "Italians of New York," Municipal Archives of the City of New York.

IHRC: Immigration History Research Center, University of Minnesota.

ITC: Institute of Texan Cultures.

JNY: Federal Writers' Project of the City of New York, WPA, "Jews of the City of New York," Municipal Archives of the City of New York.

ROHO: Regional Oral History Office, the Bancroft Library, University of California at Berkeley.

Introduction: What Do We Eat?

1. Lisa Belkin, "A Slice of New York (On Rye) in Texas," *New York Times*, September 6, 1989.

2. Terri L. Darrow, "Cowboys and Bagels," *Restaurant Hospitality* 73, 5 (May 1989): 30.

3. David B. Green, "Betting That Lots of Israelis Will Take to American Bagels," *New York Times*, July 31, 1996.

4. Octavio Paz, "At Table and in Bed," in *Convergences: Essays on Art and Literature* (Orlando: Harcourt, Brace, and Jovanovich, 1987), pp. 68–99.

5. Molly O'Neill, "Bagels Are Now Fast Food, And Purists Do a Slow Boil," *New York Times*, April 25, 1993.

6. See foreword by Murray Lender in Nao Hauser and Sue Spitler, *Bagels! Bagels! and More Bagels!* (Chicago: Rand McNally, 1979).

7. Daniel Young, "The Bagel's New York Accent Is Fading," *New York Times*, September 6, 1989.

8. Here I borrow from Daniel Boorstin, *The Democratic Experience* (New York: Random House, 1973), pp. 89–114, 145–148.

1. Colonial Creoles

1. Richard J. Hooker, ed., *A Colonial Plantation Cookbook: The Receipt Book of Harriott Pinckney Horry, 1770* (Columbia: University of South Carolina Press, 1990), p. 66.

2. Amelia Simmons, *The First American Cookbook* (New York: Dover, 1984), p. 28.

3. Quoted in Bernard A. Weisberger, "A Nation of Immigrants," *American Heritage* (February/March 1994): 77.

4. Paul Weatherwax, *Indian Corn in Old America* (New York: Macmillan, 1954), p. 84.

5. F. W. Waugh, *Iroquois Foods and Food Preparations* (Ohsweken, Ontario: Iroqrafts, 1991), p. 117.

6. Notes, Reports, and Essays (Idaho), p. 7, Box A-831, AE.

7. Quoting the Reverend Francis Higginson, in George Francis Dow, *Every Day Life in the Massachusetts Bay Colony* (New York: Benjamin Blom, 1935), p. 3.

8. Notes, Reports, and Essays (The Northeast), p. 1, Box A-833, AE.

9. Quoted in Carolyn Merchant, *Ecological Revolutions: Nature, Gender and Science in New England* (Chapel Hill: University of North Carolina Press, 1989), p. 64.

10. James H. Merrell, *The Indians' New World: Catawbas and Their Neighbors from European Contact through the Era of Removal* (Chapel Hill: University of North Carolina Press and Institute of Early American History and Culture, Williamsburg, VA, 1989), pp. 2–3.

11. People of 'Ksan, *Gathering What the Great Nature Provided: Food Traditions of the Gitksan* (Vancouver: Douglas & McIntyre, 1980), p. 98.

12. Ian K. Steele, *Warpaths: Invasions of North America* (New York: Oxford University Press, 1994), p. 14.

13. Tom Hatley, *The Dividing Paths: Cherokees and South Carolinians through the Era of Revolution* (New York: Oxford University Press, 1993), p. 97.

14. Richard White, *The Roots of Dependency: Subsistence, Environment and Social Change among the Choctaws, Pawnees, and Navajos* (Lincoln: University of Nebraska Press, 1993), p. 85.

15. Peter C. Mancall, *Deadly Medicine: Indians and Alcohol in Early America* (Ithaca: Cornell University Press, 1995), pp. 11, 67–68.

16. Ibid., p. 14.

17. Raymond Mohl, *Poverty in New York, 1783–1825* (New York: Oxford University Press, 1971), p. 211.

18. Ernesto Camou Healy, "El Maiz y el Trigo: Pilares de la cultura y la cocina campesina sonorense," in Ernesto Camou Healy, ed., *Cocina Sonorense* (Hermosillo: Instituto Sonorense de Cultura, 1990), pp. 46–59.

19. Charles Oliver Howe, *What I Remember*, quoted in Sarah F. McMahon, "'A Comfortable Subsistence': A History of Diet in New England, 1630–1850," unpub. Ph.D. diss., Brandeis University, 1981, p. 222.

20. William Woys Weaver, ed., *A Quaker Woman's Cookbook: The Domestic Cookery of Elizabeth Ellicott Lea* (Philadelphia: University of Pennsylvania Press, 1982).

21. William Woys Weaver, "Die Geschiete Hausfrau: The First Ethnic Cookbook in the United States," in Alexander Fenton and Trefor Owen, eds., *Food in Perspective* (Edinburgh: John Donald Publishers, 1981), pp. 343–363.

22. Peter G. Rose, *The Sensible Cook: Dutch Foodways in the Old and the New World* (Syracuse: Syracuse University Press, 1989).

23. Notes, Reports, and Essays (Louisiana) (contains Carolina materials incorrectly filed), Box A-831, AE.

24. Byrd, "History of the Dividing Line," in Louis B. Wright, ed., *The Prose Works of William Byrd of Westover: Narratives of a Colonial Virginian* (Cambridge: Belknap Press of Harvard University Press, 1966), p. 59.

2. Immigration, Isolation, and Industry

1. Mary Antin, *The Promised Land* (Boston: Houghton Mifflin, 1910), p. 185.

2. Joe Gray Taylor, *Eating, Drinking, and Visiting in the South* (Baton Rouge: Louisiana State University Press, 1982), p. 91.

3. George P. Rawick, ed., *The American Slave: A Composite Autobiography*, vol. 11 (Westport: Greenwood, 1977), pp. 5, 130.

4. Taylor, *Eating*, p. 140.

5. Ben Robertson, *Red Hills and Cotton: An Upcountry Memory* (Columbia: University of South Carolina Press, 1960), p. 66.

6. "Ain't Got No Screens," in Tom E. Terrill and Jerrold Hirsch, *Such as Us: Southern Voices of the Thirties* (Chapel Hill: University of North Carolina Press, 1978), p. 55.

7. Elizabeth W. Etheridge, *The Butterfly Caste: A Social History of Pellagra in the South* (Westport: Greenwood, 1972), p. 85.

8. Federal Writers' Project of the Works Progress Administration in North Carolina, Tennessee, and Georgia, *These Are Our Lives* (Chapel Hill: University of North Caroline Press, 1939), p. 145.

9. Rawick, *American Slave*, p. 64.

10. Notes, Essays and Reports—Louisiana (contains Carolina materials incorrectly filed), Box A-831, AE.

11. W. W. Dixon, "A Thanksgiving Dinner," Notes, Reports, and Essays (South Carolina), Box A-832, AE.

12. Notes, Reports, and Essays (South Carolina), Box 832, AE.

13. Ibid.

14. Ibid.

15. Harnett T. Kane, *The Southern Christmas Book* (New York: Bonanza Books, 1958), p. 253.

16. Sarah Rutledge, *The Carolina Housewife* (Columbia: University of South Carolina Press, 1979).

17. Patience Pennington (Pringle), *A Woman Rice Planter* (Cambridge: Harvard University Press, 1961), p. 446.

18. T. J. Woofter, *Black Yeomanry: Life on St. Helena Island* (New York: Octagon Books, 1978; orig. pub. Henry Holt, 1930), p. 221.

19. Nick Lindsey, transcriber, *An Oral History of Edisto Island: The Life and Times of Bubberson Brown* (Goshen, IN: Pinchpenny Press, 1977), p. 45.

20. Karen Hess, *The Carolina Rice Kitchen: The African Connection* (Columbia: University of South Carolina Press, 1992), p. 4.

21. Juan H. Almonte, "Statistical Report on Texas, 1835," *Southwest Historical Quarterly*, vol. 28.

22. Ernesto Galarzo, *Barrio Boy* (Notre Dame: University of Notre Dame Press, 1971), pp. 12–26 passim.

23. J. del Castillo, "A Menudo Party," Notes, Reports, and Essays (Arizona), Box A-830, AE.

24. Elizabeth Hurley, *Folk Travelers*, Texas Folklore Society, no. 25 (1953).

25. Dayan Dr. I. Grunfeld, *The Jewish Dietary Laws* (London: Soncino Press, 1972), vol. 1, p. 131.

26. Mark Zborowski and Elizabeth Herzog, *Life Is with People: The Culture of the Shtetl* (New York: Schocken Books, 1952), p. 371.

27. Jeff Kisseloff, *You Must Remember This: An Oral History of Manhattan from the 1890s to World War II* (San Diego: Harcourt, Brace, Jovanovich, 1989), p. 42.

28. Ibid., p. 41.

29. Joan Nathan, *Jewish Cooking in America* (New York: Alfred A. Knopf, 1994), p. 18.

30. Publication—Restaurants/Food, First Draft, reel 177, JNY.

31. Zborowski and Herzog, *Life Is with People*, pp. 361–362.

32. Greek Orthodox Ladies Philoptochos Society, *Popular Greek Recipes* (Charleston: The Society, 1970), p. 175.

33. Walter D. Kamphoefner, Wolfgang Helbich, and Ulrike Sommer, *News from the Land of Freedom: German Immigrants Write Home* (Ithaca: Cornell University Press, 1991), p. 218.

34. Notes, Reports, and Essays (Nebraska), "Bohemian Foods," Box 831, AE.

35. *Favorite Recipes* (St. Paul: Sokol Minnesota, 1988), p. 9.

36. Pat Martin, *Czechoslovak Culture: Recipes, History and Folk Arts* (Iowa City: Penfield Press, 1989), p. 115.

37. "My Czech Heritage," in ibid., pp. 38–39.

38. Notes, Reports, and Essays (Nebraska), "Bohemian Foods," Box 831, AE.

39. "Strawberry-Growing in the Pajaro Valley," oral history with Hiroshi Shikuma, by Randall Jarrell, University of California, Santa Cruz, Dean E. McHenry Libary, 1986.

40. Chiyo Mitori Shimamoto, *To The Land of Bright Promise: The Story of a Pioneer Japanese Truck Farming Family in California's San Joaquin Valley* (Lodi: San Joaquin County Historical Society and Museum, 1990), p. 28.

41. Catherine Tripalin Murray, *A Taste of Memories from the Old "Bush"* (Madison: Greenbush . . . remembered, 1988), vol. 1, p. 42.

42. See the anonymous memoir, "The Joy of Growing up Italian," in Oblate Sisters of the Sacred Heart of Jesus, Villa Maria Teresa, Hubbard, Ohio, *La Cucina dell'Amore: The Kitchen of Love* (Youngstown: Ralph R. Zerbonia, 1990), p. xxi.

43. Murray, *Taste of Memories*, vol. 1, pp. 43, 264.

44. Quoted in Cyril Ray, *Robert Mondavi of the Napa Valley* (London: Heinemann/Peter Davies, 1984), p. 49.

45. Murray, *Taste of Memories*, vol. 1, p. 118.

46. Ibid., pp. 162, 186, 216, and 199.

47. Antonio Mangano, "The Italian Colonies of New York City," in Francesco Cordasco, ed., *Italians in the City: Health and Related Social Needs* (New York: Arno Press, 1975), p. 21.

48. Murray, *Taste of Memories*, vol. 1, p. 239.

49. Leonard Covello, *The Social Background of the Italo-American School Child* (Leiden: E. J. Brill, 1967), p. 295; see also Jo Pagano, *Golden Wedding* (New York: Random House, 1943), pp. 12–13.

50. Sophinisba Breckinridge, *New Homes for Old* (New York: Harper, 1921), p. 85.

51. "The Joy of Growing Up Italian," p. xx.

52. J. S. Clark, *Life in the Middle West* (St. Paul: Macalester Park, 1916), p. 27.

53. Ibid., p. 25.

54. J. M. Burrows, *Fifty Years in Iowa: Being the Personal Reminiscences of J. M. D. Burrows* (Davenport: Glass & Company, 1888), p. 33.

55. Ibid., p. 42.

56. Mohl, *Poverty in New York*, p. 11.

57. Thomas F. De Voe, *The Market Book, Containing a Historical Account of the Public Markets in the Cities of New York, Boston, Philadelphia and Brooklyn* (New York: Thomas F. De Voe, 1862), p. 454.

58. Burroughs, *Fifty Years*, pp. 103–104.

59. Clarence Woodbury, "Our Daily Bread, the World's Worst," *Common Sense*, April 1945, pp. 26–27.

60. Calla Van Syckle, "Some Pictures of Food Consumption in the United States, II: 1860–1941," *Journal of the American Dietetic Association* 21 (1945): 690.

61. Harvey A. Levenstein, *Revolution at the Table: The Transformation of the American Diet* (New York: Oxford University Press, 1988), p. 29.

62. Mary Taylor Simeti, *Pomp and Sustenance: Twenty-five Centuries of Sicilian Food* (New York: Alfred A. Knopf, 1989).

3. Ethnic Entrepreneurs

1. Peter C. Y. Leung, *One Day, One Dollar: Locke, California, and the Chinese Farming Experience in the Sacramento Delta* (El Cerrito: Chinese/Chinese American History Project, 1984), chap. 4.

2. Moses Rischin, cited in Alan M. Kraut, "The Butcher, the Baker, the Pushcart Peddler: Jewish Foodways and Entrepreneurial Opportunity in the East European Immigrant Community, 1880–1940," *Journal of American Culture* 6 (Winter 1983): 75.

3. C. A. Clausen, ed., *The Lady with A Pen: Elise Waerenskjold in Texas* (Northfield, MN: Norwegian-American Historical Association, 1961), pp. 29, 41, 98.

4. *San Jose Mercury Herald*, October 25, 1954. p. 7, and *San Jose Mercury Herald*, September 6, 1942. Thanks to Gary Mormino for drawing my attention to these articles.

5. Murray, *A Taste of Memories*, vol. 1, p. 196.

6. Charles Ramsdell, *San Antonio: A Historical and Pictorial Guide* (Austin: University of Texas Press, 1959), pp. 164–165.

7. Carey D. Miller, "Japanese Foods Commonly Used in Hawaii," *Bulletin of the Hawaii Agricultural Experiment Station* 68 (November 1933): 11, 24.

8. John S. Hittell, *The Commerce and Industries of the Pacific Coast of North America* (San Francisco: A. Bancroft and Co., 1882), p. 238.

9. Robert Harris, "Chiles, el magnifico alimento," *El Universal*, March 12, 1944.

10. Hittell, *Commerce and Industries*, p. 209.

11. Lillian Cicio, "Mama Vita," p. 40, IHRC.

12. "Polly Ghirardelli Lawrence, The Ghirardelli Family and Chocolate Company of San Francisco," an oral history conducted 1984–1985 by Ruth Teiser, ROHO.

13. Alberto Cupelli, "The Italians in the Wholesale Food Industries," reel 260, INY.

14. Advertisement for C. Granucci and Sons, *Hidden Treasures of San Francisco* (San Francisco: Italian Chamber of Commerce, 1927).

15. "Little Italy Sours on Duce and War," *New York Times*, February 9, 1941.

16. Nathan, *Jewish Cooking*, p. 18.

17. Blatt, "Food Customs," Publication—Restaurants/Food, First Draft, p. 15, reel 177, JNY.

18. Kisseloff, *You Must Remember This*, p. 196.

19. Clausen, *The Lady with the Pen*, p. 41.

20. Thomas Pinney, *A History of Wine in America: From the Beginnings to Prohibition* (Berkeley: University of California Press, 1989), p. 203.

21. Ray, *Robert Mondavi*, p. 4.

22. Herbert B. Leggett, *Early History of Wine Production in California* (San Francisco: Wine Institute, 1940); Vincent P. Carosso, *The California Wine Industry, 1830–1895: The Formative Years* (Berkeley: University of California Press, 1951).

23. The best sources on California winemaking from the late nineteenth through the mid-twentieth centuries remain the series of interviews by Ruth Teiser for the ROHO. See also Ruth Teiser and Catherine Harroun, *Winemaking in California* (New York: McGraw Hill, 1983).

24. "The Joy of Growing Up Italian," p. xx.

25. Helen Worden, "To Market," *New York World-Telegram*, September 24, 1940, pp. 2, 17.

26. Andrew Heinze, "Jewish Street Merchants and Mass Consumption in New York, 1880–1914," *American Jewish History* 41, 2 (Fall/Winter 1989): 212.

27. Cited materials from Harriette Kershaw Leiding, *Street Cries of an Old Southern City* (Charleston: Daggett Printing, 1927; orig. pub. 1910).

28. Ibid.; Rutledge, *Carolina Housewife*, chap. 9.

29. Antin, *Promised Land*, p. 193.

30. "New York Jews in the Food Industry," Publication—Restaurants/Food, First Draft, p. 36., reel 177, JNY.

31. "The Appetizing Stores of New York," Publication—Restaurants/Food, First Draft, reel 177, JNY.

32. Andrew Schoch Grocery Co., St. Paul, "Records Undated and 1886–1943," Minnesota Historical Society, microfilm roll 8.

33. State of New York, Department of Agriculture and Markets, "List of Commission Merchants Bonded and Licensed to Receive New York State Farm Products for Sale on a Commission Basis for Year Ending June 30, 1941," Circular 596, in Reception of Food—Middle-men-Printed Material, reel 131, FtC.

34. William M. DeMarco, *Ethnics and Enclaves: Boston's Italian North End* (Ann Arbor: UMI Research Press, 1981), p. 77.

35. *Out of This Kitchen: A History of the Ethnic Groups and Their Foods in Steel Valley* (Pittsburgh: Publassist, 1992).

36. Antin, *Promised Land*, p. 350.

37. Kisseloff, *You Must Remember This*, p. 509.

38. Mary Kay Bentlage, *My Name Was Kay* (New York: Exposition Press, 1965), p. 22.

39. B. E. Lloyd, *Lights and Shades in San Francisco* (San Francisco: A. L. Bancroft, 1876), p. 181.

40. "Social Map of the Lower East Side," *New York Times*, April 3, 1910.

41. Ralph H. Bowen, ed., *A Frontier Family in Minnesota: Letters of Theodore and Sophie Bost* (Minneapolis: University of Minnesota Press, 1981), p. 213.

42. Kisseloff, *You Must Remember This*, p. 101.

43. John C. Burnham, *Bad Habits: Drinking, Smoking, Taking Drugs, Gambling, Sexual Misbehavior, and Swearing in American History* (New York: New York University Press, 1993), p. 60.

44. Perry Duis, *The Saloon: Public Drinking in Chicago and Boston, 1880–1920* (Urbana: University of Illinois Press, 1983).

45. Frank Bushick, quoted in Ramsdell, *San Antonio*, pp. 152–153.

46. Kamphoefner, *News from the Land of Freedom*, p. 472.

47. Ray Oldenburg, *The Great Good Place: Cafes, Coffee Shops, Beauty Parlors, General Stores, Bars, Hangouts and How They Get You Through the Day* (New York: Paragon House, 1989), chap. 5, cited material, p. 90.

48. Cited in Oldenburg, *Great Good Place*, p. 93.

49. Joyce Davis, "Hakala Family History," IHRC, p. 6.

50. Duis, *The Saloon*, p. 47.

51. Patrick Cudahy, *Patrick Cudahy: His Life* (Milwaukee: Burdick & Allen, 1912), p. 67.

52. Kamphoefner, *News from the Land of Freedom*, p. 346.

53. Margaret Byington, *Homestead: The Households of a Mill Town* (New York: Charities Publication Committee), p. 139.

54. Federal Writers' Project, New York, *The Italians of New York* (New York: Random House, 1938), p. 205.

55. Industry—Food Industry, draft of chapter, reel 177, p. 70, JNY.

56. Joan Nathan, *Jewish Cooking*, p. 56.

57. Leslie Prosterman, "Food and Celebration: A Kosher Caterer as Mediator of Communal Traditions," in Linda K. Brown and Kay Mussell, *Ethnic and Regional Foodways in the United States: The Performance of Group Identity* (Knoxville: University of Tennessee Press, 1984), p. 132.

58. Rose Shepherd, "Greek Wedding Feast," Notes, Reports, and Essays (Florida), AE.

59. Cited material, Harold Jaediker Taub, *Waldorf-in-the-Catskills* (New York: Sterling, 1952), pp. 48, 52, 100, 139.

60. Reuben Iceland, "At Goodman's and Levine's," trans. Nathan Halper, in Irving

Howe and Eliezer Greenberg, *Voices from the Yiddish: Essays, Memoirs, Diaries* (Ann Arbor: University of Michigan Press), pp. 300–305.

61. "Max T. Kniesche," an oral history interview conducted in 1976 by Ruth Teiser, ROHO, p. 119.

62. Quoted in Linda Schelbitzki Pickle, *Contented among Strangers: Rural German-Speaking Women and Their Families in the Nineteenth-Century Midwest* (Urbana: University of Illinois Press, 1996), p. 49.

63. Ibid., p. 2.

64. Mavis Hiltunen Biesanz, "The Story of Our Family," IHRC, p. 59.

65. Antin, *Promised Land*, p. 196.

66. Skulda Baner, *Latchstring Out* (Cambridge: Houghton Mifflin, Riverside Press, 1944).

67. Helen Barolini, *Umbertina* (New York: Seaview Press, 1979).

68. Citing Frank Bushick in Ramsdell, *San Antonio*, pp. 152–153.

69. Susan Strasser, *Satisfaction Guaranteed: The Making of the American Mass Market* (New York: Pantheon Books, 1989), p. 65.

70. Asian Women United of California, *Making Waves: An Anthology of Writings By and About Asian American Women* (Boston: Beacon Press, 1989), p. 17.

71. National Organization—Co-op Activities, p. 11, reel 177, JNY.

72. Umberto Lucarini, "Papers, 1927–60," IHRC.

73. Arnold Alanen, "The Development and Distribution of Finnish Consumers' Cooperatives in Michigan, Minnesota and Wisconsin, 1903–1973," in Michael G. Karni, Matti E. Kaups, and Douglas J. Ollila, Jr., eds., *The Finnish Experience in the Western Great Lakes Region: New Perspectives* (Vammala, Finland: Institute for Migration, Turkum 1975), p. 104.

74. "Highlights of History," *Central Cooperative Wholesale 20th Year 1937,* IHRC.

75. "Inventory to the Records of the Central Cooperative Wholesale," 1992, IHRC. p. 5.

76. V. S. Alanne, "Steps in Consumer Co-operation," Records of the Central Cooperative Wholesale, Box 13, IHRC.

77. "Introduction to Women's Cooperative Guilds," Papers, Northern States Cooperative Guilds and Clubs, Superior, Wisconsin, 1930–1969, Box 2, IHRC.

78. Photo caption, Edith Koivisto Papers, Supplement 1903–1981, Box 1, folder 142, IHRC.

79. "Cooperative Training Course: Evaluation Report, 1953," Records of the Central Cooperative Wholesale, Box 13, IHRC.

80. "Report on Florence County Cooperative, Iron Mountain, Michigan, 1946," Papers of the Central Cooperative Wholesale, Superior, Wisconsin, 1916–62, Box 3, IHRC.

81. Ivan H. Light, *Ethnic Enterprise in America: Business and Welfare among Chinese, Japanese and Blacks* (Berkeley: University of California Press, 1972), pp. 10–12.

4. Crossing the Boundaries of Taste

1. Rian James, *Dining in New York* (New York: John Day Company, 1930).

2. Thomas Lately, *Delmonico's: A Century of Splendor* (Boston: Houghton Mifflin, 1967), pp. 17–18.

3. Elsa Proehl Blum, *They Pleased World Stars: A Memoir of My Parents* (New York: Vantage Press, 1960), p. 29.

4. Jerry Apps, *Breweries of Wisconsin* (Madison: University of Wisconsin Press, 1992), p. xx.

5. Kisseloff, *You Must Remember This*, p. 101.

6. Dr. John E. Siebel and Anton Schwartz, *History of the Brewing Industry and Brewing Science in America* (Chicago: G. L. Peterson, 1933), p. 74.

7. Stanley Wade Baron, *Brewed in America: A History of Beer and Ale in the United States* (Boston: Little, Brown, 1962), p. 177.

8. Burnham, *Bad Habits*, p. 57.

9. Quoting *Rosa: The Life of an Italian Immigrant*, in Maxine Schwartz Sellers, ed., *Immigrant Women* (Philadelphia: Temple University Press, 1981), p. 185.

10. Gilman Ostrander, *The Prohibition Movement in California, 1848–1933* (Berkeley: University of California Press, 1957), p. 66; Duis, *The Saloon*, pp. 152–154.

11. Gertrude Berg, with Cherney Berg, *Molley and Me* (New York: McGraw-Hill Book Company, 1961), p. 6.

12. Lloyd, *Lights and Shades*, pp. 182–183.

13. James Dabney McCabe, *The Secrets of the Great City* (Philadelphia: Jones Brothers, 1868), p. 50.

14. Oldenburg, *Great Good Place*, p. 95.

15. Lloyd, *Lights and Shades*, p. 123.

16. Ibid.

17. Richard B. Stott, *Workers in the Metropolis: Class, Ethnicity, and Youth in Antebellum New York City* (Ithaca: Cornell University Press, 1990), p. 219.

18. Gustav Mann, "The Gustav Mann Story," manuscript typescript, 1952, Bancroft Library, University of California at Berkeley, p. 14.

19. Maria Sermolino, *Papa's Table d'Hote* (Philadelphia: J. B. Lippincott, 1952), direct quotes: pp. 40, 15, 41.

20. Ibid., pp. 15–16.

21. Edwords, *Bohemian San Francisco*, p. 23.

22. Frances De Talavera Berger and John Parke Custis, *Sumptuous Dining in Gaslight San Francisco, 1875–1915* (Garden City: Doubleday, 1985), p. 86.

23. Ruth Thompson and Chef Louis Hanges, *Eating Around San Francisco* (San Francisco: Suttonhouse, 1937), entry on "Veneto."

24. Scoop Kennedy, *Dining in New Orleans* (New Orleans: Bormon House, 1945), p. 54.

25. Lewis A. Erenberg, *Steppin' Out: New York Nightlife and the Transformation of American Culture* (Chicago: University of Chicago Press, 1984), p. 50.

26. D. Crivitsky "Night Clubs on the East Side," p. 1, Publication—Restaurants/Food, First Draft, reel 177, JNY.

27. Italian Chamber of Commerce, *Hidden Treasures*.

28. Publication—Restaurants/Food, First Draft, p. 1., reel 177, JNY.

29. Edwords, *Bohemian San Francisco,* p. 3.

30. Berg, *Molley and Me*, pp. 71–72.

31. Lloyd, *Lights and Shades*.

32. Cited materials, Edwords, *Bohemian San Francisco,* pp. 56, 30.

33. Tonia Chao, "Communicating through Architecture: San Francisco Chinese Restaurants and Cultural Intersections, 1849–1984," unpub. Ph.D. diss., University of California, Berkeley, 1985.

34. *Disturnell's Stranger's Guide to San Francisco and Vicinity* (San Francisco: W. C. Disturnell, 1883).

35. Kennedy, *Dining in New Orleans,* p. 39.

36. Richard Bankowsky, *After Pentecost: An Epistle to the Romans* (New York: Random House, 1961), p. 102.

37. Edwords, *Bohemian San Francisco,* p. 56.

38. Thompson and Hanges, *Eating Around San Francisco,* see entry for "Lotus Bowl."

39. "Di milkhome tsvishn tsap-sui un gefilte fish" (The War between Chop Suey and Gefilte Fish), *Der Tog,* August 20, 1928. Thanks to Daniel Soyer and the H-ETHNIC discussion on Chinese restaurants for suggesting this work.

40. Anne R. Kaplan et al., *The Minnesota Ethnic Food Book* (St. Paul: Minnesota Historical Society, 1986), p. 38.

41. Gaye Tuchman and Harry Levine, "Safe Treyf," *Brandeis Review* 24 (1993).

42. Benjamin Simons, "Street Vendors, 1940," Open Air Markets—Street Vendors, reel 131, FtC.

43. Industry—Food Industry, draft of chapter, pp. 22, 39, JNY.

44. Theodore Saloutos, *Greeks in the United States* (Cambridge: Harvard University Press, 1964), pp. 261–263.

45. Richard Vasquez, *Chicano* (Garden City: Doubleday, 1970), p. 124.

46. Imogene I. Lim, "The Chow Mein Sandwich: American as Apple Pie," *Radcliffe Culinary Times* 3, 2 (Autumn 1993): 4–5. My thanks to Marilyn Halter for referring me to this article.

47. Glenn Hassenplug, "Texas Favorite Now a National Craze," *Corpus Christi Caller,* Sunday, October 22, 1978.

48. Kisseloff, *You Must Remember This,* p. 63.

49. *Mogen Dovid Delicatessen Magazine* 1, 3 (January 1931): 9; 1, 4 (February 1931): 11; 1, 5 (February 1931): 5. James, *Dining in New York,* p. 28.

50. William G. Lockwood and Yvonne R. Lockwood, "Ethnic Roots of American Regional Foods," *Proceedings of a Conference on Current Research in Culinary History: Sources, Topics, and Methods* (Boston: Culinary Historians of Boston, 1985), p. 132; William G. Lockwood and Yvonne R. Lockwood, "The Cornish Pasty in Northern Michigan," *Proceedings Oxford Symposium, 1983; Food in Motion: The Migration of Foodstuffs and Cookery Techniques* (Stanningley, Leeds: Prospect Books, 1983), pp. 84–94.

51. Cited in Ramsdell, *San Antonio*, pp. 279–280, 282.

52. Cited in Mary Ann Noonan Guerra, *The History of San Antonio's Market Square* (San Antonio: Alamo Press, 1988), p. 14.

53. Timothy Charles Lloyd, "The Cincinnati Chili Culinary Complex," in Michael Owen Jones, *Foodways and Eating Habits: Directions for Research* (Los Angeles: California Folklore Society, 1983), pp. 28–40.

54. On pizza, see James, *Dining in New York*, p. 34; on bagels, see "Jews in Food Industry," Publication—Restaurants/Food, First draft, p. 35, reel 177, JNY.

55. "Polly Ghirardelli Lawrence."

56. Rebecca and Edward Burlend, *A True Picture of Emigration* (Lincoln: University of Nebraska Press, 1987), pp. 69–70.

57. Bentlage, *My Name Was Kay*, p. 24.

58. Biesanz, "The Story of Our Family," p. 55.

59. Marguerite Clausen, "Memories of a Lifelong Richmond Resident, 1912 to 1987," an oral history conducted in 1985 by Judith K. Dunning, ROHO, 1990.

60. Vasquez, *Chicano*, p. 50.

61. Hua-Ying, *Ch'u shu ta ch'uan Chinese and English Cookbook* (San Francisco: Fat Ming, 1910).

62. John Jussila, *Kokki-Kirja (Cookbook: Complete Directions for the Preparation of American Foods)* (Fitchburg, MA: Pohjan Tähti [North Star], 1903).

63. John E. Land, *Charleston: Her Trade, Commerce and Industries* (Charleston: Land, 1884), see entries on Wayne and Von Konitz and Antonio Canale.

64. C. D. Chapralis, *The Greek Americans and Greek Canadians: Information and Service Directory* (Chicago: Major C. D. Chapralis, 1948).

65. "The Greek Community in Birmingham, Mr. Nicholas Christu, February 3, 1977," University of Alabama in Birmingham, Oral History Research Office, in Saloutos Papers, Box 82, File 810, IHRC.

66. Stella M. Eisele, "From Gyros to Grits: Down-Home Cooking Serves Greek Restaurateurs Well," *Charlotte Observer*, May 3, 1993.

67. Dena Kleiman, "Greek Diners: Where Anything Is Possible," *New York Times*, February 27, 1991.

68. Grace Abbot, "A Study of Greeks in Chicago," Box 83, File 829; clipping, "The Greek Menu: Success," Box 84, File 839, Greek Businessmen after 1945, both in Saloutos Papers, IHRC.

69. Clippings File, "Schiek's Cafe-Restaurant," Minnesota Historical Society.

70. Howard Taylor, Jr., "Frank Pomilia: Still Hooked on Fishing," in Lawrence Di Stasi, ed., *Dream Streets: The Big Book of Italian American Culture* (New York: Harper & Row, 1989), p. 37.

71. Dominic Ghio, with Tony Ghio, "Fisherman by Trade: Sixty Years on San Francisco Bay," an oral history conducted in 1986 by Judith K. Dunning, ROHO.

72. Pauline Jacobson, "The Fish King," in Di Stasi, *Dream Streets*, pp. 35–36.

73. Peter Hernon and Terry Ganey, *Under the Influence: The Unauthorized Story of the Anheuser-Busch Dynasty* (New York: Simon & Schuster, 1991), pp. 8–9.

74. Cited in Marjorie Kreidberg, *Food on the Frontier: Minnesota Cooking from 1850 to 1900, With Selected Recipes* (St. Paul: Minnesota Historical Society Press, 1975), p. 18.

75. Thomas Vennum, Jr., *Wild Rice and the Ojibway People* (St. Paul: Minnesota Historical Society Press, 1988), pp. 177, 217, 236.

76. Shimamoto, *To The Land of Bright Promise*, p. 29.

77. Di Stasi, *Dream Streets*, p. 34; see also John G. Brucato, *The Farmer Goes to Town: The Story of the San Francisco Farmers' Market* (San Francisco: Burket Publishing Company, 1948).

78. "Historiographical Essay: Immigrants in Agriculture," Saloutos Papers, Box 32, File 226, IHRC.

79. Edna Bonacich and John Modell, *The Economic Basis of Ethnic Solidarity: Small Business in the Japanese American Community* (Berkeley: University of California Press, 1980), p. 57.

80. "Immigration in Pacific Coast Agriculture," Saloutos papers, Box 63, File 630, IHRC.

81. Kleiman, "Greek Diners."

5. Food Fights and American Values

1. Notes, Reports, and Essays (The Northeast), unpaginated, Box 833, AE.

2. Erik Amfitheatrof, *The Children of Columbus* (Boston: Little, Brown, 1973), p. 253.

3. Lillian Betts, "Some Tenement House Evils," *Century Magazine* 44 (1892): 315.

4. Tenement House Committee, *Report* (Albany: James B. Lyon, 1895), p. 20.

5. Quoted in Levenstein, *Revolution at the Table*, p. 105.

6. Jacob Riis, *The Children of the Poor* (New York: Charles Scribner's Sons, 1908), p. 197

7. Quoted in Desdemona L. Heinrich, "Dietary Habits of Elementary School Children," unpub. Ph.D. diss., New York University, 1932, p. 12.

8. Lucy H. Gillett, *Adapting Nutrition Work to a Community* (New York: Association for Improving the Condition of the Poor, 1924), p. 5.

9. Quoted in Levenstein, *Revolution at the Table*, p. 115.

10. "Latte Per Tutti," Education Material (Multilingual)—Printed Material, reel 148, FtC.

11. Carey D. Miller, "A Study of the Dietary and Value of Living of 44 Japanese Families in Hawaii," *University of Hawaii Bulletin* 18, 2 (December 1938): 16.

12. W. J. Rorabaugh, *The Alcoholic Republic: An American Tradition* (New York: Oxford University Press, 1979), p. 91.

13. See the cartoon, John K. Kasson, "Rituals of Dining: Table Manners in Victorian America," in Kathryn Grover, ed., *Dining in America, 1850–1900* (Amherst: University of Massachusetts Press and The Margaret Woodbury Strong Museum, 1987), p. 129.

14. Laura Shapiro, *Perfection Salad: Women and Cooking at the Turn of the Century* (New York: Farrar, Straus and Giroux, 1986), p. 304.

15. Quoted in Strasser, *Satisfaction Guaranteed*, p. 202.

16. Ellen H. Richards, *The Cost of Living as Modified by Sanitary Science* (New York: John Wiley, 1900), pp. 67, 70.

17. Ibid., p. 148.

18. Levenstein, *Revolution at the Table*, pp. 56–57.

19. Shapiro, *Perfection Salad*, p. 111.

20. Ibid., pp. 91, 93.

21. Ibid., pp. 98, 100.

22. Quoted in Harvey Levenstein, "The American Response to Italian Food, 1880–1930," *Food and Foodways* 1, 1 (1985): 10.

23. Gillett, *Adapting Nutrition Work*, pp. 36, 44.

24. Bertha M. Wood, *Foods of the Foreign Born in Relation to Health* (Boston: Whitcomb and Barrows, 1922), p. 90.

25. Jenna Weissman Joselit, *The Wonders of America: Reinventing Jewish Culture, 1880–1950* (New York: Hill and Wang, 1994), pp. 182–183.

26. Pearl L. Bailey, *Domestic Science, Principles and Application: A Textbook for Public Schools* (St. Paul: Webb, 1918; first pub. 1914).

27. Department of Welfare, Home Economics Section, "Educational Material," Education Material (Multilingual)—printed material, reel 148, FtC.

28. Marilyn Irvin Holt, *Linoleum, Better Babies & The Modern Farm Woman, 1890–1930* (Albuquerque: University of New Mexico Press, 1995), pp. 24–25, 44, 72.

29. *The Home Economics Counselor, New Mexico* 1, 4 (February 1926).

30. Shapiro, *Perfection Salad*, p. 145.

31. Holt, *Linoleum, Better Babies*, p. 59.

32. Quoted in Gregory R. Campbell, "Health Patterns and Economic Underdevelopment on the Northern Cheyenne Reservation, 1910–1920," in John H. Moore et al., *The Political Economy of North American Indians* (Norman: University of Oklahoma Press, 1993), p. 69.

33. Devon A. Mihesuah, *Cultivating the Rosebuds: The Education of Women at the Cherokee Female Seminary 1851–1909* (Urbana: University of Illinois Press, 1993), p. 92.

34. Quoted in Roy Lubove, *The Progressives and the Slums: Tenement House Reform in New York City, 1890–1917* (Pittsburgh: University of Pittsburgh Press, 1962), pp. 19–20.

35. Swiss Italian Sausage Factory, San Francisco, California, "Business Records, 1927–1973," IHRC.

36. Lenz, "Safeguarding the City's Food Supply," Reception of Food—Inspection—Research, roll 131, FtC.

37. Elita Lenz, "Getting Answers to a Number of Questions on Food Inspection, Sept. 11, 1940," Reception of Food—Inspection—Research, roll 131, FtC.

38. "The Regulation of Pushcarts," *American Hebrew* 79, 17 (1905): 415.

39. "First Avenue Retail Markets—Draft of Article," Municipal Retail Markets—Essex Street-Research, roll 131, FtC.

40. "Municipal Retail Markets—Essex Street-Draft of article," roll 131, FtC.

41. Quoted in Kraut, "The Butcher," p. 78.

42. Elita Lenz, "Color at Essex Street Retail Market," Municipal Retail Markets—First Avenue-Research, reel 131, FtC.

43. "Municipal Retail Markets—Essex Street-Draft of article," roll 131, FtC.

44. Robert Alan Nash, "The Chinese Shrimp Fishery in California," unpub. Ph.D. diss., University of California, Berkeley, 1973, p. 164.

45. Jack S. Blocker, Jr., *Retreat from Reform: The Prohibition Movement in the United States, 1890–1913* (Westport: Greenwood, 1976), p. 240.

46. Quoted in W. J. Rorabaugh, "Beer, Lemonade, and Propriety in the Gilded Age," in Grover, *Dining in America*, pp. 24–46.

47. *American Issue*, June 5, 1903, quoted in Blocker, *Retreat from Reform*, p. 167.

48. C. J. Hexamer, "Argument Delivered by C. J. Hexamer, President of the National German American Alliance: at a hearing before the Committee on the Judiciary of the Senate, March 9, 1912" (Philadelphia: S.n., 1912).

49. Ibid.

50. Jane Holt, "News of Food," *New York Times*, December 30, 1941.

51. Publassist, *Out of this Kitchen*.

52. Cited material from Natalie Kostecka, comp., *Ukrainian Cook Book: 76 Traditional Recipes for To-Day's Living* (Philadelphia: International Institute of Philadelphia, 1947), pp. 3–4.

53. "International Institute News Packet, April 1934," p. 5, National Institute of Immigrant Welfare (1933–1946), Shipment 3, Box 1, American Council for Nationalities Service, IHRC.

54. International Institute of Boston, Records, 1923–1952, Box 10, folder 113; and Box 11, folder 135, IHRC.

55. International Institute of Minnesota, Records, 1920–1971, Box 12, folder 183, IHRC.

56. "Folk Festival Council, Food Fights for Freedom, 1943–44," p. 4, American Council for Nationalities Service, Shipment 3, Box 9, IHRC.

57. Marjorie Leigh McLellan, "Bread and Glue: Celebration and Ritual in Four American Families," unpub. Ph.D. diss., University of Minnesota, p. 154.

58. Levenstein, *Revolution at the Table*, p. 107.

59. Department of Welfare, Home Economics Section, "Educational Material," Education Material (Multilingual)—printed material, reel 148, FtC.

60. "Suggested Low Cost Menus for One Week for the Jewish Family," Education Material (Multilingual)—Printed Material, reel 148, FtC.

61. John Charles Camp, "America Eats: Towards a Definition of American Food-ways," unpub. Ph.D. diss., University of Pennsylvania, 1978; Nelson Algren, *America Eats* (Iowa City: University of Iowa Press, 1992).

62. "Internal Editorial Report, Louisiana, January 30, 1942," Box A-830, AE.

63. "Editorial Report on Montana, November 26, 1941," p. 2, AE.

64. Letter to Mr. Felton, November 22, 1941, Editorial Report on State Copy, Box A-830, AE.

65. Notes, Reports, and Essays, Florida, Box A-830, and Notes, Reports, and Essays (Kansas), p. 5, Box A-831, AE.

66. "Cyprus Ridge Singing Convention," Notes, Reports, and Essays (Arkansas), Box A-830, AE.

67. F. L. Diard, "Old-Fashioned Creole Sunday Dinner," Notes, Reports, and Essays (Alabama), Box A-830, AE.

68. "The Salzburger Gathering," Notes, Reports, and Essays (Georgia), Box A-831, AE.

69. Notes, Reports, and Essays, Connecticut, Box A-830, AE.

70. "Notations" and "A Pitch-in Dinner after a Funeral Service," Notes, Reports, and Essays (Indiana), Box 831, AE.

71. "Letter to Mrs. Florence Kerr, December 20, 1941," Correspondence, December 1941, Box A-830, AE.

72. "Letter from Mark Muth to Mrs. Florence C. Kerr, November 3, 1941," Correspondence, December 1941, Box A-830, AE.

73. "Letter from Mark Muth to Mrs. Florence C. Kerr, November 3, 1941," and "Letter from S. L. Stolte to Mrs. Florence S. Kerr, December 10, 1941," Correspondence, December 1941, A-830, AE.

74. "Lutefisk Supper," Notes, Reports, and Essays (Minnesota), A-831, AE.

75. Algren, *America Eats*, pp. 59–61.

76. "Editorial Report on Southern California, January 7, 1942," Box A-830, AE.

77. "All Day Church Memorial Service," p. 5, Notes, Reports, and Essays (Georgia), Box-831, AE.

78. "Colorado Eats," p. 27, Notes, Reports, and Essays (Colorado), Box A-830, AE.

79. *Fort Myers News-Press*, January 18, 1948. Thanks to Gary Mormino for alerting me to this source.

80. Rebecca Spang, "The Cultural Habits of a Food Committee," *Food and Foodways* 2 (1988): 379.

81. "Says Charlotte Adams—Food in Wartime," Facts about Food—Printed Material, reel 148, FtC.

82. Common Council for American Unity, "Summary of Proceedings of Emergency Conference on Food and the Foreign Born," American Council for Nationalities Service, Shipment 3, Box 9, IHRC.

83. American Council for Nationalities Service, Shipment 6, Box 22, IHRC.

84. "What's Cooking in Your Neighbor's Pot" (New York: Common Council for American Unity, 1944), in folder 259, Box 28, International Institute of St. Louis, Missouri, Papers, 1919–1960, IRHC.

85. *PM Sunday*, March 15, 1942.

86. Jane Holt, "News of Food," *New York Times*, March 28, 1942.

87. Ibid., September 4, 1941.

88. Ibid., March 23, 1942.

89. Janet Cooke, "Wives Aiding in War Effort," *New York Journal-American*, February 26, 1942; "The Home-Maker's Journal," February 24, 1942.

90. *New York Journal-American*, October 17, 1941.

91. "The Butcher Explains," *New York World-Telegram*, October 9, 1942.

92. Zola Vincent, *New York Journal-American*, February 18, 1942.

93. Agnes Adams, "'Peace' Is a Wonderful Dish: Mrs. David Dubinsky Serves International Food," *New York Post*, May 29, 1941.

6. The Big Business of Eating

1. Carolyn Wyman, *I'm a Spam Fan: America's Best Loved Foods* (Stamford: Longmeadow Press, 1993), pp. 32–33.

2. Lawrence Di Stasi, "The Face That Made Spaghetti Famous," in Di Stasi, *Dream Streets*, pp. 72–73.

3. Robert Di Giorgio and Joseph A. Di Giorgio, "The Di Giorgios: From Fruit Merchants to Corporate Innovators," an oral history conducted in 1983 by Ruth Teiser, ROHO.

4. Asian Women United of California, *Making Waves*, p. 9.

5. Frederic B. Garver, Francis M. Boddy, and Alvar J. Nixon, *The Location of Manufactures in the United Sates, 1899–1929*, vol. 2, no. 6 (December 1933).

6. Wyman, *I'm a Spam Fan*, pp. 48, 52.

7. Lawrence J. Jelinek, *Harvest Empire: A History of California Agriculture* (San Francisco: Boyd and Fraser, 1979), pp. 20, 31.

8. "The Di Giorgios," p. 21.

9. Ibid., p. i.

10. Stephen Potter, *The Magic Number, The Story of "57"* (London: Max Reinhardt, 1959).

11. Robert C. Alberts, *The Good Provider: H. J. Heinz and His 57 Varieties* (London: Arthur Barker Limited, 1973).

12. E. D. McCafferty, *Henry J. Heinz: A Biography* (New York: Bartlett Orr Press, 1928), p. 105.

13. Potter, *The Magic Number*, p. 84.

14. Cited material, "The Di Giorgios," pp. 60, 50, 34, 71.

15. "The Di Giorgios," p. 92.

16. "Food Mergers—What Has Happened, and Why," *Business Week* 1, 2 (September 14, 1929): 29–30.

17. Douglas Collins, *America's Favorite Food: The Story of the Campbell Soup Company* (New York: H. N. Abrams, 1994), pp. 100–104.

18. Ron Bechtol, "Chili: A San Antonio Tradition," *San Antonio Monthly* 6, 8 (May 1987): 21–35, 91.

19. "William Gebhardt," ITC.

20. Randall Benham, "A Lot Like It Hot," *Texas Parade*, February 1976, pp. 18–23.

21. Wyman, *I'm a Spam Fan*, p. 80.

22. Ibid., p. 130.

23. Bruce W. Mario, *The Organization and Performance of the U.S. Food System* (Lexington, MA: Lexington Books, D. C. Heath, 1986), pp. 75–77.

24. National Decision Systems, *VISION Marketing Guide, Book 1* (Encinita, CA: National Decision Systems, 1987).

25. Joselit, *Wonders of America*, p. 221; Jane Holt, "News of Food," *New York Times*, March 27, 1942.

26. Nathan, *Jewish Cooking*, p. 21.

27. Nathan, "Crossover Kitchen," p. 51.

28. Nathan, *Jewish Cooking*, p. 22.

29. "Gabila's Knish Wishes Now Reality," *New York State Kosher Marketplace* 2, 1 (Spring 1994): 1. Thanks to Deborah Dash Moore for alerting me to this article.

30. Samuel G. Freedman, "Indiana Pastrami? Hebrew National Plans to Move," *New York Times*, August 27, 1984.

31. Nathan, *Jewish Cooking*, p. 27.

32. Nicholas Lemann, "The Frito: The Venerable Corn Chip Whose Life Is a Tex-Mex History Lesson," *Texas Monthly*, May 1982.

33. "Frito-Lay," ITC.

34. "La Preferida Seeks to Pique Customer Interest," *Chicago Tribune*, June 19, 1995, p. 4.

35. Frank McCoy, "Goya: A Lot More than Black Beans and Sofrito," *Business Week*, December 7, 1987, pp. 137–138.

36. Judann Dagnoli, "Campbell Stirs Goya Market," *Advertising Age* 48, 32 (August 3, 1987): 58.

37. Warren J. Belasco, "Ethnic Fast Food: The Corporate Melting Pot," *Food and Foodways* 2 (1987): 18.

38. Wyman, *I'm a Spam Fan*, pp. 40–41.

39. Nathan, *Jewish Cooking*, p. 27.

40. Lilian Ng, "Yeo Takes a Bite of American Market," *Asian Business* 25, 12 (December 1989): 60.

41. Wyman, *I'm a Spam Fan*, pp. 65–66.

42. "Obituary," *New York Times*, October 22, 1990.

43. "The Vichyssoise of Ice Cream," *New York Times Magazine*, January 1, 1995.

44. Beth Austin, "Kraft's Hungry . . . And Wants More," *Advertising Age* 58, 30 (July 20 1987): 3, 50.

45. Beth Spethmann, "Souping up Progresso," *Brandweek* 37, 3 (January 15, 1996): 16.

46. Wyman, *I'm a Spam Fan*, pp. 67–68.

47. Molly O'Neill, "New Mainstream: Hot Dogs, Apple Pie and Salsa," *New York Times*, March 11, 1992.

48. Ray Kroc with Robert Anderson, *Grinding It Out: The Making of McDonald's* (Chicago: Contemporary Books, 1977), pp. 1, 23.

49. Ray Kroc, quoted in Ester Reiter, *Making Fast Food: From the Frying Pan into the Fryer* (Montreal: McGill-Queen's University Press, 1991), p. 47.

50. John Anderson, "Food Fight," *Texas Monthly*, May 1991, pp. 90–92.

51. Pete Engardio, "Jeno Paulucci: When Chop Suey and Pizza Aren't Enough," *Business Week*, February 29, 1988, pp. 80–81.

52. Richard S. Tedlow, *New and Improved: The Story of Mass Marketing in America* (New York: Basic Books, 1990), p. 372.

7. Of Cookbooks and Culinary Roots

1. Antin, *Promised Land*, p. 90.

2. Vicki Baum, *It Was All Quite Different* (New York: Funk & Wagnalls, 1964), p. 325.

3. Wood, *Foods of the Foreign Born*, p. 2.

4. Judith Goode et al., "A Framework for the Analysis of Continuity and Change in Shared Sociocultural Rules for Food Use: The Italian-American Pattern," in Brown and Mussel, *Ethnic and Regional Foodways*, p. 80.

5. Valerie Matsumoto, *Farming the Home Place: A Japanese American Community in California, 1919–1982* (Ithaca: Cornell Univesity Press, 1993), Appendix C.

6. Joan Nathan, *An American Folklife Cookbook* (New York: Schocken Books, 1984), "Passover in Charleston, South Carolina."

7. "Jews of New York," Publication—Restaurants/Food, First Draft, p. 4, JNY.

8. "Notes on Dietary Law," p. 23, Publication—Restaurants/Food, First Draft, reel 177, JNY.

9. Extracts from M. Vaxer, *The Orthodox Union*, 1, 11 (1934): 6; 2, 3 (1935): 5.

10. Leonard Covello, *The Heart Is the Teacher* (New York: McGraw-Hill, 1958), p. 265.

11. Hawaii State Society of Washington, D.C., *Hawaiian Cuisine: A Collection of Recipes from Members of the Society* (Rutland, VT: Charles E. Tuttle, 1963), p. 32.

12. Anne R. Kaplan, "Ethnic Foodways in Everyday Life: Creativity and Change among Contemporary Minnesotans," unpub. Ph.D. diss., University of Pennsylvania, 1984, p. 129.

13. Gloria Braggiotti, *Born in a Crowd* (New York: Thomas Crowell Company, 1957), p. 237.

14. Notes, Reports, and Essays (The Far West), p. 51, Box A-833, AE.

15. Kisseloff, *You Must Remember This*, p. 499.

16. Cited materials in ibid., pp. 240, 370.

17. Lucie Germer, "The Food Their Families Eat: Cuisine as Communication among Cambodian Refugees," unpub. Ph.D. diss., University of Utah, 1986, p. 24.

18. Kamphoefner, *News from the Land of Freedom*, p. 243.

19. Arlie Hochschild, *The Second Shift: Working Parents and the Revolution at Home* (New York: Viking, 1989), p. 247.

20. Kisseloff, *You Must Remember This*, p. 370.

21. Judy Lael Goldman, "A Moveable Feast: The Art of a Knish Maker," in Michael Owen Jones et al., *Foodways and Eating Habits: Directions for Research* (Los Angeles: California Folklore Society, 1983), pp. 11–18.

22. "Even in the 90's Dinner Time Is Family Time," *New York Times*, December 5, 1990.

23. Lynne Ireland, "The Compiled Cookbook as Foodways Autobiography," in Jones, *Foodways and Eating Habits*, p. 107.

24. Margaret Cook, *America's Charitable Cookbooks: A Bibliography of Fund-Raising Cook Books Published in the United States (1861–1915)* (Kent, OH: Cookery Bibliography, 1971).

25. Eleanor Brown and Bob Brown, *Culinary Americana: Cookbooks Published in the Cities and Towns of the U.S. of America during the Years from 1860 through 1960* (New York: Roving Eye Press, 1961); Liora Gvion Rosenberg, "Telling the Story of Ethnicity: American Cookbooks, 1850–1900," unpub. Ph.D. diss., State University of New York at Stony Brook, 1991.

26. Molly Goldberg and Myra Waldo, *The Molly Goldberg Cookbook* (Garden City: Doubleday & Company, 1955), p. 5.

27. Marie Prisland and Albina Novak, eds., *Woman's Glory: The Kitchen* (Chicago: Slovenian Women's Union of America, 1963), p. 1.

28. Penn State Kappa Kappa Chapter of Dobro Slovo, *The Dobro Slovo Slavic*

Cookbook, ed. Teresa S. Wilson (University Park: Penn State Kappa Kappa Chapter, 1981).

29. Savella Stechishin, *Traditional Ukrainian Cookery* (Winnipeg: Trident Press, 1963), pp. 9–10.

30. St. Louis Bocce Club, Ladies Auxiliary, *St. Louis Bocce Club's Favorite Recipes* (Olathe, KS: Cookbook Publishers, 1993), p. i.

31. Lithuanian Catholic Pres [sic] Society, *Popular Lithuanian Recipes* (Chicago: Lithuanian Catholic Press, 1986), 9th printing.

32. The Kulm Family Association, *Kulm Cookery, 1890–1990* (Olathe: Cookbook Publishers, 1993), p. iii.

33. Golden Wheat Chapter, American Historical Society of Germans from Russia, *Golden Wheat Chapter Cookbook* (Kearney, NE: Morris Press, Fundraising Cookbooks, 1990).

34. Holy Trinity Church, Struthers, OH, *"Our Husbands' Favorite Recipes"* (1969, 1978).

35. Marguerita Fossesca and Alice Rossi, *A Legacy of Italian Holiday Traditions and Recipes* (s.l., s.n., 1991), p. 3.

36. Sisterhood of Temple Emanu-El, *From Generation to Generation* (Dallas: Wimmer Brothers, 1993), 2nd ed.

37. *Popular Lithuanian Recipes*, p. 5.

38. George Vukelich, "The Bush Recalled in Words and Food," *Isthmus*, March 1991, pp. 22–28.

39. Personal communication.

40. Helen Jakubowski Rog, *Na Zdrowie! "To Your Health"* (Buffalo, NY: The Cookbook as Legacy, 1992).

41. Helen Barolini, *Festa: Recipes and Recollections of Italian Holidays* (San Diego: Harcourt Brace Jovanovich, 1988), pp. 6–7, 12–13.

42. *New York Times*, May 12, 1990.

43. *The Melting Pot: Ethnic Cuisine in Texas* (San Antonio: University of Texas, Institute of Texan Cultures, 1989), rev. ed.

44. See also Katherine S. Kirlin and Thomas M. Kirlin, *Smithsonian Folklife Cookbook* (Washington: Smithsonian Institution Press, 1991).

45. "Editorial Report on South Dakota, November 2, 1941," Box 8–830, AE.

46. Helen R. Coates, *The American Festival Guide* (New York: Exposition Press, 1956).

47. Larry William Danielson, "The Ethnic Festival and Cultural Revivalism in a Small Midwestern Town," unpub. Ph.D. diss., Indiana University, 1972, p. 160.

48. Ibid., p. 194.

49. Woodville Lions Club, *Velkommen til Woodville: Home of the Syttende Mai* (Woodville, WI: Woodville Lions Club, 1991).

50. Sabina Magliocco, "Playing with Food: The Negotiation of Identity in the Ethnic Display Event by Italian Americans in Clinton, Indiana," pp. 107–126, Luisa

del Giudice, *Studies in Italian American Folklore* (Logan: Utah State University Press, 1993).

51. *New York Times*, May 16, 1986.

52. Nancy Jenkins, "Ninth Avenue: The Gourmet's Super Bowl," *New York Times*, March 17, 1985.

53. Vernon G. Zunker, *A Dream Come True: Robert Hugman and San Antonio's River Walk* (San Antonio, 1983).

54. See Smithsonian Institution, "Festival of American Folklife: A Bicentennial Presentation," pp. 1–2.

55. Ibid., p. 7.

56. *1993 Festival of American Folklife Program Book.*

57. Interview with Diane Parker and Richard Kurin, Smithsonian Institution Center for Folklife Programs, September 1994.

58. Interview with Barbara Strickland, Smithsonian Institution Center for Folklife Programs, April 3, 1995.

59. Rosemary Williams, "I AM Folklife," *Texas Highways*, August 1988, p. 7.

60. "Festival Puts Life into Folks," *Texas Highways*, August 1993, p. 25.

61. Interview with Joanne Andera, Institute of Texan Cultures, October 21, 1996.

62. Edna McGaffey, Claudia, "Berm Dog Gets Festival Ball Rolling," newspaper clipping dated July 31, 1977, Festivals—Folklife Festival-ITC—San Antonio, TX, ITC.

63. "Program," Festivals—Folklife Festival-ITC—San Antonio, TX, ITC.

64. Robert L. Emerson, *Fast Food: The Endless Shakeout* (New York: Lebhar-Friedman, 1979), pp. 147, 205–206, 234.

65. Lawrence A. Lovell-Troy, *The Social Basis of Ethnic Enterprise* (New York: Garland Publishing, 1990).

66. Ibid., p. 185.

67. Molly Geiger Schuchat, "Hungarian Refugees in America and Their Counterparts in Hungary: The Interrelations between Cosmopolitanism and Ethnicity," unpub. Ph.D. diss., Catholic University of America, 1971, p. 115.

68. Nathan, *An American Folklife Cookbook*, "An Italian Christmas Eve in Providence."

69. Jane Gross, "Savory Shops Give an Ethnic Flavor to a Bronx Avenue," *New York Times*, March 25, 1984.

70. Paul Bass, "New Haven's Kosher Market Closes," *New York Times*, May 12, 1988.

71. Philip S. Gutis, "A Florida Hotel Where a Rabbi Opens the Restaurant and Kosher Prevails," *New York Times*, February 28, 1990.

72. James Griffith, "We Always Call it 'Tucson Eat Yourself': The Role of Food at a Constructed Festival," in Theodore D. Humphrey and Lin T. Humphrey, eds., *"We Gather Together": Food and Festival in American Life* (Ann Arbor: University of Michigan Press, 1988), p. 223.

8. Nouvelle Creole

1. "Oral History Interview, Arturo and Elivira Coronado," August 18, 1976, Mexican Americans in Minnesota, Minnesota Historical Society.

2. Jim Unger "Herman," *Columbus Dispatch*, April 10, 1988.

3. Gloria Levitas, "Jamaica Is Source for Caribbean Produce," *New York Times*, April 9, 1986.

4. Nathan, *American Folklife Cookbook*, p. 309.

5. *Charlotte Observer*, December 21, 1993.

6. Rick Bragg, "Love This Barbecue Or Leave It, Stranger," *New York Times*, February 15, 1995.

7. Matthew Purdy, "In Poultry, Cackling Fresh Is Popular," *New York Times*, December 1, 1994.

8. Marvine Howe, "Bodegas Find Prosperity," *New York Times*, November 19, 1986.

9. Dena Kleiman, "In a New York Restaurant, Flavors and Style of a Cairo Kitchen," *New York Times*, September 11, 1991.

10. Genevieve Po-Ai Ho, "Factors Affecting Adaptation to American Dietary Pattern by Students from the Oriental Countries," unpub. Ph.D. diss., Pennsylvania State University, 1961.

11. Daryl Royster Alexander, "A Spicy Blend of Caribbean and Black-American Flavors," *New York Times*, November 19, 1986.

12. Dena Kleiman, "In Queens 'Mosaic,' Proof of the Melting Is in the Eating," *New York Times*, October 16, 1991.

13. "At the Nation's Table," *New York Times*, June 14, 1989.

14. *New York Times*, March 6, 1991.

15. Stan Luxenberg, *Roadside Empires: How the Chains Franchised America* (New York: Viking, 1985), p. 103.

16. Elaine Louie, "Behind Dim Sum, an Infernal Machine," *New York Times*, October 1, 1986.

17. Luxenberg, *Roadside Empires*, chap. 8.

18. Elizabeth Bogen, *Immigration in New York* (New York: Praeger, 1987), p. 93.

19. "A Few Fleas Are Good for a Dog," *Business Week* 1, 8 (October 26, 1929), p. 30.

20. Emerson, *Fast Food*, pp. 32–35.

21. Luxenburg, pp. 145–146.

22. Wyman, *I'm a Spam Fan*, pp. 56–57

23. Florence Fabricant, "Dining á la Cart: Street Food Mirrors the Tastes of a City," *New York Times*, April 17, 1991.

24. Suzanne Daley, "Street Beckons with International Flavors," *New York Times*, August 27, 1986.

25. Molly O'Neill, "The Chop Suey Syndrome: Americanizing the Exotic," *New York Times*, July 26, 1989.

26. Wine Spectator Scholarship Foundation, *California Wine Pioneers* (San Francisco: Wine Spectator Scholarship Foundation, 1988).

27. "Elie C. Skofis, California Wine and Brandy Maker," an oral history conducted in 1984 by Ruth Teiser, ROHO, p. 20.

28. William Lesch et al., "Lifestyle and Demographic Influences on Females' Consumption of Alcoholic Beverages," *International Journal of Advertising* 10, 1 (1991): 59–78.

29. Belasco, "Ethnic Fast Food," p. 5.

30. Sandra Atchison, "Blue Skies, Blue Corn—Golden Opportunity," *Business Week* 31, no. 48 (March 5, 1990): 20A.

31. Lockwood and Lockwood, "Cornish Pasty," p. 94.

32. Warren J. Belasco, *Appetite for Change: How the Counterculture Took on the Food Industry* (Ithaca: Cornell University Press, 1989).

33. *New York Times*, September 25, 1994.

34. Mark Bittman, "Talking Tamales," *Restaurant Business* 90, 8 (May 20, 1991): 197–198.

35. Roberta Kalechofsky, *Haggadah for the Liberated Lamb* (Marblehead, MA: Micah Publications 1985).

36. Maureen Goldsmith, *The Organic Yenta* (New York: Atheneum, 1972), pp. ix, xi.

37. Lockwood and Lockwood, "Ethnic Roots of American Regional Foods," p. 130.

38. Moira Hodgson, "Young Chefs: A Big-City Success Story," *New York Times*, January 28, 1981.

39. Scott Mowbray, "Have Memories, Will Travel," *Eating Well*, January/February 1995, p. 6.

40. Molly O'Neill, "New Mainstream: Hot Dogs, Apple Pie and Salsa," *New York Times*, March 11, 1992.

41. *New York Times*, June 7, 1995.

42. Nancy Harmon Jenkins, "It's Called Mexican, But Is It Genuine?" *New York Times*, April 23, 1986.

43. John F. Mariani, *Eating Out: Fearless Dining in Ethnic Restaurants* (New York: Quill, 1985).

44. D. Daryl Wyckoff and W. Earl Sasser, *The Chain Restaurant Industry* (Lexington, MA: D. C. Heath, Lexington Books, 1978), chap. 2; see also "Corporate Profile: Benihana of Japan," *Institutions/Volume Feeding Management* 79 (June 15, 1972): 71–78.

45. Wilbur Zelinsky, "The Roving Palate: North America's Ethnic Restaurant Cuisines," *Geoforum* 16 (1985): 51–72.

46. Raja Chaudry, "Sell-em Sizzle," *Restaurants and Institutions* 103, 22 (September 15, 1993): 12–13.

47. *Charlotte Observer*, October 16, 1996; April 20, 1994; November 3, 1993.

48. O'Neill, "New Mainstream."

49. Benham, "A Lot Like it Hot."

50. Glenn Collins, "Campbell Soup Takes the Big Plunge Into Salsa," *New York Times*, November 29, 1994.

51. Diane Mastrull, "Campbell and Pace Recipe: A Mixing of Disparate Cultures," *Philadelphia Business Journal* 13, 53 (February 17, 1995): 1, 3.

52. Collins, "Campbell Soup Takes the Big Plunge."

53. Martin Friedman, "New Products Fuel Salsa's Fire," *Prepared Foods* 162, 11 (October 1993): 73.

54. Chuck McCollough, "Nation's Appetite for Tortillas Heating Up Sales," *San Antonio Express*, September 12, 1993.

55. Richard Zelade, "Masa Marketing," *Texas Monthly* 17, 5 (May 1989): 132–141.

56. Lynda Richardson, "A Little Kitchen Help For Transplanted Cooks," *New York Times*, June 26, 1977.

57. Marjorie K Doughty, comp., *Happy in My Stomach* (New York: YMCA Refugee and Resettlement Services, 1975).

58. *Vietnamese American, Family Cooking: Teaching Vietnamese to Prepare Meals on a Limited Budget* (Minneapolis: Consumer Center, General Mills, 1976).

59. For example, Joanne P. Ikeda, *Hmong American Food Practices, Customs, and Holidays* (Chicago: American Dietetic Association and the American Diabetes Association, 1992).

60. "Pushcart War Simmers in Melting Pot," *New York Times*, July 22, 1978, p. 21; see also clippings in Theodore Saloutos Collection, Box 84, Greek Businessmen after 1945, IHRC.

61. Lisa Belkin, "For the City's Korean Greengrocers, Culture Often Clashes with the Law," *New York Times*, August 22, 1984.

62. Regina Schrambling, "Whose Food Is It Anyway?" *Newsweek*, March 11, 1996, p. 12. Thanks to Liz Pleck for calling my attention to this article.

63. Marian Burros, "In San Francisco, Classic Cuisine Is One Chef's Coup," *New York Times*, July 31, 1985.

Conclusion: Who Are We?

1. Identities, which scholar David A. Hollinger calls "post-ethnic," *Postethnic America: Beyond Multi-culturalism* (New York: Basic Books, 1995).

Acknowledgments

Like all historians, I cannot write without the assistance and support of others. Nor would I want to. I wish to acknowledge, first, the special contribution of several people who shared their thoughts with me in person. Without the insights offered by Joanne Andera in Texas, and Diane Parker, Richard Kurin, and Barbara Strickland in Washington, I might never have realized how important festivals and food have become in defining contemporary ethnicity, not just as a cultural or personal but as a commercial development. Liz Pleck also reminded me of some important leads to this, and other, dimensions of ethnic festivity. I can again thank Jeanne Chiang and Stuart Licht in Washington and Dorothy Kachouh in New York for their warm hospitality, and this time I can add thanks to Randy Dodgen and Lyn Roberts in San Francisco, and to Alex and Linda DeGrand in Raleigh, North Carolina.

It is a real pleasure as well to thank those who assisted me closer to home. Special gratitude goes to Larry Howard, Jason Moscato, and Barbara Reed, who handled library searches, interlibrary loans, and countless other research tasks with unflagging competence. As different as a chef, a psychologist, and an architect can be, they asked good, hard questions about my research, and I learned from them as I struggled to answer.

The Interlibrary Loan staff at UNC Charlotte's Atkins Library proved enormously helpful and patient with the stream of paperwork emerging from my office. I hope that my library colleagues have experimented with the new recipes they found as they handled all those spiral-ring-bound cookbooks arriving from North Dakota, Maine, New Mexico, and Alabama! Mercy College provided early impetus for this research with a faculty development grant for travel to Minneapolis. The Charles H. Stone fund at the University of North Carolina at Charlotte funded most of the remaining research and travel. I am particularly grateful for the wonderful support I received in the form of a year-long sabbatical, made possible by UNC Charlotte and the Cotlow Fund.

Jeffrey Pilcher read every word of the manuscript and offered a beach retreat when I needed it most. I thank him for introducing me to Mexican cuisine, Trinidad Sánchez, and purple prose. Marilyn Halter as always offered sound advice about manuscripts and other topics close to my heart. My son Tamino contributed his two cents as grammarian. His inimitable "sprachgefühl" also encouraged me to rethink some of my anecdotal evidence. I continue to appreciate the creativity of my co-cook, Thomas Kozak, and the sympathetic ears, spare beds, and open hearts provided by my mother, sisters, and late father.

Finally, I am grateful to Deborah Dash Moore, for giving me the chance to talk about airplane meals and milanese ala napolitana in Poughkeepsie, and to both Deborah and Suellen Hoy for introducing me to Joyce Seltzer—quite simply all one could ever dream of finding in one's editor.

My family, my friends, and I all ate very well during this project. I have always suspected that "we are what we eat," and my ability to appreciate multi-ethnic creoles and blends as well as "authentic" ethnic and national cuisines definitely increased as I did this research. I am a happier and, I believe, a more creative cook than I was ten years ago, and I see this change as a direct consequence of becoming a historian of food.

Early in my research, a colleague coyly suggested that I "weigh in" at the beginning of this project, and "weigh out" again upon its completion. So, for anyone even mildly interested in the corporeal consequences of food studies methodology, I can now offer some empirical data. I gained eight pounds during my ten years of food research. Considering that I was a bit on the thin side at the beginning of my work, for me that's good news. Historians contemplating future research in this field are free to draw their own conclusions.

Charlotte, North Carolina
October 1997

Index